The Life
of Riley

ALSO BY JOE RILEY

Walking in Lakeland
Today's Cathedral
A Lakeland Miscellany

ALSO BY GLADYS MARY COLES

(Editor)
Both Sides of the River:
              Merseyside in Poetry and Prose
The Poet's View: Poems for Paintings
              in the Walker Art Gallery
Poet's England: Lancashire
Poet's England: Cheshire
Poet's England: Wirral
Chester: a Collection of Stories (Chester Literature Festival)
Selected Poems of Mary Webb
Mary Webb: Collected Prose and Poems

(Poetry)
The Sounding Circle
Sinerva and Other Poems
The Snow Bird Sequence
Studies in Stone
Stoat, in Winter
Liverpool Folio
Leafburners: New and Selected Poems
The Glass Island
The Land Within

(Biography)
The Flower of Light: a Biography of Mary Webb
Mary Webb: a new biography

The Life of Riley

JOE RILEY
— 25 Years At The Liverpool Echo

Selected & Edited by
GLADYS MARY COLES

HEADLAND

First published in 2000
by
HEADLAND PUBLICATIONS
38 York Avenue, West Kirby,
Wirral, Merseyside. CH48 3JF

Copyright © Joe Riley 2000
Copyright © Gladys Mary Coles 2000: Selection & Introduction
Copyright © Peter Toyne 2000: Foreword

British Library Cataloguing in Publication Data.
A full CIP record for this book is available from the British Library

ISBN 1 902096 62 2

Printed in Great Britain by
L. Cocker & Co., Berry Street, Liverpool.

CONTENTS

Foreword by Professor Peter Toyne

Introduction by Gladys Mary Coles

FEATURES

SCREEN

STAGE

MUSIC

ART

COMMENT

PROFILES

FOREWORD

Unlike authors, journalists are published every day. Their columns, unlike books, may not be lengthy but they are the equivalent of 'Best Sellers' in terms of the numbers who read them. Yet, once published, they are usually forgotten - ephemera consigned to pulp.

How splendid it is, therefore, that a selection of the columns of one of Merseyside's best-selling journalists, Joe Riley, has been brought together heroically by Gladys Mary Coles in this anthology. With thousands of column inches from 25 years of articles in the *Liverpool Echo* to choose from, a representative selection has been made as a heartfelt tribute to the man who many think of not just as an outstanding journalist, but also as something of a Merseyside 'institution'.

In the best tradition of local journalism, Joe is a well-respected writer and trusted Arts critic who combines great literary style with searching objectivity and critical powers. Furthermore, he writes in plain English. And that's why he is such a valued visiting Lecturer in Journalism at the JMU Media School where he is passing on to the next generation of would-be journalists his immense journalistic experience and talents.

In publishing *The Life of Riley*, Joe's columns are no longer ephemera, they are destined for posterity - a fitting tribute to one who has stimulated, entertained, and occasionally even annoyed *Echo* readers over the last 25 years. We are both fortunate and proud to have such a 'Best Seller' in our midst.

Professor Peter Toyne DL
Vice Chancellor and Chief Executive
Liverpool John Moores University

INTRODUCTION

The idea for this book first occurred to me when I was researching the anthology *Both Sides of the River: Merseyside in Poetry and Prose* (1993) - a portrait of Merseyside, present and past, through literature. Looking through issues of the *Liverpool Echo*, I was impressed by the wealth of material in Joe Riley's columns. Ultimately, I selected two of his major features for my Merseyside anthology, but would have liked to have included many more if space had permitted. It was then that I determined to make a selection from Joe's columns which would represent all aspects of his achievement as a journalist with the *Liverpool Echo*. Clearly, such a collection would be fascinating to compile. It would also be a celebration not only of Joe's work but of Merseyside itself - an interesting and appropriate book to follow *Both Sides of the River* in which one of my principal aims was to widen public perception of Liverpool, and Merseyside as a whole, going beyond the clichéd images.

I searched through almost fifty volumes of Joe Riley's archive of articles, reading every word he has written in the *Echo* during the 25 years from 1974 to 1999. My intention was to bring together a collection of his finest pieces from features, interviews and profiles, and from his work as an Arts critic covering Screen, Stage, Music and the Fine Arts. The research was absorbing, the selection process difficult, with such a wide diversity of pieces from which to choose. I was aware, too, of the responsibility of my undertaking, and its importance - the material I was selecting and shaping into a book offers a unique view of the last quarter of the Twentieth Century.

The contents of the Features section are not arranged chronologically but have been grouped for interest. They range from those capturing historical moments, events of national and international interest such as the first Moonwalk, the visit of Pope John Paul, the completion of the Anglican Cathedral (the largest Gothic cathedral in Europe), to some of the most exciting and influential developments in the Arts world such as the opening of the Tate Gallery Liverpool. Many of these features have a strong Merseyside emphasis, reflecting the rich creativity of the region, and of Liverpool in particular, its significant contribution to the artistic life and culture of the nation.

As the *Echo's* Arts Editor, Joe Riley has interviewed most of the leading actors and directors of the last 25 years, and reviewed the major shows, concerts and exhibitions in the region. From these I made a representative selection, and for reasons of space had to exclude many pieces of equal interest which were vying for inclusion. The resulting miscellany will, I hope, appeal to a wide range of tastes and preferences.

Always crisply written, Joe's writing is consistently witty and informative. He has a distinctive voice and style not curbed by constraints of length, and is invariably pithy and exact (and sometimes provocative). Fortunate for Merseyside that this talented journalist has dedicated his career to his birthplace.

To assemble some biographical details, I put Joe Riley into the unaccustomed position of interviewee. He was educated at Merchant Taylors' School, Crosby (where he won the Public Speaking Prize); and on reaching the crossroads of career choice, although teaching was an option, Joe had no hesitation in choosing journalism. He joined *The Crosby Herald* on 12 June 1967 as a cub reporter, moving after 18 months to *The Southport Visiter*. In April 1970 he joined the *Daily Post* as a sub-editor, progressing to Leader Writer and Feature Writer. On 1 January 1974, at the age of 26, Joe Riley became the youngest Arts Editor in Britain when he was appointed to the *Liverpool Echo*.

Joe has won many national awards for his journalism. He was the first winner of the Press Awards 'Feature Writer of the Year' (1972), and won the National Arts Campaigning Award in 1978 (which he received from Richard Attenborough). In 1980 he was 'Cinema Writer of the Year' and, most recently, was awarded a B.T. Prize for Feature Writing.

A Fellow of the Royal Society of Arts (elected in 1976), Joe is also a musician in his own right, a member of the Royal College of Organists. Frequently an adjudicator at festivals of music and theatre, and a narrator, he has presented the St George's Hall carol concerts in Liverpool for the past eight years.

Joe's work has taken him all over the world, from America to the Far East. His American television review of the premiere of Paul McCartney's *Liverpool Oratorio* was seen coast to coast by an audience of 60 million. His travels have included more than 20 foreign tours with the Royal Philharmonic Orchestra. This year he travelled to Prague to cover the orchestra's performance in the Spring Festival. As a Senior Visiting Lecturer in Journalism at Liverpool John Moores University, he brings a wealth of experience to Media students.

This collection of Joe Riley's writings will, I hope, be a source of enjoyable reading for many years to come, as well as an enduring record of our times.

Gladys Mary Coles

For his valued encouragement and interest in this project, I wish particularly to thank Professor Peter Toyne, Vice-Chancellor of Liverpool John Moores University.

I am grateful for the generous support of
 Griffiths & Armour (Liverpool)
 Mace and Jones (Liverpool).

For their part in the production of the book in its various stages, my thanks are extended to:
 Richard Lloyd-Jones for design, cover, and typesetting
 Carole Baldock for typesetting and helpful suggestions
 Stella Lloyd-Jones for additional typesetting
 John Donnelly and Jim Grimes of L. Cocker & Co. (Liverpool) for their care and expertise in printing.

           G.M.C.

ACKNOWLEDGEMENTS

Grateful acknowledgement is made to the Liverpool Daily Post and Echo Ltd for kind permission to reproduce Joe Riley's articles, and also photographs from the *Liverpool Echo* archive.

Joe Riley dedicates this book
to the memory of his mother and father

FEATURES

FAREWELL, TALL SHIPS

It was one of the great spectacles of the world. Be in no doubt about that. Hopefully, it was also the time that Merseyside rediscovered itself - not just through the looking glass of history, but for a better future too.

The Grand Regatta Columbus - involving 8,000 crew from no fewer than 40 countries - showed Merseyside sunny side up. Five hundred years of nautical tradition galvanised into five days. As those 70 magnificent tall ships sailed over the horizon into the sunset of a glorious summer Sunday, you realised that the passage of time means nothing. Tomorrow's adventure is everything. Yet with those valiant ships went seven years of organisation and four months of physical endeavour.

It had been a long weekend of Champagne and Coca-Cola, of cartons of chips and plates of the finest beefsteak. But whether you came by Rolls Royce or push-chair, by plane, train or on foot, it scarcely mattered. Because, in all, more than a million people made the pilgrimage. Some had travelled from the ends of the earth. Others from the end of the street.

High in the sky, vintage aircraft soared where only hours earlier fireworks had crackled and sparkled. And beneath it all, the stately galleons came and went, enriching the lives of all who saw them. When historians come to tell this particular tale of the river-bank, they will see it as one of Merseyside's finest declarations of intent. And even Liverpool, once the second city of the Empire, will find few chapters to surpass this testament of international excellence.

Nothing could quite match the finale - The Grand Parade of Sail - as vessel after vessel took centre stage down the Mersey Channel. Leading the way, the four-masted Spanish Royal Naval training ship, *Juan Sebastian de Elcano*, was honoured with the great arch of a water cannon salute. Then other giants - like the Russian ships *Kruzenshtern, Sedov* and *Mir* - sailed alongside smaller, but no less worthy participants.

Christopher Columbus had but three ships. Yesterday's crowds had three score plus ten. The entire panorama resembled a painting by Canaletto. It could have been 1792 rather than 1992. These ships had constituted the greatest fleet assembled since the Battle of Trafalgar. But these are friendlier times. There had been a host of 'hellos'. Yesterday, however, it was time for goodbyes. This leaving of Liverpool was marked by both laughter and tears. And the hope that the Tall Ships will return to the Mersey. As the 1992 crews headed majestically for their home ports, the message from Merseyside was loud and clear: *God Speed - and Haste Ye Back.*

[17.8.1992]

OPERA SPECTACULAR

GRAND REGATTA COLUMBUS

The gods were kind to Britain's biggest-ever opera spectacular - performed in an 'instant' amphitheatre at Liverpool's Kings Dock last night. Despite the forebodings of Michael Fish and Co - 'Cloudy with drizzle' - and the Duke of York's own last minute aside - 'I hope they've brought their mackintoshes' - King Juan Carlos and Queen Sophia of Spain presided at a crisp and dry run of the ultimate gala of song to mark the Merseyside presence of the Grand Regatta Columbus.

Beneath a mackerel sky, and by the light of a silvery moon, an international audience of 14,000 were taken on a three-hour journey from straight Classical, through Flamenco to Broadway glitz. And the extravaganza ended with the entire assembly joining with soloists and the Royal Liverpool Philharmonic Choir and Orchestra in Liverpool's adopted anthem, *You'll Never Walk Alone.*

That finale, backed by a river skyline bright with fireworks, formed an image that will not fade for many a year in the minds of those present. But the eventual audience will be universal. For quite apart from the Welsh channel, S4C, presenting it live with the frightening title of *Cyngerdd Columbus A'r Byd Newydd*, and a concurrent relay on Radio 2, the rest of the world awaits the spectacle on film.

A quest which started out in the minds of its producers as a Philharmonic Hall concert - and then just grew and grew. More than seven months of detailed planning, and just three weeks of physical building turned the Kings Dock into a powerhouse for sound, complete with enough wattage to light a town the size of Birkenhead. On a stage framed by two 3,600 sq ft screens and a pair of 200ft ship's masts, the participants voyaged forth under the watchful eye of Master of Ceremonies, Sir Peter Ustinov.

And topping the bill with the sort of voice that could cut a diamond, the world's most recorded opera star, Montserrat Caballe, reportedly here for a mere £10,000 - said to be one fifth of her usual fee. A glittering line-up read like a *Who's Who* of opera, completed by Wallasey's own Rita Hunter (who had travelled from Australia); Alfredo Kraus; Dennis O'Neill; Julia Migenes; Justino Diaz; Mario Frangoulis and Dmitri Hvorostovsky.

The crowd had begun assembling more than two hours before the concert, and there was disappointment when a set of high gates by the royal reception tent were closed immediately prior to the arrival of the Spanish King and Queen. Queen Sophia wore a ravishingly beautiful lime green outfit, while the King's concession to fashion was a prominently pink tie. Minutes earlier, the Duke of York had been cheered when he arrived in company with the Lord Lieutenant of Merseyside, Henry Cotton.

Sir Peter Ustinov struck a blow for those who protest at the popular historic image of Christopher Columbus as a great explorer. The concert, he said, was an antidote 'to desperate cruelties'. But on a lighter note, he reminded the Spanish Royals that their ancestors didn't have the monopoly on patronage. 'John Cabot got £10 from Henry VII for discovering Canada,' he said.

The audience included no fewer than seven ambassadors as well as many visitors from America and Japan, who were guests of the Merseyside Development Corporation.

[15.8.1992]

EMPRESS OF IRELAND DISASTER

14 MINUTES...AND 1,012 PERISH

When the *Empress of Ireland*, a 14,000-ton Canadian Pacific liner sank in the St. Lawrence River on May 28, 1914, en route for Liverpool, mankind was on the brink of a war of unparalleled destructiveness. There were more important issues to fill the front pages of newspapers than the saga of her fate and the public inquiry that followed. Yet it was the greatest sea disaster of all time - more frightening in lives lost than the sinking of the *Titanic*.

The Liverpool registered ship, built on the Clyde for service on the Atlantic run - a task she and her sister *The Empress of Britain* undertook with new standards of speed - was not outstandingly large, nor outstandingly fashionable, despite the string orchestra which played daily for first and second class passengers amid a profusion of potted palms. Most of her passengers were East European migrants. The world was unlikely to pay the same sort of attention to this tragedy as it had to the sinking of the *Titanic* two years earlier when a substantial part of the New York social register had been snuffed out. And the *Titanic* had been the world's largest liner, regarded as unsinkable, and undertaking her maiden voyage. Nor were there the immense political repercussions that followed the later sinking by torpedo of the *Lusitania*, sent to her watery grave in 20 minutes.

But of this trio of nautical disasters, the loss of the *Empress of Ireland* brought the greatest passsenger death toll in the shortest space of time. After she collided with the Norwegian collier, *Storstad*, near the St. Lawrence riverside town of Rimouski, it took just 14 minutes for the liner to disappear to her final resting place 150ft. beneath the ink-black calm waters.

The mathematics of the disaster were shocking: of the 1,477 people who had sailed from Quebec nine-and-a-half hours earlier, 1,012 were to die. 840 were passengers and 172 were crew (compared with 807 and 696 respectively in the *Titanic* and 785 and 415 in the *Lusitania*). 90 per cent of the *Empress's* crew came from Liverpool. The news struck with appalling force in the closely-knit street communities. Crowds gathered at the CPR offices on the waterfront as information trickled in. As in Canada and London, the ordeal was made worse by the early baseless report that all on board had been saved. The terrible truth was that hundreds of passengers, especially in the third class accommodation down in the bowels of the ship, had died instantly as water flooded into the 350 sq.ft.wound in the ship's side at a rate of 60,000 gallons a second.

Even Captain Henry Kendall, with more than a quarter of a century of experience behind him, was unable to save her. At that moment, he may well have contemplated a bizarre version of Kipling's poem, *If,* which had been his life-long creed. If only the *Storstad* could hold her position in his ship's gaping side, she may hold up. If only he could beach her on the nearby coast. Both hopes were dashed. In the scramble that followed, few lifeboats could be launched because of the rate of the ship's demise. One boat was overwhelmed as the *Empress* rolled over. At that moment, Kendall was flung from the bridge into the sea, among hundreds of his floundering, drowning crew and passengers. He was one of the lucky ones. He survived, as did the young New Brighton born wireless operator, 23-year-old Ronald Ferguson, who seconds before had been sending out a distress call, until the ship's list had become so great as to tip the acid out of his stand-by batteries.

In those few moments, a legion of gallant, horrific and ironic stories were in the making. There is the account of the actor, Laurence Irving (son of the legendary Sir Henry Irving, who played many great roles on the Liverpool stage) kissing his wife as they disappeared beneath the waves. And the tale of Sir Henry Seton-Kerr, one-time Unionist MP for St. Helens and married into the Pilkington family, giving his life jacket to a fellow passenger.

The bringing together of all this information has been undertaken by London writer, James Croall, whose truly excellent book, *Fourteen Minutes*, is the first comprehensive account of the events of that awful night. Of course, such dramas demand inquests, and the man sent to Canada was John Charles Bingham, the Liverpool-born First Baron Mersey, who was to end up with the ominous distinction of heading enquiries into the *Titanic, Empress* and *Lusitania* disasters. The debate over exactly what happened, and which Croall examines in detail, was long and complicated. Suffice to say here that it centres on shipping's 'rules of the road' in relation to vessels' warning lights, and the movements of the *Empress* and *Storstad* in a blanket of fog.

But a unique epitaph to the whole affair was supplied by a quiet Irish ex-soldier, described as appearing rather toilworn, as well he might. For not only had he escaped from the *Empress's* stokehold with the river water foaming at his heels, he had also escaped under similar circumstances from the *Titanic*. Willam Clarke was cruelly qualified to compare the scene: 'There was no waiting for the *Empress*. The *Titanic* went down straight like a baby goes to sleep. The *Empress* rolled over like a hog in a ditch....' he told reporters.

[27.6.1980]

BLITZED! BUT WE NEVER CLOSED

70 SHIPS WRECKED, AND STILL THE PORT KEPT WORKING

The May Blitz of 1941 - seven successive nights on which the airborne might of Germany was thrown at Merseyside, ended with dockland smouldering in ruins. But the Port of Liverpool had remained open to keep up the vital flow of Britain's food and arms. The sinking of a ship in the Rover channel could have seriously impeded the flow of craft to quaysides, and the men who led this fight to keep the waterways clear belonged to the Marine Surveyor's Department.

As early as November 1940, intelligence reports indicated that the Germans were to end night raids on London and switch their main offensive to Liverpool. The Marine Department hurriedly consulted counterparts in London, Southampton and Plymouth. The 'team' at that stage - alarmingly small - was 50 men. The first real taste of what was to come was ladled out by the enemy on the night of March 11 - 12, when Birkenhead and Wallasey were heavily attacked. Further heavy raids followed on Bootle. But nothing was to equal the Luftwaffe fury of May 1941. Many craft were sunk or damaged in that week alone, and among those salvaged was the 10,000 ton captured German liner, *Europa*. To salvage vessels was crucial as every available pound of scrap metal was needed.

The Nazis were using a new weapon extensively for the first time - the land-mine. They were mainly designed to sink ships, but on ground, the blast devastated large areas of buildings. During this series of raids one of the Marine Department's main fears was realised. The floating crane, *Mammoth*, then the second largest in the world, was sunk at Birkenhead. The Germans knew that she was the only one in Britain capable of handling the great weight of battleship guns for replacement. The crane settled upright on the dock bottom and divers sealed up holes made by the bombs. A difficult task in water thick with oil and bombing debris. But the *Mammoth* was lifted and continued her essential work.

By the end of the May Blitz, the Marine Department had 70 wrecked ships on their hands. The river, and particularly the docks, were littered with them - 57 sunk in one ten-day period. The berths, many of them occupied, were of the utmost importance, as were their cargoes. During the week before the May raids, 145,000 tons of cargo were landed at the port. The following week, only 35,000 tons could be landed. It seemed only time before the port would be out of action. Then the raids stopped. One of the men in charge of the salvage operations recalls: 'It was hard to believe that the Germans didn't know what tremendous damage they had caused, and just gave up out of belief that they could never bring Merseyside to its knees.'

But it says much for the men and women who survived the ordeal that, a month later, the docks were once again capable of handling 108,000 tons in a week. The tonnage of wrecked and damaged ships dealt with by the salvage forces that May had been 207,000 dead weight. As the flickering curtain of flame stretched from the Gladstone system to Huskisson Dock, the staff of the Marine Department succeeded in defying Germany's wish to cripple the Mersey. Like the Windmill Theatre, it never closed.

[6. 9.1979]

THE BATTLE OF DERBY HOUSE

FRONT LINE: WHEN MERSEYSIDE WENT TO WAR

Winston Churchill described the Battle of the Atlantic as a war of groping and drowning, of ambuscade and strategy, of science and seamanship. Later, he admitted that what most frightened him about World War II was the U-Boat menace. On this war at sea hinged Britain's fortunes. Allied shipping brought vital supplies, and if German Grand Admiral Doenitz's fleet cut the lifeline, Britain would almost certainly sink.

Merseyside was the core of that lifeline. The Western Approaches Command, whose job was to ensure safe passage of Allied shipping, had other sea-going bases, but none more important than Gladstone Dock. The heavy bombing which Merseyside had endured and the harrowing losses at sea only strengthened resolve to beat Doenitz.

At the beginning, the U-Boat captains held the initiative. Doenitz had said in 1940: 'I will show that the U-Boat alone can win this war. Nothing is impossible to us.' Merseyside had taken a battering, but could dish it out too. Captain Johnny Walker, ace U-Boat killer, from Devon, who came to regard Bootle as a second home, reflected that determination as he set sail in sloops based at the Gladstone system, to the sound of his signature tune, *A Hunting We Will Go.*

If Walker was the killer captain, the plan's architect was Admiral Sir Max Horton, Commander-in-Chief, Western Approaches. He arrived on Merseyside in November 1942, already a naval legend. During the First World War, in command of submarine E9, he was the first British officer to sink an enemy warship. Eventually he lost count of the craft he accounted for. This stocky, determined man, who once lived at Betws-y-Coed and went to school at Llanrwst, had a simple brief: to sweep the Doenitz submarines from the ocean, to give safe passage to manpower and supplies for Britain.

He was based at Derby House, Liverpool, the main plot and operation room of the Battle of the Atlantic. This headquarters below ground was protected by steel doors and 12 feet of concrete. Facing the great map boards, where every shipping movement was plotted, were the 'choir stalls' from which duty officers watched. Above them in the 'upper stalls', Horton analysed the battle day and night.

Derby House, or 'The Citadel', as it was called by the forces' men, had its own radio for communication with ships and aircraft. It was connected by cable with the U.S.A. and other countries. During the war, staff handled more than 30 million coded messages. Horton took over command at a crucial time. He planned to surprise the enemy in mid-Atlantic with co-ordinated counter attacks by several highly trained frigates, working in groups with carrier borne and long range aircraft. The plan was two-fold. First, to launch a main offensive by naval and air striking forces to destroy the U-Boats clustering around the convoys in mid-ocean. Secondly, a subsidiary offensive by shore-based air forces to destroy U-Boats in the Bay of Biscay, to delay them in transit, to attack them in their bases and to destroy morale.

Rear-Admiral W. S. Chalmers, author of the book, *Max Horton and the Western Approaches*, recalled 25 years later: 'The hard truth of war was brought home to sailors and airmen alike - neither could exist without the other. Victory at sea came suddenly to the Allies, but it would have gone the other way if there had been no convoy system to ensure that the right force would be sent to the right place at the right time. It can be said with certainty that Horton's success in the Battle of the Atlantic will live in history as a classic example of the correct application and complete vindication of the ancient principles of war.'

But the grim battle had its humour. Close to Derby House, in Exchange Buildings, was housed the tactical training unit. This was an anti-submarine school in which miniature battles were fought daily with model ships and submarines deployed on the floor lino. Sometimes the battles were blacked out - to simulate darkness or fog. Officers under instruction had only the information of ASDIC signals.

One, Captain Gilbert Roberts, who ran the school, announced that he had devised a new method of sinking a U-Boat. Horton challenged him, and three times his toy U-Boat was sunk. No one dared tell him that the ship that sunk him three times was being operated by a Wren Third Officer working blind in another room.

But nothing could simulate the realities. The Battle of the Atlantic went first one way, then the other. There was near despair at the toll wrought by the U-Boats, but then jubilation as escort and support ships coming home reported more and more success.

Captain Walker played the prime part, backed up by air support. The R.A.F., in the form of the 15th Group, came to Derby House from Plymouth in 1941. It organised anti-U-Boat operations and covered the hunting and final sinking of the *Bismark* (plotted throughout from Liverpool), and dogged blockade runners. Its range widened, and in May 1943, the great area known as the Atlantic Gap, initially outside aircraft reach, was closed. No fewer than 40 U-Boats were sunk that month, and Doenitz sent out a signal recalling home his sea wolves - or what was left of them. It was a message acknowledging defeat.

And so, on May 23, 1943, the tide turned - a date in British naval history to rank equal to that of Trafalgar. The lifeline of Britain was kept intact. During 68 months of war, Allied shipping brought 19 million tons of food, one million tons of shells, bombs and ammunition, 66,000 tons of tanks and war vehicles, as well as petrol, cotton, iron and steel into Liverpool Docks - a remarkable achievement. Even more importantly 3.5 million British and 1.2 million American fighting men and women were transported from Liverpool.

Horton retired in 1945. He was later given Honorary Freedom of the City of Liverpool - an honour which he said he shared with 100,000 officers, men and women. Five years later his funeral cortège passed through Liverpool, accompanied by 500 naval ratings. Huge crowds gathered. In Leece Street, a veteran sailor decked in medals wept unashamedly: 'My old boss,' he told an *Echo* reporter.

Later that afternoon, an admiral's ashes were placed in a niche in the South-East transept of Liverpool Cathedral - The Cathedral of the Western Approaches.

[7. 9. 1979]

THE DAY THAT CHANGED THE WORLD

LIVERPOOL'S KEY ROLE IN MAKING THE A-BOMB

On the sixth day of August 1945, mankind stepped over the threshold into the shadow of 'The Bomb'. The 9,000lb 'Little Boy' atom bomb went off above the Japanese city of Hiroshima. Altogether, 78,000 of its inhabitants lay dead or were doomed to die in that awful elimination. Three days later, the Allies dropped the larger 'Fat Boy' bomb, and a second name, Nagasaki, was added to Hiroshima in the history books.

This action by American Air Force craft effectively put an end to the Second World War. But it has also meant that, ever since, man has possessed the means to destroy the world. Yet had it not been for the profound, if dangerous, strides made in Liverpool five years earlier, the Allies may never have had the bomb.

The role played by Professor Sir James Chadwick and his team in research at Liverpool University is one of the most dramatic stories of science. Chadwick had startled colleagues in 1932 by discovering an uncharged particle, the neutron, and thereby completely transforming the conception of the constitution of matter. Chadwick's discovery, for which he received a Nobel Prize, was fundamental. For the neutron is the agent which causes the atomic bomb to 'work'. It has no electric charge of its own, and is able to penetrate the nucleus of atoms, thereby causing disintegration.

Chadwick was appointed Lyon Jones Professor of Physics at Liverpool University, and in 1939, installed a cyclotron. A huge machine, occupying the whole of one floor, it was used to accelerate particles to speeds at which they split any atom they hit. For the work, Chadwick collected about him a team of young scientists working along similar lines. They included the Polish exile, Joseph Rotblat, later to become secretary of 'Pugwash', an international group of scientists dedicated to promoting world peace; another exile, Otto Frisch, from Austria; T. G. Pickvance, St Helens-born and J. R. Holt from Runcorn.

The original plan was to undertake 'pure research for its own sake'. However, developments were soon to alter this. Intelligence reports indicated a growing fear that Hitler's Germany was about to stumble on the atomic truth (not until near the end of the war did the fear diminish). Meanwhile, the Americans had almost given up the idea of an atom bomb. No doubt they were surprised when visiting Chadwick and his team to find that the British calculations meant the bomb was theoretically feasible. The Liverpool team moved almost wholesale to America, although it took some special string-pulling in Washington to allow Rotblat to enter. Once installed at their base at Los Alamos, the Americans made sure they wanted for nothing. On one occasion they indented for a dentist's chair as a joke, and it duly arrived.

The result of the Los Alamos project saw the first bomb test exploded in the New Mexican Desert on July 16, 1945. Six years later, in 1951, Chadwick was to contend that the production of the bomb was delayed for about 12 months because of failure to achieve full co-operation between American and British research workers. But the stage was now set for the fateful day at Hiroshima. Two thousand American airforce men were interviewed for duty, and one third rejected. The rest took part in a rigorous training programme. Eventually, in practice runs, crews could hit a 500ft circle from 30,000ft.

And so the Atomic Age was ushered in, and all former methods of combat made dated by the crew of *Anola Gay*, a B29 Superfortress aircraft. Their mission was to become the greatest single act of warfare ever perpetrated. It was Rotblat who provided a moving postscript: 'Human imagination can only take in a certain amount of horror, and this was a new chapter in horror ... One always hoped that it would not be used or that one had made a mistake and the bomb would not go off.'

But it did. Experiments at Liverpool University had helped change the course of mankind.

[24.10.1979]

CAPTAIN JOHNNY WALKER

HERO OF THE HIGH SEAS

As a lad, in the days when you could go down the docks for a Sunday treat without being suspected of terrorism or smuggling, my Dad used to take me to the West Wall of Gladstone Dock, and tell tales of a brave man called Johnny Walker.

My father was in no doubt that he was a Naval hero as great as Drake or Nelson. For Captain Frederick John Walker, ace German U-boat killer, had masterminded victory in the Battle of the Atlantic. And had not Mr Churchill himself said that without triumph in this quarter, Britain may have lost the war? So while other boys took their heroes from the pages of fiction (Flash Gordon was the favourite), I had a real hero.

There were real reasons too: not least, because my grandparents had been Mayor and Mayoress of Bootle in 1941-42 and had become close friends of the Walkers. Indeed, when the already legendary Captain died from exhaustion, aged just 48, in the old Liverpool Naval Hospital, on July 8 1944, it was my grandfather who broke the tragic news to his wife. The death certificate gave the cause of death as cerebral thrombosis, but in less clinical terms, there was no doubt that Walker burned himself out. In between missions, he used the mayoral parlour at Bootle Town Hall as a personal retreat, and would often be found there, simply asleep. Not that there wasn't time for fun, even in the dark days of war: one of Walker's party tricks was to drink a tankard of ale while standing on his head!

But there was vital work to be done, and Johnny Walker told my grandfather: 'They're giving me a free hand, and I'm going to show them what I can do.' He became 'U-boat killer number one.' His name today is associated with two ships, *Starling* and *Stork*, and he took as his signature tune, *A-Hunting we will go*. Each time he returned to the 'sheltering arms' of Gladstone Dock (letter, March 16 1942), the melody would ring out on the quayside. But under his wing as commander were other support vessels, all with bird names like *Wild Goose, Wren, Kite, Cygnet, Woodpecker* and *Magpie*. He referred to them as his 'Chicks'.

There are, however, acts which set men apart: Captain Walker's most dramatic gesture was to order the hoisting of the General Chase, which could be decoded as 'Every Man For Himself'. In the whole of British Naval history, this had only happened twice before: it was used by Drake when he chased the Spanish Armada from the Channel, and by

Nelson when he defeated Napoleon's fleet at the Battle of the Nile.

All of these things - and so much more - are honoured and remembered each year on Merseyside. And so it was with considerable pride that I took Captain Walker's wartime letters aboard the Duke of York's ship, the destroyer *HMS Edinburgh*, yesterday, berthed in Bootle in honour of Walker and his men, and on an occasion when, once again, fathers brought children for a day out of remembering. Lt. Comdr. Angus Ross, who had organised *Edinburgh's* visit to Liverpool, told me: 'Our visit has been a real pleasure, and although this is in many ways a public relations exercise in peace time, we are nevertheless in perpetual readiness for work in the equator northwards.' It is, one feels sure, a readiness which Johnny Walker would never have devalued.

[8.5.1989]

MONTY

ON THE DAY THE QUEEN MOTHER UNVEILS HIS MEMORIAL STATUE, A PERSONAL PORTRAIT OF THE HERO OF ALAMEIN, THE ACTION MAN WITH THE HUMAN TOUCH

Joe Riley talks to Tom Bigland,
the man who served as liaison officer between Field Marshal
Montgomery and the American General Omar Bradley from the
D-Day Invasion campaign until final victory in Europe.

Tom Bigland will be 70 on Monday, but last night he was in London with his old Army pals celebrating the anniversary of the D-Day invasion, 36 years ago to-day.

Mr Bigland, who reached the rank of Lieutenant Colonel in the Royal Artillery, and was awarded the D.S.O. during the Libyan Campaign, now lives in retirement in the Wirral village of Willaston. He has worked as a stockbroker and in wine trade management in Liverpool, but his love of the Army and scouting have run like a silver thread through his life. And because of his liaison duties during the last war, he was as near as one could be to the heart-beat of battle strategy.

Everyone has their stories about the legendary Monty, but many are second or third-hand. Tom Bigland, however, had the job of reporting on the day-to day plans that led to final victory. If Churchill inspired the Home Front, then Monty, equally, inspired the battlefront.

'Even if you were a junior officer, as I was, Monty came across as very human and easy to get on with. But even if you were a senior general, you had to be on the network or not. He did say more than once that it was his job to win the war, and if he thought a particular general could carry out what he wanted, he would employ that general. He used to say that although the other chap might be equally good, there was no time to find out at that moment. He wouldn't have people around who were fat and unfit. I can well remember before D-Day he sacked a very nice and very able chap who'd come back from the Middle East, and several people were very upset at this. But Monty simply said that he was too fat. It was going to be a tough invasion and he couldn't have people around who might crack. This chap may have been as good as some other people, but he wasn't fit.

Monty was a most amazing man, and I think he will go down in history as the man who defeated the Axis Powers in the war. It was amazing, because he was never really the top commander. At Alamein, where it all started, he was under Alexander, and this continued through North Africa, Sicily and Italy. He was then under Ike in Europe, and for this campaign never commanded more than 17 divisions, which was all we could raise in the last year of the war, compared with 63 American divisions, with Bradley commanding over 40 for most of the time.

Whenever 21st Army Group had to be strengthened, it was always with American divisions, and although the most friendly and cooperative relations were established, it can also be said this was not always popular with the Americans. Of course, Eisenhower's great achievement was in getting the Americans and the British working together so well. I think there was mutual respect between Monty and Ike, but I think Monty disagreed a great deal with his ideas on how to win the war. Bradley and Georgie Patton were just as fed up with Ike at times. He would never make his bloody mind up and was never up to date with the battle. I can well remember in Luxembourg when one of his planning staff went back to Paris with three plans and said: "For God's sake, Sir, say 'yes' to one of them!".

Meanwhile, Monty was relishing the charisma that had surrounded him since the desert campaign. Although he neither drank nor smoked, he was famous for carrying cigarettes to hand out to the troops. Mind you, I'm sure he had a glass of champagne at the dinner following the signing of the surrender. And I still maintain he had some Rothschild wine at one of the late dinner parties. I've no real grounds for saying this, but I always felt that Alexander deliberately let Monty take the limelight. We needed someone in the Middle East to counter Rommel, who was something of a myth in the desert. Monty loved it. I don't think he was theatrical about it. He just saw it as part of the job.

He had a very great ability to communicate. Before D-Day he went round every unit and spoke to them personally. He also went round the factories and spoke there. It was publicity, but publicity with an object. The initial invasion was entirely under Monty's command and it was magnificently done. It should be emphasised how wonderfully the Americans worked with him and how very good he was at achieving this.

Come what may, Monty would go to bed early but demand to be briefed at 6.30 am the next day. He was a man of very great control. After all, once a plan has been drawn up and started, there's not much you can do about certain things.'

Tom recalls how, though he didn't drink or smoke, Monty loved a bet. 'He kept a betting book, and I remember having to ask him for £5 he owed to General Sibert over a bet as to when the war would end. I got him to sign the £5 note - and within half an hour I should think there were a hundred copies.'

Monty believed the war in Europe would not be over until June 1945. In fact, it finished in May.

[6.6.1980]

THE GLORY THAT IS ST GEORGE'S

People were sentenced to death there for piracy, poisoning and street shoot-outs. It contains a priceless mosaic floor and a unique and massive concert organ. And for good measure, there's a cat buried in the basement. Even in this week of Tate grabbing headlines, St George's Hall cannot - and it seems, will not - be upstaged.

The great neo-classical pile, designed by a young man who had never been to Greece or Rome, opens all of its doors to the public next Monday. Which means that everything, from the deepest prison cell to the loftiest decorated vaulting, will be on view for the first time since 1984, when the law courts moved out, the Home Office grants ceased, and the Hatton administration, blind to anything which smacked of inherited wealth, shut up shop. For the Hall, still at the hub of the City, was the epitome of Liverpool's nineteenth century prestige as the second city of the entire British Empire.

It was built between 1841 and 1854, at a time when corporation was trying to out-do corporation to gain the municipal laurels. Liverpool Council came top of the league. It gave the city - nay, the nation - what was described in an architects' journal at the time as 'the greatest building in the world.' If that seems a little over the top, then perhaps we can accept the late Sir John Betjeman's twentieth century assessment of it as 'the finest neo-classical building in Europe.' By any standards it has a magnificence which even in present day Communist Bloc countries would not be allowed to deteriorate.

And so, in the nick of time, Liverpool's newly aware Labour council, in conjunction with the Museum's aptly-named Large Objects Department, has agreed to cast aside the dust sheets for a summer of concerts, workshops, theatre performances and audio-visual tours.

The flavour-of-the-month bosses at the new Tate, faced with their own cash-flow crisis, may take heart from knowing that St George's Hall came into being a quarter of a million pounds over budget - it cost £380,000. The architect was only a novice, 25-year-old Harvey Lonsdale Elmes. He did not commit suicide, as popular local myth has it, 'because the hall was built the wrong way around.' Yet tragically, he did not live to see his greatest creation completed, for he died from tuberculosis in 1847, aged only 33, and leaving a wife and only son penniless.

As to whether the giant pillars of the hall's main frontage that overlooks Lime Street, should have faced what is now St John's Gardens, remains a point of conjecture. But what is known is that the foundation stone was laid 18 months before the architects' design competition was held, and is nowhere near the building!

Inside, the three great treasures are the decorated floor, comprised of 30,000 tiles, and now uncovered for only the ninth time this century; the great 7,000-pipe Willis organ, originally the largest instrument in the UK, and still the third largest (the largest is now in Liverpool Cathedral); and the delightful small concert room, completed by Elmes' successor, Charles Cockrell. But the law courts, famous as the scene of the death sentence passed on Florence Maybrick in 1889 for allegedly poisoning her husband, are also much in demand by passing film makers.

Who needs to build scenery for a good gallows period piece when you can hire the real thing? In recent times, it is the film industry and TV which have prevented St George's Hall from being completely mothballed. The new internationally screened Coca Cola advert (complete with massed choir of local children) was made there, part of a Granada TV *Sherlock Holmes* episode was filmed there, and only last month the BBC's *Antiques Road Show* was filmed there for transmission early next year. Presenter Hugh Scully described it as 'the most fabulous setting the show had ever had in 20 years.'

Tea dances, political rallies, charitable bazaars, comic shows and exhibitions have all graced St George's Hall, in addition to the once renowned organ recitals given by the legendary W. T. Best, who had the habit of plunging his head into a basin of cold water after concerts, and once shooed Queen Victoria away from the console until he had finished playing. A First Lord of the Admiralty, Sir John Graham, was also refused entry by a door-man 'because he didn't look as if he was there on business.'

Charles Dickens gave readings at St George's Hall while waiting to sail to America from Liverpool, but it was a lesser-known writer, Maud Budder, who immortalised the building in verse:

> Assizes judges as they go
> Beneath the massive portico
> Are heard to mutter: 'Bless my wig,
> This hall is really rather big.'

Surprising facts about St George's Hall:

- On plunging 82 feet from the roof in the 1850s, a workman got up, told his mates he'd had a 'great fall' and then fainted. He returned to work two weeks later.
- If 2,000 people attended a concert (as they did for the inaugural

ceremonies), they would need 20 million mouthfuls of air.
- Organ loving pussy-cat Mr Jinks is buried in the basement of the hall. During organ tuning sessions, the cat was to be found purring contentedly, his whiskers blowing in the breeze from the pipes.
- The chandeliers, each of which weighs three quarters of a ton, were originally lit by 140 gas jets, and described as 'quite electrical' when first seen. During the opening ceremony they received a round of applause.
- The supports for the star-spangled chandeliers are modelled on the prows of Greek ships.
- Each pair of brass doors in the hall weighs 43 hundredweight.
- 1855 saw an outburst in the press about the 'scant clothing' of some of the hall's statues. It was the patron saint of thieves and merchants, Mercury, who came in for most criticism.
- The barrel-vaulted ceiling is one foot wider than the Baths of Caracalla in Rome, which inspired it.

[27. 5. 1988]

FANFARE ENDS 74 YEARS' TOIL

A CATHEDRAL IS BORN

It's not every day that new cathedrals are completed. But the final dedication of Liverpool Cathedral today, in the presence of the Queen, was in every way a unique occasion. Beneath the glare of television lights, which gave magnificent relief to the pink sandstone of Sir Giles Scott's architectural masterpiece, Liverpool inherited the first mother church in the Northern province of England since the Reformation.

It is the fifth largest church in the world - the last of Britain's great cathedrals, and the biggest in the Anglican Communion. But this Goliath on the skyline of the city of the Orange and Green, was today the focus of an ecumenical act of worship, imposing a vision of unity which itself symbolised the Queen's later meeting with other churchmen on Merseyside. The great service - described as a drama in three acts, and using every inch of the vast interior - represented the beginning, the continuing and the completion of an enterprise spanning 74 years.

The bells, more than 200 feet up in the tower, rang out, the mighty organ roared and trumpets and drums sounded. Everyone in the 2,500 strong congregation, drawn from a cross-section of diocesan and community interests, sang mightily. There was a sense of pageantry and an eloquence of language to equal anything in the history books, but today this was clothed within a wholly 20th century fabric, built to last 1,000 years.

The Queen's entry into the cathedral, watched by waving crowds who swarmed around St. James' Mount, was heralded by a fanfare. She was accompanied by Mr Malcolm Harrison, chairman of the cathedral's executive committee, and the Archbishop of York, the Most Rev Stuart Blanch. The Queen was conducted to a seat near the steps to the choir by Dean Edward Patey. It was then, with two verses of the National Anthem, that the majesty of the service was truly struck up - that unmistakeable Liverpool Cathedral sound echoing through every arch.

Half an hour earlier, three hundred clergy from parishes in the diocese as well as chaplains, layworkers, deaconesses, readers and canons *emeriti*, and visiting clergy from near and far, including many bishops, had entered in procession. It was a special and great moment for the £5 million enterprise.

At the very heart of the service was the bond of friendship between Liverpool's two cathedrals - a friendship that would have seemed impossible at the turn of the century. The Archbishop of Liverpool, the Most Rev Derek Worlock presented Dean Patey with a Jerusalem Bible 'in the name of the Roman Catholic community in this city.'

For the final part of the service, the Queen, with the Archbishop of York, was conducted to a seat beneath the nave bridge for the climax of the day - the historic words of appropriation. Mr Malcolm Harrison told the Dean: 'On behalf of the Liverpool Cathedral Executive Committee, whose responsibility it has been to direct the building of this House of God, I ask you to take into your charge the third bay of the nave, near which we now stand, and thereby a completed cathedral.' The new section was then dedicated by Bishop Sheppard, and after the resounding premiere of *A Song of Creation*, composed by former chorister John Madden, the Queen unveiled the Completion Stone to commemorate her presence at the service. But to the waiting crowd outside, the ultimate spectacle must have been that of a reigning monarch emerging from a freshly minted Gothic cathedral in 1978 AD. At last, the work is finished.

After the service, the Queen attended a private reception in the cathedral's Western Rooms, where she met members of staff and those involved in the building work. During the reception she was presented with a commemorative plate by Mr Harrison. She also received a specially bound copy of my book, entitled *Today's Cathedral*, published to coincide with the completion of the cathedral. Before leaving, the Queen signed an illuminated scroll to mark her presence at the service of dedication and thanksgiving.

[25. 10. 1978]

POPE JOHN PAUL

HE CAME, HE SAW AND HE CONQUERED

'Thank you very much ...' The most heartfelt emotions can be summed up in the simplest of phrases, and those four small words were all that the Pope needed to prove to the Church Omnipotent and the world that he had taken Liverpool to his heart.

They appeared on no programme or service sheet. They were the spontaneous and loudly proclaimed thanks of the 246th successor of St Peter as he concluded his blessing at the altar of Liverpool's Anglican Cathedral, facing the largest ecumenical gathering ever assembled on Merseyside. Only minutes earlier, in Toxteth, as he made his way from Liverpool Airport to the largest church in the Anglican communion, he had turned to bless a small pocket of Protestant protestors still recalling the words of John Ryle, the first Bishop of Liverpool. 'Beware of countenancing any retrograde movement in the country towards Rome.' But once at the great west doors of this great cathedral, he was made aware of man's willingness to bury differences in what was once the city of the orange and the green.

There to greet him was David, sixth Bishop of Liverpool. And as the massive doors of the cathedral were flung open wide to the sound of brass fanfares and organ music and singing, the pages of the old history books were firmly closed. Within seconds the loudest noise in the building was that of clapping hands, acclaimed by the Psalmists of old. The tanned, slightly stooped figure of a man in a white skullcap was dwarfed as it made its way up the Nave beneath the highest Gothic arches ever constructed, designed by Sir Giles Scott, himself a convert to Roman Catholicism. Above, in the tower, the world's loftiest peal of bells rang out.

There could be no greater setting for John Paul, Superstar, to set the seal on the story of Hope Street, where at either end two great Christian families had raised their hopes to the skies as twentieth century acts of faith. The Pope was overwhelmed by the grandeur of the event and overcome by the enthusiasm of his welcome, and at no time was his smile more telling than when, with characteristic unpredictability he moved from the altar steps to congratulate the choir, under their director, Ian Tracey, on the singing of a Christmas carol from his native Poland.

The congregation, too, was as spontaneous as the Pontiff as they added further dimension to all the clapping and the singing with three resounding cheers. The ecumenical service at Canterbury Cathedral on Saturday may have been the standard bearer for Christian unity in Britain, but it was in Liverpool Cathedral that the Pope most truly felt the groundswell of support for that initiative. And it was from there that he left for an historic journey down Hope Street, to be with his own flock at the Metropolitan Cathedral on the fifteenth anniversary of its consecration.

It was the late Cardinal Heenan, then Archbishop of Liverpool, who two decades ago inverted the title of Liverpool's famous road and incorporated it into the oft-quoted phrase of 'a street called Hope'. For a time, the spirit of ecumenism went little beyond lip service, but latterly it has grown into a unique phenomenon in British Christian kingsmanship, with both cathedrals exchanging preachers and choirs and visitors. John Paul's journey down this road, also known for its colleges and arts venues and pubs, was the full blossoming of that spirit of togetherness.

Outside the Metropolitan Cathedral, a crowd of 2,000 young people raised their voices in song: 'Let there be love shared among us, let there be peace shared among us,' they proclaimed. When he faced the capacity congregation inside Frederick Gibberd's more modern Space Age cathedral, the Pope was immediate and eloquent in his appeal for reconciliation. 'The sin of disunity among Christians, which has been with us for centuries, weighs heavily upon the church,' he said. 'A restoration of unity among Christians is one of the main concerns of the church in the last part of the twentieth century. This task is for us all. No one can claim exemption from this responsibility.'

In his welcome to the Pope, Archbishop Derek Worlock, the man most responsible for salvaging the Papal trip from the entanglements of a war 8,000 miles away, said that he hoped that the Hope Street journey would light a torch for reconciliation. Meanwhile, the Pentecostal Mass, like everything else on this most memorable of days, was lit by bright sunlight and warmed by an outside temperature of 75 degrees Fahrenheit.

But it was not just the temperature that made the Pope feel as if he was home among the more familiar Vatican pilgrims. It was the vocal strength and unity of the crowds who lined his route and whose enthusiasm more than compensated for a smaller turn-out than the organisers had expected. Many had stayed at home to watch the Liverpool visit on television, perhaps put off by the anticipation of crowds so large as to obscure a glimpse of the Pope from lesser vantage points. Yet, as it was, many people were able to leave the Anglican Cathedral and move down Hope Street in time to see the Holy Father's arrival at Brownlow Hill. Even at the Airport, the attendance had been about half of what was expected. But 150,000 people are still capable of making a welter of noise — and they did. From the minute the Pope stepped from his helicopter and his skullcap blew off, you could tell the Liverpool visit was going to be different. And within minutes the Pope was demonstrating his outstanding ability at splicing together the formal and informal aspects of his British visit.

For while he is well capable of kissing babies and even stopping to pick up a person's dropped rosary beads, he is also a man of serious words. At the Airport, he had a message for Merseyside's 128,000 unemployed 'and all people of goodwill'. He told the crowds: 'In many countries unemployment has risen sharply and caused hardship to individuals and families. It tends to sow seeds of bitterness, division and even violence. The young feel unable to find a job, feel cheated of their dreams, while those who have lost their jobs feel rejected and useless.' This was an apparent reference to the riots in Toxteth less than a year ago, and minutes later, the Pope was driving through those troubled streets, now sunny and filled with newly leafed trees. But this was not a muted political ploy on a pastoral visit. The Pope's route through Toxteth had been planned well in advance of the troubles. It had arisen almost two years ago, when Derek Worlock issued his invitation following the National Pastoral Congress of Catholics in Liverpool.

Let it never be forgotten that this was the genesis of the rejoicing in Liverpool today, and rejoicing that began - and for many culminated - in the story of a street called Hope. Nor let the masters of St James' Mount or Brownlow Hill forget the words of the man whom the Pope came to represent: 'Tu es Petra ... Thou Art Peter and upon this rock shall I build my church.'

[1. 6. 1982]

TERRY WAITE

THE WORLD REJOICES

At last - a happy ending to the nightmare that has lasted almost five years. News of Terry Waite's imminent release, is, of course, a triumph for international diplomacy.

But it is also a triumph for the individual spirit. A freedom which has come as much from firm Faith and undying Hope as from physical endurance. Furthermore, it is a battle which has been almost as hard fought here in the North-West as in distant Beirut. For Terry Waite, whose father was a Cheshire policeman, went to school at what is now Bridgewater High School at Appleton, near Warrington. His mother, Mrs Lena Waite, still lives in the quiet countryside of Lymm. And those communities, like tens of thousands of other individuals in the wider family of the Church, have been unceasing in their prayers for Terry's well-being.

Yet during the seemingly endless days and nights since the Archbishop of Canterbury's Special Envoy was snatched on January 20, 1987, it was Terry's own unshakeable belief in God which saw him through the hell of it. Similarly, his wife, Frances, who has deliberately shunned publicity, declared from the start: 'In God's time, Terry will return.' Indeed, one of the things she packed in her husband's suitcase prior to his fateful departure was a Bible.

Yet Terry Waite, now 52, was never a 'rowdy' Christian. On the contrary, he had a great respect for other beliefs. Which is why, also in his luggage that day, was a book on the Druze faith - the faith of those he had befriended in Beirut, and who would serve as his bodyguards. His style had always been one of quiet competence, based on many so-called 'Missions Impossible'. In Uganda, he had learned what it was like to look down the wrong end of a gun barrel on several occasions. He had gone there to negotiate with the bloody regime of Idi Amin - a man once rumoured to have cooked a bishop and had him served up for a dinner party. And Terry had also been ushered into the company of the equally feared Ayatollah Khomeni; squatted on the floor of the tented homestead of Colonel Gaddafi, and done the diplomatic round of South Africa - where he bravely flouted the state emergency laws

Less then six months prior to his disappearance - on a much more enjoyable mission - he had been to Liverpool to receive an honorary Doctor of Laws degree from the University, on July 11, 1986. When I spoke to him on that day - we sipped sherry together in the peaceful surroundings of the Philharmonic Hall - Terry was philosophical rather than evangelical about his role on behalf of the then Archbishop of Canterbury, Crosby-born Robert Runcie. 'I have always had to be careful. You never know what's going to happen,' he told me.

Little did anyone know that his third trip to Beirut - ironically, to negotiate for the release of hostages Terry Anderson, Chief Middle East Correspondent of Associated Press, and Thomas Sutherland, Acting Dean of Agriculture at the American University there - would be his last. In the months that followed, there were all sorts of wild reports of his impending release. Others said that he had been killed, and one talked of him being 'sentenced to death.' But now the scaremongers have had their day. Terry Waite is to be freed at last - and all the Church, in every corner, shouts 'Amen!'

[18.11.1991]

PRINCESS DIANA

CHANCE IN A LIFETIME MEETING

Diana was every inch the magical princess of the children's story books. A being beyond reach in the aspirational sense, but very much in touch with people, often spurning formality to bring that very special 'something' to the unexpected moment. It was at such a time that I met her quite by chance.

She had come to Liverpool Cathedral - not on the now-famous occasion when she was photographed with Prince Charles for one of the last times - but on a less formal visit. The Princess genuinely loved Liverpool Cathedral and was visibly awestruck by its monumental sense of space. She was once given a personal and private tour of the building by the Dean, The Very Rev Derrick Walters, and the cathedral organist, Ian Tracey, played music especially for her.

My own experience of meeting her was prior to that. I had decided to make my 'escape' from the building using a little-known route beneath the cathedral Nave, along a corridor bordering a reception area known as The Western Rooms. I simply rounded a corner, and there she was; no time for formal introductions. I knew who she was, of course; she looked at me somewhat less decidedly and must have wondered who I was and where I was going. But as is Royal style, she smiled and was the first to say hello. I responded likewise and remember asking whether she was enjoying the day. A fatuous question maybe, but what else do you do when suddenly confronted by a magical princess?

She was standing side on when I first saw her, and I remember thinking just how very, very slim she was (this was before any talk of bulimia). She looked like a delicate china doll, her high cheeks slightly rouged, the hair immaculate, the eyes sparkling. We talked for all of what must have been 90 seconds. It seemed much longer. Yes, she did like the cathedral. 'Amazing' was the word she used to describe it - twice. And then she was gone. A chance encounter with the fairy tale princess was over, but never to be forgotten.

[1.9.1997]

DANCE HALL DAYS

'We may now have two cathedrals, but there's only one Grafton,' says Lizzie, fuschia pink from blue rinsed roots to spangled shoes, as she glides across the dance floor to the sounds of Glen Miller. And Lizzie is most definitely *In The Mood*. It might as well be 1939 as 1999.

When the real Glen Miller's plane disappeared over the English Channel, the Grafton was in its heyday. Britain's most famous *palais de dance*, built for £15,000, was a refuge from the ravages of war for service men and women and civilians alike. As the sirens sounded, there was the choice of carrying on dancing or heading for the shelters. Hundreds stayed dancing: *Land of Hope and Glory, We'll Meet Again*, Union Jacks waving.

When, a generation on, rock 'n' roll wreaked havoc with the former graces, and later still, managers fought falling receipts with cabaret boxing and Madonna videos, it seemed that the Grafton was permanently on the verge of falling into moribund ruin. But what goes around, comes around - not least the glitter ball in the ceiling. It's renaissance time. Once again, on Wednesday afternoons, the programme is strictly ballroom: waltz, foxtrot, tango. No longer demoted to the call-signs of taxis, but reclaimed as three very good reasons for putting on a posh frock and going for a twirl.

There was a time when 2,000 underfloor springs would have aided Our Lizzie's musical progress. But even the replacement flat dance floor cannot obliterate the memories. And they were queuing up to prove it. Folk like Christine and Derek Lowkes, and Eva and George Smart, all of whom had travelled from Wirral for the ballroom revival: 'We saw it advertised in the *Echo*,' said Christine.

There's a chorus of approval from the others waiting to pay a quid a head (including free raffle ticket) for the privilege of shaking a leg. 'We used to come here every Thursday and Saturday afternoon,' recalls George Smart. 'This is the first time we've been back in 40 years.'

That's music to the ears of Grafton manager, Allan Cannon - 'a hundred last week, more this week.' Not bad. When the Beatles played here in '63 for the princely sum of £45, only 200 turned up. Allan notably described his building on telly as a 'fantasy factory'. And for thousands of intentionally amorous Scousers, spanning 75 years, that's true. Those whom the fragrance of *Coty l'Aimant* and the whiff of *Brylcreem* have joined together, let no man put asunder. They danced to the bands of Jack Hylton, Salvador Scala, Roy Fox, Henry Hall, Ambrose, Joe Loss and Victor Sylvester. One night, Duke Ellington came over after a concert at the Empire and played into the small hours.

And who remembers Wilf Hamer, the man whose band included the largest piano in the world - an instrument brought to the Grafton by Liverpool firm, Rushworths? Hamer was one of the immortals. His brother John, rechristened in showbiz as Malcolm Munro, managed the Grafton for three decades. Malcolm, who died aged 80 in 1971, was the UK's leading ballrom dance teacher - and the subject of a more sober BBC documentary called *Dancing Life*.

When the Grafton opened in January 1924 with no speeches, the National Anthem and immediate swing music for the fashionable Flappers, there was a temperance café in the balcony. Someone who remembers it is Maurice Finlay, a retired barber born in Smithdown Road, now 89, and back at the Wednesday sessions. 'It's the first time I've been through the doors since 1938,' he told me. 'The balcony was at the back of the hall and even the bands used to play down that end sometimes.' Like Alf and May Fieldsend from Kensington at the next table, Maurice is game for any of the dances during the four-hour session: 'We think the TV series has let Liverpool down,' says Alf, 'We're glad there's still another side to the Grafton story.'

And some have come a very long way to make the point - like May Flanagan (neé Disley), a former shop assistant at George Henry Lee's, who emigrated to Toronto in 1955. She's here for a month visiting her sisters: 'I used to do tap dancing. I was in shows with Ken Dodd.'

From her handbag she produces a photo of herself with a youthful-looking Doddy.

Today's spot prizes for dancing to the CDs of DJ Eddie 'Rock Steady' Parry, a 30-year old Roman Catholic lay minister from Everton, include a silver-plated picture frame, six mugs, a clock, a doll and a pottery piano. There are also bottles of bubbly, and trophies winners can 'put on their tables for the afternoon.' Back in '24, you could win a leather wallet for keeps in a Charleston contest. But the new customers love it all just as much. Eddie says he keeps the music 'at a decent volume', adding: 'I know what they want because I listen to people.'

So no chance of a scratch mix, then Eddie? Not on this occasion anyway. Today, those enfolding each other with aging arms have a date with history.

[28.3.1999]

THE NO. 1 CITY OF THE 60s

During the 60s, Liverpool - once the second city of the Empire - was reaching for the sky in a different way. Things were looking up again. Never more so than at the close of the decade, when St John's Beacon completed the now familiar city skyline at 480ft.

However, the natural geography of St James's Mount meant that nothing quite beat the still evolving Anglican Cathedral, its Gothic tower rising 700ft above the Mersey, and joined in '67 by the futuristic glass crown of the Metropolitan Cathedral, immediately labelled 'Paddy's Wigwam'. All this could still be viewed from New Brighton's red-brick Tower Building, the roof reached by ski-like bucket seats. But what was it about that 60s skyline that was completely different?

The answer is soot. Liverpool still held the patent on creating a good yellow smog. A three-day pea souper, with flag-bearing folk walking in front of vehicles wasn't uncommon, until the smokeless zones put paid to the great coal yards of Bankhall. There were steam trains at Lime Street, and the London loco ran twice a day down the line to Exchange Station, collecting the businessmen of prosperous Blundellsands. The Liver Building, St George's Hall, the municipal clock tower in Dale Street, the museum - all were black.

We had winters too. It always snowed. You could skate on the canal, more full of ice-entombed iron bedsteads than barges. And we didn't need gritters. We had veteran Labour MP, battling Bessie Braddock, to clear any obstruction, political or otherwise. Incredibly, the City Council was Tory, and run by Alderman Sir Harold Macdonald Steward. The nouveau riche were Ford workers, and the car was king. No pedestrian precincts. You could drive past George Henry Lee's to a true city centre that had not yet been turned into a bus rank. Queen Square and Williamson Square, like so many areas, were made up of cobbled streets, many still bearing tram tracks. Alas, the last tram departed in October '57.

At the Stork Hotel, theatregoers would take a nightcap, served by waiters in white jackets and waitresses in frilly caps. The poshest hotel was still the Adelphi. In the tea salon one day, the great Russian pianist Vladimir Ashkenazy announced his defection to the West. For those of stouter constitution, there were four Yates's Wine Lodges, and one bar, The Spanish House, which made the Lodges look like health clubs. Red lino and sawdust was the decor. We all did the conga out of there on the night man landed on the moon.

Another path was cut by Vera Bray, the Mayor of Bootle. She declared the road to the docks over Miller's Bridge, to be 'Export Highway' as part of the *I'm Backing Britain* campaign. That said, anyone could go to the docks without being thought a pimp or a drug runner. It was a day out for local kids; the great liners in the dry dock at Gladstone: the Cunard, Blue Funnel and P and O boats. There was also the world's largest floating crane, the *Mammoth*: capable of lifting 200 tons and boasting the slogan: 'If a ship can hold it, Merseyside can load it.' The great dredger, *Leviathan*, kept the Mersey clear, prior to the silting up of the estuary with the coming of the Seaforth container terminal in '68. There was even a channel kept open for the cruise boats to Llandudno.

Sitting on the beaches at New Brighton and Crosby (amid the wartime tank traps which still hadn't sunk out of view) was a leisure option. The hardy took the plunge at New Brighton open-air baths. For football fans, the glory years were dawning. At Goodison and Anfield, there were trophy rooms to be filled. And there was world class boxing at the Stadium.

Glory of a different kind, as Liverpool began to take stock of its role in the Battle of the Atlantic, only 20 years earlier. The names of Captain Johnny Walker, U-boat destroyer, and Admiral Sir Max Horton, officially entered the history books.

On a dark note, who could have guessed that Britain's last execution would take place at Walton Jail in August '64? Of no significance at the time, it made four paragraphs on the front of the old-style broadsheet *Echo*.

Side by side with the street newspaper sellers were the flower girls. Most famous among them, selling daffs outside Central Station in all weathers, was Lizzie Christian. The streets were filled with the neatly uniformed pupils of the Liverpool Collegiate and Institute schools. Boys still wore caps, and raised them to ladies like Lizzie.

The most famous hat in town was the cocked trilby worn by the *Echo's* George Harrison. He (not the other chap) was THE George Harrison to local folk. His nightly column, *Over the Mersey Wall*, was called after the revetment wall, built to control tidal flows mid-river. The ruins of these dumped stones, held together by concrete, can still be seen.

Meanwhile, Liverpudlians looked to the hammerhead cranes of still flourishing ship-building at Cammell Laird. From Wirral, residents saw that now completing sky-line in Liverpool. But under the river, a new tunnel was being dug that would open the next decade.

The epitome of a top night out 'in town' was a meal at the Oriel Restaurant, where the fish on your plate had been swimming in a nearby tank minutes before the leather-bound menus arrived. No fish in the river, however. The days of clean water had yet to arrive.

But there was the Mersey Sound. To some, that meant Ronald Settle and Joan Ovens playing piano duets in the pit at the Playhouse; to others, the radical spoken words of actors at the newly formed Everyman. To still others, a visiting American rock star like Guy Mitchell at the Empire.

But in Mathew Street, something big was brewing. Four lads were about to shake the world. They did. And so much else of what was 60s Liverpool has since sadly been eclipsed.

[8.2.1999]

42

SCOUSEOLOGY AWARDS

JOINING SOME FAMOUS FACES,
RAISING A GLASS TO A UNIQUE CITY AND ITS PEOPLE

Get this for a laugh. Here's a photie of me with some of me bezzies. We'd 'ad a few scoops like, and thought that as it's getting close to Chrissy, we'd 'ave our picture taken together to celebrate all of them being legends in their own lunchtimes. Torkin of which, we 'ad chops with red and white vino because it was the thing to do. When, in fact, for the Whitbread Scouseology Awards, presented in partnership wid de *Echo*, some of us 'ad expected our lamb to be dressed as mutton, and, before you could say 'Aunt Mary 'ad a Canary', be turned into a pan of Scouse.

For I ask you: are we, or are we not, one big family, all named after, and made equal by, the boiled remains of someone else's dinner? I know, before yoos all start on at me, that the residents of Eccles are never referred to as Cakes, nor their surrounding Lancashire neighbours as Hot Pots. But we *are* Scousers, and have been since the reign of Queen Anne, when, as some people will have you believe, the chair leg was invented. Now would I pull your leg? No way. Scouse arrived here in 1706, when Liverpool's seafaring connections were well on the way to making us the second city of the Empire. Ee-aye-o! Ee-aye-o! Pull the other one! (Note for the benefit of our wider readership, this article will now continue in English).

Seriously, Scouse takes its name from the Dutch word 'Lapskous' or the Norwegian word (also found in Danish and German) 'Lapskaus'. So thank the sailors who brought it here, and take your pick...

According to Ken Dodd, this culinary delight made Liverpudlians - or 'Liverpolitans', as the middle classes liked to be known - the first true Europeans. And we certainly appear to be ready for 1992 and all that. For on arrival at the Scouseology lunch, Gerry Marsden kissed Tommy Smith - and no one had scored a goal. When I say kissed, what I really mean is, embraced with user-friendly facial contact: in the way that Scousers always have, ever since the days when the word 'Mates' meant nothing more than the people you went to the boozer with.

'Scousers are very clannish,' says Gerry, who, although he took the ferry across the Mersey, still lives near Chester. 'I once got off a plane in Perth, Australia, and the first voice I heard was that of a bouncer from Walton Road.'

Small world. But none smaller than the cupboard under the stairs, where poet Gladys-Mary Coles, accepting a theatre award on behalf of her cousin Pauline Collins, had spent the summer writing a book. 'It was the coolest place,' confided Liverpool born Gladys-Mary, fully realising that the Greenhouse Effect could bring about the return of sun-tanned Scousers in exile.

Some, like writer Willy Russell, never wanted to get away. 'I'm not still around because of some romantic notion. I've put roots down with my family, and anyway, it's only 200 miles from London. Besides, when I first met you, Joe, you were going to live in the Lake District. That was 15 years ago, and you're still here...'

That's right, Willy. Tell it like it is. Don't fall for these trick loyalty questions from the media. Every day, folk like Billy Butler, Wally Scott, Johnny Kennedy tell it like it is on the wireless. According to *Brookside* actor Bill Dean, Wally has replaced Ena Sharples in the affections of ordinary people. We're still trying to work that one out! Put it down to our legendary sense of humour. As when Gerry Marsden says that to be a true Scouser is to read the *Echo* - and enjoy it. Good one, Gerry. 'It's also optimism,' says Doddy, who adds that 'my summer season this year was one that I'll never forget.'

Yes, we are survivors, and we know our rights. Like the Scouser who was stranded on Crewe station in July, as British Rail staff began one of their weekly 24-hour strikes. He pointed out that his ticket was from London to Liverpool, and got the station manager to sign for a taxi the rest of the way: 'Do ya wanna lift, mate?' 'Oh yes,' says Gerry Marsden. 'Scousers will help each other out in everything from a scrap in a pub to finding water in the desert.'

You find them in all forms. While Cilla is having 'a Lorra, Lorra laughs' on the telly, Peter Sissons, an ex-Institute pupil, is reading the Six o'clock News; while Paul McCartney is still singing around the world, Simon Rattle is conducting the world's top orchestras.

Recently, movie-makers were at the Town Hall filming a crowd scene with extras from local job centres. When one gent tripped over, the others continued unabashed as instructed, but not before a voice was heard to shout: 'Be sure you purina a claim!'. I think they call it 'character building'?

Yet Billy Butler, who took this year's award as Top Scouser of '89, got it right when he said: 'I don't mind being Scouser personality of the year. But Top Scouser isn't something I can be on my own. We all know people who do so much to raise money for charity to help others and to make life better, from all over Merseyside. They are the Scousers of the Year.'

We all drank to that, as indeed we would, the drink being free. But we clapped as well, and we are the most cynical of tribes when it comes to applause. But in congratulating Billy and all the other winners, we were saying thank you to all those people who make this city and its suburbs a unique place to be. For being Scouse is much more than a meal ticket. Knoworrameanlike?

[4.12. 1989]

LIPA

FAME AT LAST!

No more sitting on the old school bench for Paul McCartney - or any of the now greying pupils who once passed through the imposing gates of the Liverpool Institute. A school for boys where, for 160 years, sons followed fathers for a grounding in godliness and good learning. A posh Victorian pile, turned ruin, eventually overshadowed by a great Gothic cathedral. So much for the past. Now, a different type of pupil walks the freshly-painted corridors...

A new Institute , the Liverpool Institute of Performing Arts (LIPA) - already nicknamed 'Paul McCartney's Fame School' or, even more glibly, the 'Macca University' - is up and running at last. And when the ex-Beatle takes centre stage in the old assembly hall for the official opening next Tuesday, he could be forgiven a tear or two of nostalgia. Not only will he be standing where his headmaster once intoned morning prayers in mortar board and gown, he will also look out at the 500-seat theatre which is at the heart of a dream to provide talented students with a passport to the world of entertainment. And that means everything, from drama and dance to music-making and management.

It's taken seven years - including a million pounds of his own money - for McCartney to head the trek to this particular Promised Land. One where the roll-call is not only international and cosmopolitan, but where the latest students are as likely to be female as male. The first 200 hopefuls - out of an eventual 700 - are already in class. Full-time and part-time courses will combine to make LIPA a unique experience.

Steve Mathurin, 24, doing a three-year BA honours degree (validated by the neighbouring John Moores University) is typical of the new-found enthusiasm: 'I like the ethos of the whole place. There's none of the stuffiness you get with other music colleges. Here, it's about becoming a complete entertainer by hooking up to other skills and making friends and contacts worldwide.' For Londoner Steve, who's already been a singer with a couple of soul bands, joining LIPA is a serious business. 'I've given up a £20,000 a year job as a telephone engineer to be here. I'm not playing around,' he says.

Sarah Driver, 19, from Manchester, and Sarah Langton, 20, from Ormskirk, are both specialising in acting, with video, sound and lighting as extra studies. And like Steve, they also think Liverpool is the ideal student city. Meanwhile, down in the canteen - cut into former bedrock - it's a case of His Master's Voice. A McCartney CD plays over the speakers as students munch lunch (but no meat, mind you, by Macca decree!)

'Attention all GROOVERS' beams a video message at reception. If 'groovers' sounds old hat, all else is gleaming afresh. Modern concrete, steel and glass enmeshed with the original Victorian facades are set off with art deco lighting designs. At the main entrance, the gates, the classical columns, the imposing staircases, and the giant oak-rimmed clock are reminders of a sterner regime. One can almost hear the fast-clicking heels of ghostly schoolboys scurrying late to Latin. When that era of tuck-shop and prep ended during the mid-80s, the old school fell into disrepair - not least because there was a restriction on it being used for anything other than education.

Says LIPA publicist Alison Holbourn: 'When the renovations started, we discovered some real horror stories. You hear about Victorian buildings and how "they don't build them like that any more." Well, perhaps it's a good job they don't. In one place, an arch had been built over some unstable muddy ground, with the whole weight of the building bearing down on it.'

The transformation has cost more than £12m, with the Queen (who'll visit in June) making a personal donation. Apart from the McCartney £1m cheque, £4m apiece has come from the government, European funding and the private sector. Typical of ordinary well-wishers are brother and sister Rachel and John Bowes, aged 12 and 9, from Wirral, who have raised £50 to buy a theatre seat.

For LIPA will truly be an institute for the *performing* arts; a place for plays, musicals and rock gigs - open to the public. Which takes us back to the motto of the old school. Translated from Latin, it reads: 'Not for ourselves, but for the whole world, we were born.' Those words remain in their rightful place - emblazoned on the great arch above the main entrance. Now, they are the motto of a new and even more famous Liverpool Institute.

[25.1.1996]

BLOOD BROTHERS WOWS BROADWAY

The Liver Birds were the highest flyers on the Manhattan skyline today. Willy Russell's musical *Blood Brothers*, which began life as a school play 12 years ago, wowed Broadway. The 1,000-strong capacity audience instantly stood up as one to give the show a seven-minute standing ovation. It was a triumph for Merseyside enterprise in the world capital of showbusiness. And not least for writer/composer Russell; producer/director Bill Kenwright, and leading title-role actors, Skelmersdale's Con O'Neill and Wallasey born Mark Hutchinson. Top British critic Jack Tinker of the *Daily Mail* - a veteran of dozens of Broadway first nights - told me: 'I have never witnessed anything like it before. It is the first time I have ever seen actors recalled from their dressings rooms to take an extra curtain call.'

Certainly, the production, which travelled to New York from the Liverpool Playhouse, via Toronto, has totally won public support here, both at the previews and at the official premiere. After the applause finally subsided, men and women - many of them reduced to tears by the emotional tale of twins separated at birth - queued up to embrace Willy Russell. Word of mouth has been so good - and there is already one million dollars in the kitty - that today's mixed review in *The New York Times* is for once thought unlikely to affect the overall prospects. *Blood Brothers* is likely to have a long life in offshoot productions right across America, while Bill Kenwright was sufficiently confident this morning to predict that one of the next stops could be Australia.

The show - played against a backdrop of the Liverpool waterfront, and boasting graffiti that includes 'Scousers rule', 'Everton for the Cup' and 'Up the Reds', has been the talk of New York TV and radio in the lead-up to the official opening. Bill Kenwright, now London's leading producer, as well as executive producer for Liverpool Playhouse, has risked £2.6 million of his own money on the Broadway run at the Music Box theatre, once owned by Irving Berlin, and where Humphrey Bogart first appeared in 1925. It's a gamble made possible by the success of the eight shows Kenwright has on in the West End, as well as six others on tour in the UK.

'I still find it hard to believe that we are here,' he says. 'I never used to have New York ambitions, but the way we have opened makes me think that maybe I would like to stay here and do a dozen shows. The theatre world here is a village - maybe two blocks, with just 13 or 14 shows. In London, there could be 60. But for me, this is the natural progression: to bring *Blood Brothers* to America, via Canada, after the Liverpool run.'

Yet when Kenwright first came to Broadway with Richard Harris' play, *Stepping Out* (which he commissioned), he got his fingers burnt. But on that occasion, he clashed with the director, while with *Blood Brothers*, he has gone it alone. His confidence has also been boosted by one of his productions, *Dancing at Lughnasa*, winning a Tony award last year. And a bonus this time is that Willy Russell has become an established major force in America with the film and play versions of *Shirley Valentine*.

The stunning reception for *Blood Brothers* rode in on the back of a sunny Sunday afternoon here, with temperatures in the mid-70s. By 5pm, the crowds were four deep on the pavement outside the theatre, which is just off Times Square, and but a few blocks from where Liverpool's most famous musical son, John Lennon, was gunned down.

Mounted police controlled autograph hunters as New York's theatre elite arrived, dressed to the nines. Among early celebrities were the film stars Stephen Rea from the smash hit *The Crying Game*, and Kevin Bacon (*Flatliners* etc). The older generation was represented by folk like Vaudeville comedian Joey Adams, while UK supporters included TV and radio presenter Gloria Hunniford.

Many people seeking late return tickets were disappointed, but seemed pleased to be getting their faces on television as camera crews mingled with first nighters in the humid heat. And after it was all over, Con O'Neill, who 12 years ago was selling programmes at the Playhouse, joked: 'If you want an official quote for the *Echo*, I still haven't got one.' But the actor, who had been watched by proud mum and dad, Kate and Gerry O'Neill, adds: 'seriously, though, all this just hasn't sunk in at all yet, except to say that my finest memories are still playing in the show at the Playhouse.'

Meanwhile, his stage 'twin', Mark Hutchinson, who started his career dancing in amateur shows at the Floral Pavilion, New Brighton, admitted, 'I am just amazed to be here. To think I saw *Blood Brothers* four times over the years, without ever thinking I would be in it. Then Bill Kenwright saw me in a revue in a London pub and invited me to audition.'

But that's showbiz. And as the famous song, *New York, New York* immortalised by Ol' Blue Eyes himself, Frank Sinatra, says: 'If you can make it here, you can make it anywhere...'

[26.4.1993]

TIME GENTLEMEN PLEASE

JOE CLOCKS ON TO PUT THE LIVER CLOCK BACK

When I was a child, I spoke as a child. I used to stand in front of our hall mirror going: 'Ding-dong, ding-dong, ding-dong, ding-dong. I was, of course, Big Ben. 'BONG! BONG!' And *News at Ten* hadn't even been invented. But in the early hours of yesterday morning I went one better: I put the Liver Clock back one hour to good old Greenwich Mean Time.

And each of the Liver Clock's four faces (three in the West Tower one in the East) are two-and-a-half feet wider than Big Ben. In fact, they are the largest public clocks in the land, yet in the private ownership of the Royal Liver Friendly Society, whose own humble origins as a burial club back in 1850, with headquarters in a front parlour in Pickup Street, off Vauxhall Road, belied the magnificence of what lay ahead. Today, Building Manager Philip Alcock quite rightly says: 'Everyone in Liverpool wants our present address.' If the Government ever privatises the Palace of Westminster, one feels sure that Royal Liver, with accumulated funds of more than £535 million, will lead the bidding to get themselves a prize pair of clocks. But Liverpool's Liver timepiece, adopted symbol of our city and a world-renowned landmark, leads the way.

Its real name is Great George, as it was set in motion on June 22, 1911, at the precise moment that George V was being crowned in Westminster Abbey. That was only three years after the foundation stone of the granite-clad building had been laid. The lightning rise of the entire edifice had been made possible by the then revolutionary use of iron and concrete frameworks, which required no massive load-bearing outer walls. Nevertheless, it was the clock that came out King of the Statistics:

- The faces, 220ft above road level, are 25ft in diameter.
- The weight of the clock mechanism is four tons.
- The combined weight of iron-work and opal glass in the dials is 16 tons.
- The weight of the four pairs of hands is two tons, with the minute fingers, 14ft long and 3ft wide, each weighing five hundredweight.
- The hour marks are each three feet high, and there is a 14-inch space between each minute.

All quite mind-blowing, especially when you confront it all at close quarters, and are made to feel like an inhabitant of Lilliput. However, *Gulliver's Travels* ain't got nothin' on this trip: lift to the ninth floor; staircase to the roof, with its keeper's house and centre building chasm of a well; then more stairs to the whitewashed and spotlessly clean clock chamber (you could eat your dinner off the floor, as they say). The intrepid may then continue upstairs to the first lantern gallery, and, with a goodly head for heights, even onward up the spiral iron staircase to the top lantern. That brings you out just below the strapped-down 18ft Liver Birds, who haughtily hold their mythical heads 322 ft above the Dinky Toy traffic of the Pier Head. But one disappointment, I'm afraid....Despite Quasimodo being in residence at the Everyman Theatre right now, there are no bells. The chimes, installed in 1953, are struck by hammers on piano-wire type lengths, picked up by microphones and then blasted out through eight huge speakers in the lower lantern gallery of the West Tower. Not to worry, though. It's all very impressive just as it is.

Liverpool's full-time Mr Liver Clock is John Atkinson, of Hunts Cross, my companion on this lofty perch for the hour-changing ceremony. It all works off a small master clock. But how does that work? 'I phone TIM, and my watch keeps good time,' says John, who looks at the paint-splashed dial on his wrist. So now you know. What TIM says, John's watch says; what John's watch says checks the master clock; what the master clock says, you read. And that's accurate to within half-a-second a day.

'Mind you, sometimes, the wind blows so strongly that it pushes back the fingers of the clock and we have to make minor re-adjustments,' confides John. No wonder the glass in the dials is made to withstand pressures of an incredible 11 tons per square inch. And even then, they lose the odd pane every so often. It's enough to give you the pip. The Greenwich Pip, that is.

*Okay, Okay! There is a technical mistake in the feature. Before anyone writes in, let me say that 'Big Ben' is the name of the bell in the clocktower at Westminster, and not the clock. BONG!

[24.10.1988]

WHEN WE WERE ALL OVER THE MOON

July 20, 1969. I remember it as though it was yesterday. A most pleasant summer's evening, the temperature settling back to just below 70 degrees. For a Sunday, Liverpool's city centre pubs were unusually full. Most had hired televisions and placed them high up on makeshift rickety shelving above the heads of drinkers. No big screens then: a 19-inch cabinet set rented from Rediffusion if you were lucky, and luckier still if you were viewing at less than 20 paces. It was just after eight o'clock. By that time, the attention of every short-sleeved reveller was fixed on black and white pictures being flashed to earth from more than a quarter of a million miles away. Man was about to land on the moon.

The previous evening, there had been a 34-minute telecast of the lunar surface. Astronauts Neil Armstrong and Buzz Aldrin had transferred from their Apollo-11 spaceship into a moon module called Eagle. Four days earlier, they had been blasted into space from Cape Kennedy, Florida, in company with third crew member, Michael Collins. Collins' job was to pilot the command module. Armstrong and Aldrin were destined for the greatest privilege in history: to become the first men to step on to an extra-terrestrial surface.

And we were with them - every one of us who crowded into the lino-floored old Royal Court pub at the corner of Queen Square, by day the site of a flourishing fruit market, by night, the crossroads of Liverpool's theatreland. There was similar expectation all around, not least in the nearby packed lounges of the Stork Hotel. At the bar, the rounds had been getting bigger and bigger for the past hour or so - ever since Armstrong had declared: 'The Eagle has wings' as the tiny module separated away and began the final descent in the moon's own gravitational pull.

The television had been turned up to blaring point over the growing din. Someone made a joke about how this was a much more compelling story than the newly released *Where Eagles Dare*, which had opened two days earlier at the ABC on Lime Street. At 17 minutes past nine precisely, Armstrong's voice, distinctly American, very clear, but undeniably emotional, declared: 'The Eagle has landed.' Then, almost immediately it seemed, another voice, presumably Aldrin, calmly reported what was for me an even more sensational sentence, with its own sense of shorthand poetry: 'Tranquility base, we have touchdown.'

At that very moment, Liverpool had lift-off. There went up a roar and a cheer I shall never forget. Hugging, dancing and kissing all around. Strangers embracing strangers. Folk rushed into the cobbled square to sound their car horns. People seemed to be streaming out of every door of every building - out into the open for some sort of impromptu carnival. A conga-line formed that stretched from outside the Royal Court Theatre, across the square, past the Stork, down past the Spanish House, and round the corner towards the tunnel entrance. Surely they weren't going to dance their way to Birkenhead?

The *Echo*'s legendary columnist of the day, George Harrison frequented the Court bar for stories. That day, for his next *Over The Mersey Wall* diary, he had been writing of how a 66-year-old farmer from Ince Blundell, about to be honoured by the Royal Agricultural Society, still milked his cows at dawn before a hearty breakfast. But he had scrapped it because this dawn had been different. It was a day that would change things for ever.

As Dr Wernher Von Braun, director of the Marshall Space Flight Centre, assured *Echo* readers of man's eventual victory over death, local Labour MPs Eric Heffer, Walter Alldritt, Simon Mahon and James Dunn were preparing a rebellion against increased charges for spectacles and false teeth. Clearly, inter-stellar immortality was still some way off. 'Life on earth goes on as normal,' reported George Harrison, with his usual dry sense of fun. And indeed it did. A Mrs C. Baggs of L15, took her own small step for mankind. She warned in the *Echo*'s letters column of the danger of hiking in sandals, having just returned from three weeks in a Plymouth hospital after an adder attack on Bodmin Moor.

Amid all this, the *Echo*'s banner headline foresaw the significance of what had, and was about, to happen. SALUTE TO A NEW WORLD, it roared in the largest type-face that the technology of the day afforded. Unable to join Armstrong on the moon, *Echo* reporters did the next best thing: they interviewed all the residents of Apollo Street, Liverpool 6, who were clearly over the moon to a man.

Who would have thought then that Liverpool Museum would one day contain not one, but three pieces of moonrock and three lunar soil samples. They were brought back to earth by Apollo missions 15, 16 and 17 during the 80s, and are on loan from the Physics and Astronomy Research Council. The rocks are thumbnail size, and look not unlike pieces of coal or coke. They take their rightful place in the Time and Space Gallery in William Brown Street and are seen by thousands of visitors every year. But, they are not flavour of the month at the moment. At the planetarium, they are gearing themselves up to the next monumental event in the heavens - the eclipse on August 11th.

'It will be 91% in Liverpool. There's lots of interest,' reports museum publicist Stephen Guy. And he adds: 'If it's still the moon people want, then they should come and see our Jupiter display. That's got 16 moons!'

[17.7.1999]

DAY THE SUN WENT OUT

June 29, 1927 was the day Liverpool became the centre of the universe. At 6.24 am, the first total eclipse in England for more than 200 years was due to pass overhead. The city, together with Formby and Southport, was on the midline of this startling event - in the same way that Falmouth and Plymouth are for the coming eclipse next Wednesday.

The line of totality ran from Criccieth in North Wales, across the summit of Snowdon, to Merseyside and on through Lancashire to the Yorkshire village of Giggleswick, where the astronomer royal, Sir Frank Dyson, had set up special recording instruments at the village's famous public school.

Excitement - and a little fear - was rife. These were the days before a wide understanding of astronomy. There was no *Sky At Night* on television and few college science courses. Some people still believed that an eclipse was a portent of doom. At the time of totality, a woman on New Brighton promenade screamed: 'It's the end of the world,' and rushed towards the sea causing panic. She was pursued by uniformed nurses from Leasowe Hospital.

A gramophone in the crowd outside Wallasey Cricket Club played *Abide With Me*. Two women fainted. Elsewhere, the mood was less tense, more joyous. The anticipation had been building up for months. The LMS railway ran 100 extra trains to the area. A special sailing of the Isle of Man steamer, *Manxman*, was arranged and many aircraft chartered from Liverpool Airport.

Southport - the town at the epicentre of totality - was hailed as the UK's eclipse capital. Thomas Cook offered a train from Euston to Southport - the return journey, plus a night in a top hotel, costing three pounds (contrast that with a now fully-booked Concorde eclipse-chasing flight offer this time of £1,550 per person, and other charter trips at around £500 per person). To match its celebrity status, Southport even laid on all-night cinema shows and concerts. Hotels served pre-eclipse breakfasts from 4am.

In Liverpool, the city centre was thronged with massive crowds. The parks were crowded to capacity. People queued for admission to rooftops, including the Royal Liver and Cunard buildings, and to the high southern terraces of the cathedral, then still minus its tower. City centre stores and hotels - most notably the roof of the Adelphi - were seen as great vantage points. On Wirral, 50,000 people climbed Bidston Hill. Fifteen thousand more were on the uplands at Caldy.

Every one of those who still remember - and they now need to be at least in their mid-70s - has a personal story to tell. Typical is Iris Cawthorne, now living in Formby, who was nine at the time: 'We were then living in Litherland,' she recalls. 'Our parents took me, my brother and two sisters, to the top of Hatton Hill Road, which was the best local vantage point and still surrounded by country fields in those days. We waited with bated breath. Everything went quiet and still, and the colour of the atmosphere turned crimson and the temperature dropped suddenly.'

The diary of railway signalman Richard Rigby of Rainford, where visibility was the best in the region, reports: 'The spectacle was unforgettable. Everyone was stricken by the wonder of it all and one was aware of the insignificance of oneself amid such majestic grandeur.'

That day, the *Echo* reported: 'The first supernatural fading of the light had an instantaneous effect. Many were not prepared for it and stopped short in the middle of jokes and laughter. There was a sudden on-rush of darkness and a strange hush descended upon the city. The crowd looked like troops in the grey morning light. One felt a quickening of the heart and a vague panic. Almost as quickly as the light had been taken away, it was restored.'

Others were not so lucky. Patchy cloud made the intensity of the eclipse a hit-or-miss affair. Those from Merseyside who had travelled to Snowdon for a special train up the mountain, were met with a curtain of mist and visibility of only 30 yards. Whatever and wherever, that generation fondly looked back at that midsummer's morning with awe. It became known locally at 'the day the sun went out'.

For people like Iris Cawthorne, the prospect of a second major eclipse is just as exciting: 'It won't be total here this time, but I'm sure it will be just as wonderful to a new and younger generation,' she says.

[6.8.1999]

54

A SHOW WHICH CAN'T BE LICKED

Postal strike? Forget it. The mail has got through - even if it has taken 400 years. On show in Liverpool tomorrow will be a letter written by Elizabeth I, back in 1588. It is just one of the exhibits in a literally priceless display of stamps and written communications at the city's museum - the largest of its kind ever held, and covering more than 6,000 square feet.

Ironically, this tribute has come to the Post Office at a time when public feeling is a little perforated around the edges. Had the Liverpool workers and management sorted themselves out sooner, it had been hoped to run an 18th century mail-coach through the city to launch the show. This little gesture of goodwill, has, however, had to be cancelled. No matter. All else is in place, delivered on time, and available for public scrutiny.

Apart from rare stamps of incalculable value, there are historic letters from all corners of the land, and from the seabed. The latter were recovered by divers from the wreckage of the *Empress of Ireland*, which sank on May 29, 1914. 1024 lives were lost out of 1467 on board. And timely for this particular display, come November 5, is a list of people arrested for the Gunpowder Plot of 1605. It was probably posted to other plotters to warn them of their imminent arrest, say the experts.

Never let it be said that History doesn't have a contemporary relevance: also on show is a letter to Oliver Cromwell marked 'Post Haste with Speede'. It was delivered during the English Civil War, and every time the postman stopped, the letter was signed with the date and time. Incidentally, to send a letter across the English Channel at that time cost you an average of 4d every time. And that's when 4d was 4d. There are two more royal letters - this time from Charles II - and the last letter written by condemned rebel William Jenkyns before his execution on September 30, 1685. Equally startling, from modern times, is a letter from Liverpool to Western Australia, and franked: 'delayed en route - aircraft hi-jack.'

So how long has all this posting been going on? Before 1635, there was no official mail service for the public. Royal Mail ran from 1482, and the first public mailcoach ran between London and Bristol in 1784. The first post office in Liverpool was opened in 1691. Prior to this, the city was served on foot from Chester, and later by horse post via Warrington. But by 1801, Liverpool had its own penny post. Mail was collected and delivered by bell men for 1d, and receiving houses were opened from 1824 onwards in Great Howard Street, Old Hall Street,

Scotland Road, Everton, London Road, Edge Hill and St James. By 1707, the city had it own postal mark, spelt LEVERPOOL, becoming LIVERPOOL in 1717.

Soon, thousands of letters passed through the city, due to the growth of the shipping trade. As they were handed in to be franked, this justified the Post Office making an extra charge (so what's new?). Yet soldiers and seamen below commissioned rank were allowed special rates. A floating receiving house on the south landing stage was opened on August 18, 1849. It was no more than a small wooden hut, but it meant that letters could be posted for the New World up to a few minutes before a ship sailed.

Says Carolyn Fleming of the museum's press office: 'Liverpool certainly enjoyed a unique postal history. Six of the stamps on display are so valuable, we're not going to tell you how much they're worth!'

Obviously, it's a show which can't be licked... or can it? The Black Penny was the world's first adhesive stamp, issued in May 1840. And one of the letters here bears a Penny Black used on May 6, 1840, and posted from Liverpool.

[21.9.1988]

STEAM DREAMS

It was a way of Liverpool life that has passed into the looking glass of history. Tomorrow marks the anniversary when Britain's last main line steam train pulled out of Lime Street Station 30 years ago. Those aboard the 45110 on August 11, 1968, were experiencing the last chapter of an international story that had begun just a couple of miles down the track.

In 1829, the first locomotive trials took place at Edge Hill. Most remembered from those distant days - now five generations past - was the first rail fatality: the death of Government minister William 'Free Trade' Huskisson, whose mausoleum now stands in the shadow of Liverpool Cathedral. But the significance of the Edge Hill experiment was global, contributing directly to Liverpool's place as the second city of the British Empire, handling more than 40% of world trade.

Once ashore, steam was the carrier: a miracle for commerce as well as for those who were not yet called commuters. Passengers travelled in great style - if they had the money. London was less than 200 miles and six hours away. Liverpool's rail links, the most complex in Britain at the time, were as vital to ocean cruising visitors from the New World entering Europe, as they were to industrialists. So that final journey of steam rightly took place where it all began. Driver Jack Hart, fireman Brian Bradley and guard Harry Crossland proudly took up their posts for the last time. The story of life on the footplate had gone full circle.

And it was also the reason why every little boy wanted to be a train driver. The distant rumble, the clanking of iron, the rush of steam, a plume of smoke, the shrieking tuneless rising pitch of the whistle, the clatter of carriages over the points, and the aftermath of falling smut, which left specs on spectators. Everyone and everything - including the Liver Building in those days - ended up blackened by soot. There was even the smell of the steam train. It was all part of the magic. And for the enthusiasts, it was apparently everywhere. Apart from Lime Street, there were mainline Liverpool stations at Central and Exchange; dockboard steam trains shunted beneath the Overhead Railway; steam locos set off through the sandhills towards Southport, and cross-country to the Pennines. In goods yards and coal sidings, through factory gates and along the waterfront, steam thrived. One of the most popular sights each year was the 'specials' arriving at Aintree for the Grand National.

A map of the Liverpool rail system showed the vast and famous 'Grid Iron' - 60 miles of track capable of handling 2,000 goods wagons in any 24-hour period. Garston, for instance, was famous as the prime UK importing centre for bananas. So now you know why that new sculpture, *Super Lamb Banana*, is so called, and so symbolic of the city's trading past. Many factories had their own trains: even Crawfords had their own 'biscuit loco'. But by 1955, diesel was beginning to replace steam on many main routes.

Liverpool's unique place in the saga of steam is now available on a video, researched and produced by Martin Jenkins, one of the founders of the Everyman theatre. Among the 25 film-makers featured is the late George Gregeen, a former editor of the *Echo*, who was a lifelong steam enthusiast. There's also footage by Sir Neil Cossens, once a student at Liverpool University and now director of the Science Museum.

By 1967, there were only four Dock Board locos left. The following year, all Liverpool main line steam had gone. For those lucky enough to remember, the memories come flooding back. For those too young, the excitement remains on film.

[10.8.1998]

NONE THE WISER
AFTER A DAY AT THE RACES

What follows is written in haste. I have just spent a day among the nags and am none the wiser...Decoded, this means I have been at Aintree for the Liverpool Meeting, which, as more than 600 million folk world-wide will testify, culminates tomorrow in the joining together of two of the most powerful words in the English language: The Grand National.

In order to undertake this venture, (how could the *Echo* not be there?), I decked myself out in enough county tweed to qualify as a slice of Battenburg cake. But it's not like sauntering around Wimbledon or taking to the waters of Henley. Here, you're meant to know what you are doing. From childhood, I recalled the cry of TV's fastest-talking man with a microphone, Peter O'Sullivan: 'And now over to Peter Moore on the rails.' I have never met Peter Moore, if indeed he still exists. But it always sounded a most uncomfortable place to be.

And if you were off the rails, then that was something else. But to this day, it's where the bookies hang out, hoping for the sake of their own mortgages that your judgement will fail, as the horses are placed under starter's orders. I was told - after what seemed like enough rain to launch the movie, *Noah II* - that the going was 'heavy'. I had mud on my brogues and was inclined to agree. Everyone was studying form; what happened 'last time out'. This chap called Charlie Walsh from Aigburth gives me a tip: '*Bank View* is going to be trying tomorrow...' What he doesn't realise is that, as a closet drama critic out for a few paragraphs of 'atmosphere', I know much more about pantomime horse than the ones with steaming fetlocks. But note that he doesn't say that *Bank View* is going to win. Everyone is very cagey. In fact, very unsure. Which is why all bookmakers are very rich.

I opt to play an extra in a crowd scene. And why not? The National Meeting is as much about absorbing as partaking. At this stage, better mutter than flutter. This year, nostalgia is the best runner. 150 years of The Big Race at Aintree, if you bear in mind that the first two Nationals were run at Formby. What a mine of information this column can be. And did you know that one year, *all* the runners, bar the eventful winner, fell during the race? Well, there's a poser for you. Which year was it? All part of tittle-tattle which contributes to the occasion.

I may go back tomorrow or I may not. I may just leave it to the experts. But I remember once asking astrologer Russell Grant why he didn't use his powers of foresight to predict the winner. He told me that astrologers had a sort of agreement never to use observations for their own self gain. But it may be to yours. And if you know the answer, give me a call...

[7. 4. 1989]

SHAGGY DOG STORY

No eyes turned as a long-haired terrier made his way to the *Echo* for an exclusive interview. How was anyone to know that this was Bothie Twisleton-Wykeham-Fiennes, the only canine on earth to have been to the North and South Poles? Bothie may be a wild rover, but he's no ordinary Rover, being the prize possession of explorer Sir Ranulph Fiennes and his wife, Virginia. The World's Most Widely Travelled Dog was in Liverpool for a three-day break - his first visit to the city, in fact, now that his aunt, Arabella McIntyre-Brown, Lady Fiennes' sister, is living in our midst.

'Phew, it's a dog's life,' said Bothie, speaking through an interpreter. 'I've heard that all newspapers like doggy stories, especially now in what's known as the silly season, so here I am. Not bad for 91 am I?'

Obviously dogs, like old soldiers, enjoy boasting of their age, and although Bothie has been around for 13 or so human years, in his own cold-nosed terms, he's a nonagenarian.

His existence has been eventful to say the least. Bothie reached the North Pole during Easter '82. 'The South Pole was about 18 months earlier. Both were very cold, but I have this marvellous coat you see. It's very thick. Ranulph and Virginia had these special booties and wraps made for me, but quite frankly, I spurned them. I like to run with the elements, which, incidentally, reminds me of the time I actually chased penguins in Antartica. I also had my photograph taken with a pack of wolves. They couldn't make out what I was. They'd never seen anything like it before.' Auntie Arabella nods in agreement, confirming that this is no tall story, even though the wolves were a lot taller than Bothie.

'I'm named after a man called Peter Booth, who introduced me to the Fiennes household, where I was adopted. It also means that where they go, I go, and they do get around a bit. They consulted the RSPCA and that sort of thing, and they said it would be okay, so off we went on a trans-global expedition. Broke every record in the *Guinness Book of Records*. It fell to me to keep everyone happy through the Roaring Forties. The only bit I didn't do was Africa. Far too hot. In Antarctica, I was good company for Virginia. She still maintains I kept her sane. Apart from the expedition party, there was no-one else around, you see. The place is completely uninhabited.'

As Bothie lapped at a bowl of water, I asked about diet: 'Oh, just straight dog food, and perhaps the odd gastronomic delight sent down from human dining tables. But nothing too rich. I can't afford to be sluggish or over-weight. At home there are also six huge black dogs called St John's Water Dogs. They come from the Arctic and are the Alaskan equivalent of St Bernard's. They actually jump into the icy waters and rescue people. It's in their genes. As for me, I have a bit of a killer instinct, being a terrier. And although I love humans, I take it out on squeaky toys. I've been through dozens of yellow elephants and pink frogs. If you throw a ball for me, then that's it for the day. I'll just keep bringing it back. Care to try?'

I explain that the deadline is looming. Bothie looks somewhat disgusted. 'Oh yes, I forgot. You're involved in the human rat race. Dreadful thing. You've got to leave time for your personal life.'

And what of yours, Bothie? 'Funny you should ask. I'm actually besotted with Auntie Arabella's cat, Lightning. It was love at first chase. We like to go streaking together in Aigburth, where I'm staying.'

And what do you make of Liverpool? 'Marvellous. there's a distinctive smell to the place, which in canine culture, is a compliment, not an insult. And I've met some interesting people, including a Polytechnic student by the name of Jamie Riley. No relation of yours. He's been a fan of mine ever since I appeared regularly on *Blue Peter*. He feels that he's grown up with me. I read a quote from Guy Mitchell in your column the other day, saying much the same thing about his fans.'

So do you read the *Echo Diary*? 'Never miss it. Auntie Arabella sends copies to me, so they'll love this when I get home. Ranulph's always being interviewed, but I hope I've been able to give you something of the story behind the stories. Of course, other people have tried to interview me over the years. I bit Russell Harty, but quite liked David Frost. Mind you, neither of them got a word out of me. I have only agreed to speak to you now in view of your allegedly excellent shorthand. And just to prove I can be outspoken, I bet I'm the first person - sorry dog - to ask why you wear those rather silly glasses and peer over the top of them.'

I tell Bothie to sit and give me his paw. 'Sorry, that's what all dogs are expected to do. You'll be wanting to tickle my tummy next. I'm afraid I'm an extremely independent chap. I'll always do what you least expect.'

As Auntie Arabella gathers him up - 'why walk when you can be carried?' - Bothie lets out a bark. Obviously, the interview was over.

[10.7.1989]

MYSTERY MONSTER TOUR

The Scottish Tourist Board had, in their wisdom (and generosity), presented me with a bottle of *Glenturret*, a delightful malt, distilled and bonded at Crieff, in what used to be Perthshire, since 1773. An excellent form of personalised central heating for touring the Highlands in a chauffeured minibus, during the very week winter decided to make a comeback. Yet, good grief! Here we are now, a couple of hundred road miles northward, peering into the murky peat-laden waters of Loch Ness, looking for a prehistoric creature first spotted by man more than a thousand years before, during the seventh century.

I must stress that the contents of the bottle have no bearing on what follows...

Ms Linda Lowe of the Scottish Tourist Board, proclaims 'It exists!' And adds: 'Even Nicholas Witchell believes in it!' Well, I ask you. Could the *Six o'clock News* from the BBC in distant London be read by someone who is deluded? Of course not. And then there's Peter Scott, a man close to Nature if ever there was, and who has actually produced a picture of what he thinks Nessie looks like.

I intend to stay on first-name terms with the alleged creature, not just because 'monster' is an ugly word, but also because, back in 1933, just after the Lochside road from Fort Augustus to Inverness opened the area up to tourism, Nessie was reported by *The Observer* newspaper as being 'SEEN WITH LAMB IN ITS MOUTH - PEOPLE ALARMED.' Better to be spotted for a sheep as a lamb, I say.

'Why kill the monster that laid the golden egg?' asks a reporter from York. 'It's a bit of a chicken and egg situation,' adds another from

Burnley, cautious, not least, because back home he has to mind what he says about the Witches of Pendle Hill. Well, we are mixing our metaphors, gentlemen, and I can feel a metamorphosis coming on....

Is it a log I see before me? Or is it ? No, just a ripple of the imagination, out there in Urquhart Bay, by the castle ruins. Apparently, this is the spot where most of the sightings have occurred, the most spectacular in recent times being on May 21, 1977. That photograph, complete with head and long neck, is now a collector's item on those little cards you find in the bottom of boxes of teabags.

'There's 263 billion cubic feet of water out there,' intones our driver. 'More than enough to submerge the entire population of the world twice over. In places, it's more than 700 feet deep, and at the lower levels, the water stays at a constant 43 degrees Fahrenheit all year round.'

So come on, let's be charitable: in unchanging conditions over thousands of years, something could have survived, and there could be a whole family of them. After all, Loch Ness is just one of more than 30 Scottish lochs said to contain prehistoric creatures. Most of the others are inaccessible by road, although Loch Morar, on the west coast, near Mallaig - with an incredible depth of 1,200 feet - can be visited. It was there, in 1858 that a vast creature was spotted by a nun from Liverpool. You can't get more gospel than that!

And what about Nessie? Spotted by priests, surgeons and scientists, and not just by hoteliers who might be considered by the more cynical to be on the make. There have also been sonar soundings, mass underwater camera searches, and even attempted net dredgings, some with official 'results'. But nothing today, it seems.

'It's like looking for a needle in a haystack,' says the man from Burnley with all the perception of a well-known cliché. 'And if I do spot it, I'm the only one without a camera. Nobody will believe me.' I assure him I'll sell him the negatives for enough money to start my own distillery. I have to report no such luck.

Yet, as you make your way along the A82, you canna help scanning the waters. What's more, the Nessie-spotting season is almost upon us: May is a very good month, I'm assured. But as they say in this land of 300 golf courses: 'It's a long shot, laddie.'

[26. 4.1989]

THE LAKES

It was the morning of the first frost, and overnight the trees and bracken had begun to turn from green to gold, brown and red. More than a thousand feet below, Lake Windermere glinted like a piece of silver paper, and the low elevation of the morning sun gave relief to every crag and peak. There wasn't a soul to be seen. On my Landrover radio, a recording of the *Last Night of the Proms* and six thousand voices were singing *Jerusalem...* 'And did those feet in ancient time, Walk upon England's mountains green...', Such moments, built from so many coincidences, are few. Yet they are unforgettable.

Down in the valley, the picture was somewhat different, as a season which had seen two million visitors to Lakeland was drawing to a close. Here, you are more likely to hear a Radio One D.J. shouting from a carried transistor set.

The Lake District may be England's biggest National Park, but it is just 30 miles long by 25 miles wide, and the truth is, it's just too popular. Windermere town and Bowness, which started out as hamlets before the railway arrived, look more like Blackpool at the height of the season. Coaches spill cargoes of trippers onto the pavements. Off they go to buy souvenirs, ranging from varnished pebbles to entire slate fireplaces. Every other shop is selling tweeds and waterproofs, often at inflated prices. The rest brew tea and serve meals, as the natives engage in a love-hate relationship with the invaders. What's needed, they argue, are fewer people spending more money. But with petrol prices rising, more coaches seem certain. Add to them caravans, cars, bicycles and boat trailers, all passing through streets and lanes more suited to ponies and traps, and you begin to appreciate the problem. Ambleside - even Tarn Hows, the central beauty spot that adorns every tea towel and table mat in creation - has gone over to one-way traffic. Tiny Hawkshead, where Wordsworth went to school, has a by-pass.

All these tourists have come to walk, climb, sail, swim, ski, drive or simply feed the ducks. In the winter, the now tame ducks roam the streets in gangs looking for food. A man has been employed to catch them. The most famous of all Lakeland ducks, however, is called Jemima, a creation of Beatrix Potter, who lived on the other side of Windermere, at Sawrey. She disliked children and people in general.

More people. Some munching Kendal Mint Cake (as eaten on Everest and at the South Pole), others stuffing their faces with Buttermere fudge and toffee: very fattening, this love of Lakeland sweet-stuffs. Perhaps the streets will burst one day with bloated tourists. But you can't beat a good Cumbrian breakfast - straight off the farm and onto the plate, so to speak. And one place you get that is at Greenbank Guesthouse, Hawkshead, run by Albert and Mary Hart. The Harts moved up here in 1970 after running a village store in the Rossendale valley.

'It's a hard slog at times,' says Mr Hart. 'You're working 12 hours a day, seven days a week, for seven, maybe eight months of the year. But we've made many friends and our regulars come back year after year. We both like meeting people, and it's a challenge.'

To many people, a day or a weekend in the Lakes begins and ends in these southern lowland areas. They are prone to venture no further. Americans bent on doing the district in a day left spare between Chester and Edinburgh, rush into historic buildings bearing cameras. 'You do the inside, I'll do the outside,' wife yells to husband. Then off they go, lenses pressed to steamed-up coach windows, still clicking away.

But it's not all like that; not everybody up here is selling bric-a-brac, turning mattresses or frying bacon and eggs for a living. There is still the shepherd - and his sheep, guided into pens or off to market by the skilled collie dogs. They all have short, sharp names like Jed, Floss and Shep. Not one of them, I swear, is called Jemima.

They also quarry slate in these parts - Westmorland Green has faced buildings and covered floors all over the world. It doesn't all end up being turned into ashtrays and clocks with 'A Present from Grasmere' written across it.

And mention of writing brings me to graffiti - there isn't any. The worst crimes for the local police are thefts from cars. 'People go walking up the mountains and come back to find cameras and binoculars missing,' says one village Bobby. Mugging, thank heaven, is virtually unknown and pub scuffles at closing time, together with rowdiness and damage to property, are largely confined to the Bank Holidays. Some people even manage to lock themselves away from all that. In the sailing club at Windermere and in the golf house, times don't change as everyone swaps tales of long ago, before the riff-raff arrived to spoil it all.

There's every indication that the latest trend in Lakeland tourism is for shorter stays. Inflation hits the customer as well as the hotelier and this year, aided by a poor summer, vacancy signs, normally a rare sight in peak season, have been popping up in windows. During one week in August, an Ambleside hotel with seventeen bedrooms had only six guests. That's why the Cumbrian Tourist Board is doing all it can to promote winter holidays. At the same time, they are trying to interest people in the outer areas around Broughton, along the coastal plain and up to the Border forests.

The Board lists its members in a special Where to Stay guide, but many small B and B businesses are highly sceptical about the impact this has. They say that the Lake District virtually promotes itself by word of mouth. If people are offered good, clean accommodation, they tend to return and to recommend it to others, without the need for any 'outside' help. However, those who are establishing new businesses say that the Tourist Board, regarded as a mixed blessing by most of the residents, can be most helpful. Without doubt, the outer areas of Lakeland have great potential that has yet to be realised. More tourism there would create badly needed jobs.

But for most of the trippers, the sixteen major lakes, especially Windermere, ten miles long and four times as deep as the Mersey, will remain the prime attraction. How they park all those extra coaches, hide all those extra caravans from view, and at the same time, keep everyone happy, is the major challenge of the future.

Meanwhile, I'm sure that Beatrix Potter is turning in her grave.

[24.9.1979]

MURDER MOOR REVISITED

A blood-red sub-zero dawn broke over Saddleworth Moor this morning, and at first light I took the winding road that climbs from the village of Greenfield and disappears over the horizon into West Yorkshire. At the coming up of the sun, they were being remembered afresh: the child and teenage innocents slaughtered by Ian Brady and Myra Hindley a generation ago.

In the watery moonlight that preceded the first stirrings of the new day, a mile-long line of police 'no waiting' cones caught in my headlights were the only intrusion upon raw Pennine nature that had by morning also deposited a powdering of snow above 1,800 feet; a polite reminder that men would shortly be at work. Then they came, with dogs and shovels and metal rods.

For the locals, who had seen it all before, it was like a Hammer Horror time warp. Their children had grown up with tales of murder and mystery above the valley treeline But now it was a reality once more. As one shopkeeper put it: 'the Moors murders are our Chernobyl. The effects have been, and will be, felt for years to come. They are stamped on other people's awareness and perception of the area too.'

Brian Snooks, proprietor of Nont Sarah's Hotel, 1,200 feet up on the old Roman road that runs from Saddleworth to Huddersfield, was quite to the point: 'folk around here will never forget. You still get the families and friends of the children coming in from time to time.'

True to say, nobody I spoke to in Greenfield or neighbouring Uppermill - the two villages nearest the old (and probably new) grave sites - talks in terms of parole for Myra Hindley.

'We'd string her and Brady up from the nearest tree,' said a fellow drinker in what was fast becoming a public conversation.

The area which Hindley has now identified to police looking for the bodies of Keith Bennett and Pauline Reade covers up to 3,000 acres on either side of the A635 near the spot where it is crossed by the Pennine Way walking route. It was close to here that the bodies of Lesley Ann Downey and John Kilbride were discovered 21 years ago. This particular location is said to have had a fascination for Brady. Certainly, looking west, the views before you reach the peat bog plateau are impressive. The valley below cuts a deep channel holding the waters of the Yeoman Hey reservoir, against the backcloth of a long ridge that takes a sudden dive to a glistening carpet of factory and street lights below. It's almost picture postcard. Before the industrial revolution, it undoubtedly was. The moors themselves have changed little. They are still largely unchanged and inhabited more by sheep than people.

'You've got to be careful out here,' said the barman at Nont Sarah's. 'It's like the desert. The ground shifts and slides, especially after heavy rain like we had earlier this week. You've got to be sure that you don't put your foot through the top crust.'

'You know,' said Brian Snooks, 'people come and take the peat for their gardens, but it's so acidy, all it does is burn up the roots of their plants.'

Thus, unlike some commentators, locals are not at all certain that any bodies may have survived a 20-year burial in such conditions. They fear that it may hamper and prolong the police search, despite the use of specially trained sniffer dogs.

'The moors are not much use for anything,' adds Brian Snooks, 'apart from grazing sheep around the edges, and we do have a local shoot.'

Until Tuesday of this week, one of the big topics of conversation locally had been rising rates that had seen off half-a-dozen small businesses and hit hotels and restaurants already reeling from the effects of a bad summer season.

But now the media circus has come to town again. This morning, the streets of Saddleworth, their limestone architecture reminding you of one-time Victorian opulence, were busier than usual. The buzz had changed once more to what was going on up in the surrounding hills. How long it will take to end speculation over this most dire and unhappy chapter of events is anybody's guess.

If the weather breaks, then the search may have to be put off until the spring. Last year, the snow came on bonfire night when they ended up knee deep in the stuff. And it didn't disappear until April. Now that dusting of snow is a timely and ominous reminder that the elements are what set the pace up here.

[20.11.1986]

AN ENGLISHMAN AT THE EISTEDDFOD

'YOU HAVE TO BE WELSH TO ENJOY BEING A BARD...'

It's National Eisteddfod week in Wales and the Welsh are gathered at Machynlleth to celebrate in song and verse. We sent an Englishman to look at this unique occasion, where English, like the demon drink, is forbidden and there are all sorts of strange rituals, including the crowning and chairing of various bards.

According to George Thomas, man of Rhondda, Methodist teetotaller, Speaker of the House of Commons and late of the Royal Wedding lectern, where he read about faith, hope and love, this is a happy eisteddfod.

'I sense it,' he told me, perhaps because people had been rushing up and asking for autographs. It was marvellous, he went on, how all these people came from villages and valleys, from north, south, east and west. 'This cultural feast,' he began ... as if about to do his own version of Shakespeare and finish ... 'this Wales.' But he didn't. Instead, he almost answered questions about the survival of the language, the arrival of the demon drink on the fringe of the showground (although one pub was only serving locals) and his job at

Westminster. 'I've been Speaker for so long that I'm impartial about everything except the Lord's Prayer.'

And two more jokes: 'That's how I've kept alive for so long - by giving answers like that ... it does demand a price from you. For a Welshman to have to keep his mouth shut is harder than for an Englishman ... I never minded demonstrations (when Secretary of State for Wales) provided I thought I was winning.'

The new Secretary of State, Nicholas Edwards, was somewhere around, but not keen to talk. It was a private visit. So thank goodness for Mr. Speaker, who was obviously trying hard to convince the small lobby of English 'foreign' correspondents that the Welsh were not a dour race living in a land of wool shops and dry stone walls. For here we all were on the banks of the Dyfi River in North Powys, walking around amid the music and poetry, the litter, the smell of chips and the scurrying kids: a week of artistic endeavour which, according to Mr. Thomas, is without equal in the Western World, and where the speaking, writing or reading of English is scorned. Even the listening bank, nestling amid the 330 trade stands, is only heard as a *Banc y Midland.*

The honour of the National Eisteddfod had once again come to bunting-strewn Machynlleth - or to be precise, to a cow field six miles to the east. Welshmen from as far away as Patagonia, and folk from Brittany, were all jabbering away in what sounded like the last letters of the alphabet. Why are the French here? 'If you want to get your head kicked in, go and ask them if they're French,' said my Welsh mole. 'They're Celts.'

So far, it had been a trying day. We were labouring under what the man on Radio 4 had called 'the remnants of a cold front', and that, with the help of the nearby 2,900 ft Cader Idris mountain, translated as mist and drizzle. It had probably been much the same when Owain Glyndwr held the first and only Welsh Parliament at Machynlleth in 1404, but it was enough to make the bards and druids of 1981 forsake their stone circle (built for the 1937 Eisteddfod here) and opt for Plan B, which was a get-together in the local school. They crammed onto the stage, where they looked set for a Nativity play. One of their number, one Emrys Deudraeth, let go a lighthearted ode about Lady Di, which included a joke about themselves looking like 'Arabs without camels.' What a relief that was, for five pages of notes earlier I'd scribbled 'Arabs - most - wearing severe looking specs.' Now he'd agreed, I need have no qualms about using it.

There were first rung green bards, middle rung blue ones and white robed top notches, or Druids, all backed up by crimson clad trumpeters. Presiding over all was Archdruid Jams Niclas (James Nicholas to you), a retired inspector of schools from Bangor. He wore a nice gold hat and a great chain, and everyone clapped when he said that the Welsh should guard against carelessness with their language. He told the story of Steithenyn, a harbour guard who fell asleep while the flood-gates burst. Yes, parables are alive and well and living in Wales.

All the cloaks, which you can hire like university gowns, billowed and swirled with approval. We sang hymns from our 280 page programme, went through what sounded like a set of religious responses and watched in awe as a 6ft sword held horizontally aloft was thrust thrice into its sheath. A bit Freudian, thought we English. A blue bard then sang about the area, and a white druid conducted the community efforts with what looked like a gold propelling pencil. Frances Mon skilfully plucked her harp and new bards were installed. Certainly the Archdruid must be the most enthusiastic and vigorous hand-shaker in all of Wales.

Later, when the weather had brightened, the ceremonial reached new heights. Now, back on the field, and in the eisteddfod pavilion, which looks like a prefabricated factory, the Archdruid crowned the bard of the hour, 24 year old Sion Aled from Bangor, who'd written a free metre poem on the theme of 'Faces.' Judging by young Sion's face, he was happy as he faced the television cameras and rose from the crowd like a transfigured saint to the tune of *Men of Harlech*, played on a great computer organ. Less happy was a man in a blue suit, who just managed to stop flower clad schoolgirls walking into the wrong seats, and was so upset that one druid was wandering around without a chair, that he grabbed one of the Press seats. How the mighty had fallen!

So what's the eisteddfod all about? Obviously, it's not about the tourist ashtrays and glasses sporting images of ladies in stove pipe hats which sell on the side stalls. It's not even about making money, for this year's little do has cost £70,000 and will probably make a loss of £90,000. And it's not even about tourism, because too many concessions to cosmopolitan taste would rob it of its Welshness. 'No it's a celebration, a meeting,' said my guide. 'You walk around the field and meet old friends. It's like your Wembley, but you can't really equate a great cultural event with a football match. The trouble with you English is that you've been Americanised, although you don't know it. Our culture is purer. Many of us can express ourselves better in Welsh than in English. And our whole outlook is different. Our tolerance rate is different, and even our news is different. A £7,000 robbery is headlines here, but in Liverpool it probably happens every day. The eisteddfod is a totally Welsh experience, and you've got to be Welsh to really understand it.'

But whilst the causes of nationalism and the language are always to the fore (albeit under peaceful guidelines), one voice confessed: 'There's talk that the success of the Royal Wedding has set the Nat's cause back ten years.'

And then, there's always the thought that a culture under threat is always made stronger. Looking at the sheer elation of the crowd at the chairing ceremony, that gut reaction of being Welsh first and British second is a prime one. As the people rose to welcome their new bard, I expected dear old George Thomas to shout 'Or-der, Or-der.' But, alas, not today.

As a lad, George had walked over the hills of the Rhondda to his first eisteddfod. Today, like most others, he'd come by car; a symbol of the Westminster establishment yes, but foremost to clap when the Celtic delegates from afar affirmed: *Cymru am Byth!* Wales for Ever!

[6.8.1981]

GLITTERING PRIZES

Ron Callender's advice is worth its weight in gold. But don't expect to strike it rich overnight. It's for the love of life and travel that Ron's gold prospecting has taken him all over the world. He is now the leading British author and expert on the subject, and a former secretary for the World Gold Panning Championships.

What's more, this affable Scotsman, now Merseyside based, has made me an irresistible wager: that within a couple of hour's drive from Liverpool, we would find gold. And we did. Seven tiny specks taken from the gravel of a river-bed during a single afternoon.

Our journey took us to the Dolgellau Gold Belt in westernmost Wales: a still wild place, where 160 years ago, men dreamed of making fortunes by commercially mining gold from the ore-bearing crags that link Snowdonia to the uplands of Cader Idris. But just as the mythical magician Merlin failed at alchemy, they too failed to become tycoons. Mining was abandoned in 1914.

Today, the barracks and offices of Cefn Coch, 500ft above the Mawdach valley, are a roofless rockery to thistles and ferns. The rail line is broken and rusted. Ron hopes that one day such sites will be cared for like cathedrals and castles. They are as much a part of our heritage. 'This is industrial archaeology,' he says, pointing at a large flat stone beside a white foaming river that descends in a series of spectacular cascades and pools. To the uninitiated, it looks like debris from the Ice Age. But it is an 'arrastra', used to grind down rubble and reveal the gleaming precious metal of pharaohs and emperors.

Gold has fascinated Ron Callender ever since as a schoolboy in Lanarkshire - literally in the shadow of the Ravenscraig steelworks - he heard that the Scottish Crown had been made from local gold. 'It seized upon my imagination, and the fascination has never left me,' he admits. Since then Ron's prospecting travels have taken him from sunny California to the Arctic Circle. He has met men whose staking of claims have turned them into millionaires. Alas, he says, that cannot happen in Britain, where the flakes of gold are small.

Ron shows me his collection, made internationally over the past decade: perhaps enough if melted down, to make three gold rings, he says. 'People like me do it for the fun and the wonder of it all. To think that the gold we find today - however small in amount - came out of the earth's core, and has been waiting to be collected for three million years.'

But why did gold become the means of regulating the world's economy? 'I suppose mankind could have decided that coal was the most precious commodity,' admits Ron. 'But gold is relatively scarce, wonderful to look at, easy to work and it doesn't oxidise, so it keeps its shine.'

But beware of fool's gold: iron pyrites. One sure test, says Ron, is that while pyrites will float, gold, by virtue of its weight, will always sink. But the proof is in the producing. Ron puts water and soft gravel from downstream of large boulders (collected either by hand or suction pump) into a wooden pan made in Bolivia. He swirls the dish gently and examines the sediment carefully. The process is repeated several times. After 20 minutes - perhaps less - there is a tiny, tiny glint. It sinks. Ron has struck gold.

'What's it worth?' I ask. 'That depends whether you're buying or selling,' says Ron with an even bigger glint in his eye.

'No, seriously,' I enquire.

'Seriously, about £1,' says Ron.

To think, wars were fought over this stuff. Thousands were slain. Throughout Britain during the last century, there grew a rumour that gold was someway linked to the fourth degree west of longitude on the map. For it was found in Cornwall, West Wales, Cumbria and Scotland. But Ron — author of *Gold in Britain* — insists that it's a coincidence. 'We are talking about completely different types of rock formation where the various gold is found. In Wales, for instance, it is associated with quartz-bearing rocks.'

All of which goes to prove that some romantic tales are not worth passing on to the next generation. And just remember. All that glitters is not ...

[3. 9.1994]

AGATHA CHRISTIE

THE QUEEN OF CRIME

Torquay is the place to be this weekend. You can even get there on the Orient Express. For the world's most famous train has been diverted in honour of the world's most famous author. Agatha Christie was born in the Devonshire seaside resort 100 years ago tomorrow - the daughter of an American father and English mother. The visiting train, star of her best known novels, is but one of the gestures in honour of the quiet, diligent, dependable and unassuming writer, who acceded to the title of 'Queen of Crime', and is still outsold only by copies of the Bible and Shakespeare.

When she died in 1976, Christie's unparalleled reign had bequeathed to mankind: 78 crime novels; 150 short stories; four non-fictional works; six romances (written under the pseudonym Mary Westmacott) and 20 plays. So far, on the printed page, that adds up to two billion sales in 100 languages. On the stage there have been millions of spoken words too. Many of them to audiences of *The Mousetrap*, still enjoying a 38 year unbroken run in the West End, having generated £15 million in royalties. Indeed, that single, phenomenal mystery - originally requested as a radio play by Queen Mary, no less - has been performed in 44 countries before eight million people. Not bad for a girl who had no formal education, chose nursing as a career, and whose first novel was rejected by six publishers. However, *The Mysterious Affair at Styles* did eventually see the light of day, in 1920. It was inspired in the dispensary in Torquay where Agatha worked during the First World War. Not only does it explain her abiding fascination with poisons, but the presence of Belgian Refugees in the town gave birth to one of her two abiding fictional detective characters - Hercule Poirot.

The other, of course, is Miss Marple, prim to the point of being proper, and capable of solving the most perplexing crimes from the comfort of an armchair. The Christie genre became an inextricable part of the British scene in 1926, when *The Murder of Roger Ackroyd* was serialised in a national newspaper. Her style was one of clever and complete analysis. Everything was written into its place, all loose ends were tidied up. The pages were littered with inspectors, vicars and majors and spinsters. All very tee-hee and tra-la, but bolted together with the inevitable intrigue of whodunnit?

Yet there are two outstanding Christie mysteries to which answers are still being offered. The first concerns the ability of an 'average' writer to achieve such profound status: for instance, the *Oxford Dictionary of Quotations* does not contain a single Christie entry! It's down to the plots, say most. They, at least, are superb. The second Christie real-life mystery concerns the writer's disappearance following her first husband's adultery: Colonel Archibald Christie ran off with a woman called Miss Neele. Agatha Christie, much upset, vanished the night she got the news. For nine days, just prior to Christmas, the nation searched every field and hedgerow for the lost celebrity. Her car was found abandoned in Surrey. There was talk of suicide - and worse. A woman's right shoe was found, then a powder puff. A chemist said the writer had often discussed with him the many ways of committing suicide. Even her husband volunteered that she had once boasted that she could disappear without trace.

As it happens, on December 13, 1926, Agatha Christie was found - staying in a hotel in Harrogate. None of the guests had recognised her. The official explanation was that she had lost her memory. The less charitable called it a publicity stunt. The latter reason was unlikely. For Agatha Christie shunned publicity all her days, insisting that if she must make speeches, they should be no longer than two minutes. In September, 1930, following her divorce, she married Max Mallowan, an archaeologist she had met in the Middle East. They lived, as the best stories say, happily ever after.

But Agatha Christie's death 14 years ago - just five years after becoming a Dame of the British Empire - in no way stemmed the tide of appreciation. This year, one million of her paperbacks are expected to be sold in Britain alone. A great centenary tribute to a nice lady who, in life, had also earned the honours of CBE, and Doctor of Literature. Hercule Poirot was even immortalised on a stamp by Nicaragua. Agatha Mary Clarissa Christie died peacefully on January 12 1976, having immortalised herself as the best-selling author in the world. What's more, she still is.

[14. 9.1990]

THE IMPORTANCE OF BEING NEIGHBOURS!

I've put my Genius into my Life;
I've only put my Talent into my Works - Oscar Wilde

When Oscar Fingal O'Flahertie Wills Wilde sailed out of Liverpool on Christmas Eve, 1881, he had already gained a public reputation for witty conversation as fulsome as the private name on his Irish birth certificate.

And now, Oscar the Oxford graduate was off to America - on the good ship *Arizona* - to give the mentally impoverished Yanks the benefit of his mind. This he did for an entire year, often with no frills attached. For instance, when the outlandish folk of Griggsville sent him a wire asking: 'Will you lecture us on aesthetics?' Wilde simply replied: 'Begin by changing the name of your town.'

But from New York to San Francisco, Oscar was singularly unimpressed by America and Americans. Among their principal faults, he maintained, were bad manners; a complete lack of ceremonial - and an obsession with catching trains. However, had he been around three quarters of a century or so later, he may just have had a grudging admiration for one of their number: James Douglas Morrison.

Let us hope so. For in death, they are near neighbours. Wilde the leading dramatist, and Morrison, leader of The Doors rock band, are both buried in Pére Lachaise cemetery in Paris, where I spent a refreshingly pleasant day this week. No, I am not a ghoul. I like my steak well done, and I never kill spiders. But this magnificent site in the heart of the world's noblest city is back on the tourist map. Oliver Stone's film, *The Doors*, released here today, has rekindled the flame of eternal youth, which Morrison epitomised before dying of heart failure in 1971, at 27. Pére Lachaise is also 'home' to composer Frederic Chopin and the singer Edith Piaf. But it is Jim and Oscar who attract most visitors.

Nothing, though is sacred. Graffiti is a feature of both sites. And even Oscar cannot escape mediocrity. One such scrawl reads: "You are the greatest writer - Morrissey told me so.' To which, if he could, Oscar may well have said, as he did during one of his American lectures: 'Save me from my disciples.' No matter. Disciples he has a-plenty. They pay homage in a curiously silent way, compared to the antics at Morrison's plot. 'Here's a present from my mum,' says a Hippy, pouring the dregs of a bottle of wine onto the gravel of the grave. Yes, a Hippy! Risen, as it were, from the dead, complete with beads and waist-length hair.

Suddenly, one realises that the unifying spirit between Morrison and Wilde - apart from the stuff in a bottle - was style. And here are people attempting to emulate the deceased as if style has gone out of fashion. Perhaps it has. A century ago, who else but Wilde walked down the road in knee-breeches, silk shirt and green smoking jacket, complete with button-hole of sunflower or lily? And who, in the late 1960s, was being quite so outrageous - even in tight leather trousers - as Jim Morrison? Both greatly enjoyed scandalising society. Although neither could have forseen that their list of shared distinctions would include convictions for lewd behaviour and sentences of hard labour. By the vagaries of American law, Morrison escaped from serving his term. Oscar was less fortunate. Two years in prison broke his spirit, even if it did produce the masterpiece that is *The Ballad of Reading Gaol*. He died at 46, in a Paris hotel, hating the wallpaper and expiring with the memorable line: 'One of us had to go!'

Morrison died in his bath-tub. Or did he? For his wife, Pamela, who was killed in a car crash in Africa three years later, had sealed the coffin and obtained a death certificate by the time Doors manager Bill Siddon arrived from LA. The rumours thus started that Morrison had done a bunk, changed identity, and started a new life. Yet to him, Death would be a new life. It fascinated him. Oscar, on the other hand, when asked what happened to good Americans after death, replied that they ended up in Paris. Jim Morrison sure did. And what's more, he's in the very best of company.

[10.5.1991]

SCREEN

MERYL STREEP

WOMAN ON EVERYONE'S LIPS

Right now, Meryl Streep is quite simply the hottest property in the celluloid world of films. And nothing the critics might write tomorrow is going to alter that, despite the fact that *The French Lieutenant's Woman* which gets its British premiere tonight, is Miss Streep's first major film role. For she *is* the *Lieutenant's Woman*, and the *Lieutenant's Woman* has been a cult figure for the past 11 years, ever since novelist John Fowles had the book published.

But the box office pull doesn't end there. Harold Pinter, no less, has done the film script, a director of the calibre of Karel Reisz has succeeded where Fred Zinnemann, Franklin Schaffner and Mike Nichols did not, by actually putting it in the can, and Miss Streep's leading man, Jeremy Irons, has this week been whisked to telly stardom by appearing in the grand and costly series, *Brideshead Revisited*. All of which has left dear Meryl rather overwhelmed. She may have done films like *Julia, The Seduction of Joe Tynan, Manhattan* and *The Deerhunter,* as well as winning the Golden Globe Award as Best Supporting Actress in *Kramer Versus Kramer,* but the clamour of interest surrounding *Lieutenant's Woman* is truly unsurpassed. What's more, it's given to its shooting location, Lyme Regis, a mythical Camelot quality.

'Perhaps it's because it's come after so much summer fluff like *Raiders of the Lost Ark* and *Clash of the Titans*, and here, at last, is something to think and write about,' says Miss Streep by way of searching for an explanation. Before her other films, Reisz had seen her as Kate in a stage version of *The Taming of the Shrew* and knew that there was the intellect and power he needed to create the character of Sarah Woodruff, a turbulent, passionate spirit, born a Victorian, but belonging to the twentieth century.

'But you don't expect this response,' says the blonde American herself. 'When I was at college, the breadth of my ambition was just to stay employed. I was a Jack of all trades person and I'd studied religion, literature and science. I'd even been for voice training and ended up in a Broadway musical called *Happy End*, which got rave notices but which nobody came to see. Yet here I am, being offered the most incredible film roles in the world. Five years from now, it might be different, and therefore my stage career will remain a constant. I can go back there for ever.'

At first she was 'paranoid' about doing Reïsz's film. She worried about her accent and 'felt that every British actress must have hated me for getting the part ... I was so nervous we had to reshoot the first day's work.' And a party she'd thrown for the cast and crew ended in tears in the back kitchen. 'I thought some local gatecrashers were taking a rise out of my New Jersey accent, until I realised that that was how they spoke in Dorset.'

There was more serious upset when an American newspaper started rumour mongering about a real life affair between herself and Jeremy Irons during filming. 'Everybody who knows me and knows him knows it's untrue, but the great American public didn't know that. I couldn't take out a newspaper ad or anything, but it did prove to me that there were people out to get you.'

Yet there was a happy ending. Just everybody wanted to know about the movie. Miss Streep even came out with the memorable quote that she thought it was better than *Gone with the Wind*, the all time best seller. 'In the end, however, I wanted to stand in the middle of Time Square and say: "It's just another film, folks. It's not the Second Coming."'

One of the things that had most pleased her was Pinter's script, a marvellous piece of editing and control. 'It was so nice to be able to lie back on the script and rely on it, rather than having to improvise which is a big thing over in the States. The location was so nice too. There's nowhere in the world quite like that.'

But today in America, Meryl Streep is paying the inevitable price for that fame. She can't walk down a street in New York without being pestered. 'In London, I can, however. Because of the film, they all think I've got red hair. I guess that luxury now is peace and quiet. I wish I could say that I go to the Studio 54 disco and dance all night, but I can't. The money is wonderful, but the loss of privacy is horrible, and so security and insecurity have to exist side by side.' But one senses that she's largly unaffected by the temptation to go on any mad spending spree. 'I wouldn't pay outrageous prices for St Tropez type fashions. The clothes I'm wearing now are from *Kramer Vs Kramer*, because one of the nice things is that you get to keep them. I'm not one of those people who believe you have to walk round in furs and have facelifts every five minutes to prove anything.'

She has no secretary, but an accountant does the taxes and buys up New York bonds from time to time. She doesn't smoke, but likes a glass of wine, and reads non-fiction. Back in 1972, she was just another American teenager who came to Britain for the first time on a back-packing holiday. 'I'd like to travel more over here. Perhaps I will ...' But for the present, she's battling with a new film in which she plays a Polish Catholic girl. 'I can't do it yet, but I'm working on it,' she says with determination that would do credit to Sarah Woodruff.

[15.10.1981

JOHN CLEESE

THE MAN BEHIND THE BRITISH TWIT

I was in a Soho restaurant yesterday, having as discreet a lunch as is possible with a man as instantly recognisable as John Cleese, when up comes a television chap and asks Cleese to smack him in the face with a cherry gateau. This wasn't your pantomime custard-pie trick with shaving foam. It was a real cherry gateau, fully paid for. Cleese didn't even flinch: perhaps it happens all the time? So, with nothing to lose, he let fly, and the man (from Birmingham, I think) ended up with a ruined suit but very happy with the stunt. Even the head waiter didn't seem to mind the odd blob of cream on the carpet.

Extraordinary. But so is John Cleese, harbinger of the zany Monty Python humour of the early 70s, closely followed up by his rude television hotelier, Basil Fawlty, and roles in equally talked-about films like *The Life of Brian*. But now there is another talking point: the film version of Peter Nichols' award-winning play, *Privates on Parade*, in which he takes the part of Major Giles Flack, officer in charge of a 40s Army entertainment platoon in the Far East.

The backers include ex-Beatle George Harrison, who obviously sees the potential of such revelry, even if it was filmed around Aldershot, instead of deep in the steaming Malayan jungle. But producer Simon Relph was quick to assure me, it's not a film about fauna and flora - although there is wild life in abundance. It centres on the antics of the troupe, and provides as funny and outrageous a movie as you're likely to see for a long time. A touch of what Bette Midler would label as 'divine decadence'.

Cleese is called on to epitomise the British twit. It's now 12 years since he did his immortal *Ministry of Silly Walks* sketch on the small screen, but here he is again, double-jointing every limb, turning himself into Pipe Cleaner Man. Major Flack is also oblivious to an outbreak of blatant homosexuality among his troops. Cleese's co-star,

Denis Quilley (who played the West End title role in *Sweeney Todd*) portrays the wonderfully vulgar Captain Dennis, who calls his male cohorts by girls' names and tells them: 'Come in, if you're pretty!'

Quilley also took this part in the West End stage production. He says his daughter, who was only 16 at the time, laughed until she cried, watching dad slapping up and dragged up, doing his Marlene Dietrich and Carmen Miranda numbers. Quilley, and the only girl in the cast, Nicola Pagett (as a half-Welsh half-Indian beauty), had also joined in our somewhat extravagant lunch, but had moved on before the cherry gateau incident.

As for John Cleese, supporting a new full beard and the sort of outfit more benefitting a benevolent schoolmaster rather than a film star, well, he was left to do most of the explaining. He went to public school, and then went to Cambridge to read law, so it's almost inevitable that he's been stuck with this image of being 'good officer material'.

'It was a minor public school in Bristol, actually,' he says almost apologetically. 'We were taught to vault horses in the gym, to run across fields and through rivers, with some time left when Friday afternoon came along. As for the film, I didn't think the part was going to be too difficult, although I'd never been through a whole film before. When we did the Python films, I was only involved in sketches. But it's been marvellous, particularly the director, who always managed to see that something extra in a situation.'

Major Flack provides ample opportunity for wide (and wild) interpretation. He believes that his men are undertaking God's work, fighting a holy war against the new gospel of St Marx. Ironically, the real John Cleese has to admit: 'I'm a dreadful coward. I have a considerable fear of confrontation. I find it difficult to say to anyone: "this is not good enough".' And when people do get upset he always hopes that 'they'll sit down and talk about it'.

The nature of his work has brought plenty of chances for that to happen. 'I used to get far more uptight about it, but then I realised that if people want to be offended, they can always find something to pick on. Two days before I did the *Ministry of Silly Walks* sketch on television, a BBC man stopped me in New Bond Street and asked if I'd bothered to consider that the parents of spastic children might think I was making fun. Then in *Fawlty Towers*, when we had dead bodies appearing around the place, other people said that those who had just been bereaved could be hurt.'

He's even more definite in his words about *The Life of Brian*. 'Brian was not meant to be Christ. He was merely a Christ-like Messiah figure. The humour was about the reaction of his followers.' John Cleese says that he has never been impressed by organised religion, as it can detract from the essential purpose. 'I think it was best summed up in our sketch about Vice-Pope Eric, who said that in order to have a church that preached poverty and humility, you need a very powerful and very rich organisation to do it.'

As for his latest filmic swipe at the establishment, he says he fears that many people do make the assumption that all officers are as stupid as Flack, but he adds that his own meetings with soldiers have shown them to be 'very unselfish, very straight, very on the ball.'

No doubt about it, underneath the manic persona of Cleese the comic, there's a much quieter and very thoughtful Cleese. Indeed, he's just finishing the second draft of a book which he hopes will be of help to people. 'I've written it with my own ex-psychiatrist,' he said. 'I was on therapy for three years when my last marriage (to actress Connie Booth) began to go wrong. The working title is *Kitchen Shrink*, but I don't like that. For although it's got humour in it, I don't want to sell it on that.'

Cleese says it's amazing to discover how many people are paranoid about something or other. He thinks that right now the Conservative and Labour Parties are paranoid about the S.D.P. because the new party is threatening to break up the age-old private fight. He has harsh words too, for the Americans in San Salvador. But, as if stepping from within his latest film, he declares: 'I am totally against Communism, and I agree that a war is going on. I even think that if they could take us over they would.'

Having talked about himself and the world, he returns to himself: 'I am constantly trying to plan my life to allow time for the things I really enjoy, like reading.'

[28.1.1983]

RICHARD ATTENBOROUGH

GANDHI'S SECRETS

'No I don't think I want to make *Gandhi Two*,' says Sir Richard Attenborough, who has just given 20 of his 59 mortal years to immortalising the Indian man of peace. That film, just plain *Gandhi*, will have cost £22 million when everything, including interest on loans, is totted up, but already it's heading for universal sell-outs and Oscar nominations. In London it's already done seven weeks capacity business. In New York, the crash barriers are out as multitudes head for the cinema doors. And in Liverpool, where it arrives next month, they predict round the block queues.

Ironic, then, that when three bullets from a Hindu fanatic's gun felled the frail Mahatma exactly 35 years ago this coming Sunday, the sum total of his worldly goods could have been placed on a tea tray. Ironic, too, that via the three hours of Attenborough celluloid, the world is only just reawakening to the hypnotic effect of this little man, who despite his epic campaign to dismantle the British Empire, was an essentially private person, most content when at prayer or spinning thread. How he would have viewed this outbreak of 80s euphoria, it's hard to tell: He was neither proud nor ambitious. But how Attenborough has viewed him, via actor Ben Kingsley, the half Indian son of a Liverpool doctor, is vitally important in the context of documentary film making. For it is a film which is as notable for its omissions as its message. Attenborough admits that to most people 'Gandhi is a vague and shadowy figure.'

Indeed, back in '62, when someone at the Indian High Commission first suggested he made the film, Attenborough himself knew little of Gandhi. His subsequent image was built up by books and people, newspaper cuttings and news film clips. There were influential contacts too. Four times Louis Mountbatten came to Attenborough's aid in bridging gaps and acting as a go-between. Mountbatten spoke to Pandit Nehru, and it was Nehru, the first Premier of the new India, who told Attenborough to be careful of deifying Gandhi, of placing him on a plinth. There was even the Indian lady who thought that no actor was worthy of playing the Mahatma, and that he should be seen in the film merely as a moving shaft of light. And there was Attenborough's famous reply, which holds good to this day: 'I'm not making a film about bloody Tinkerbell.'

Nevertheless, the Gandhi he shows us is a contrite character. There is only a glimpse of the bad temper of his early years, the briefest of references to his sex life, which by all accounts was unusual, while his role as a father appears exemplary. However, Attenborough freely admits: 'He was a bloody awful father in terms of our concept of parenthood. He refused to treat his family as different or special from anyone else.' Elsewhere, one of the few concessions to Gandhi's more worldly traits is a benign, if concise, sense of humour - the sort you'd have expected from Noel Coward if he'd been one for tranquilisers. According to Attenborough, the omissions of sex, family and frailer temperament are forgiveable. To have included them would have coarsened things. 'The other problem is that if you try to say everything, you end up saying nothing,' he says.

The other bone of contention is the portrayal of British imperialism as almost totally a source of evil. We see massacres, yards of footage devoted to exposing blatant racism, and eavesdrop on twee British chat, courtesy of actors as distinguished as John Gielgud, Edward Fox and John Mills. Yet even here, it could be argued, there are important gaps. Only at the Press jamboree does Attenborough mention that General Dyer, the man who ordered guns to be turned on a helpless crowd, was treated as a hero back home.

So what we have is a very selective film, but one which is bound to stir emotions and deep-fry consciences. Certainly, its cast of thousands (quite literally) were impressed. Kingsley says it made a profound impact on him; Martin Sheen (who plays a newspaper reporter) gave his entire Hollywood type fee to Mother Teresa, and South African civil rights playwright Athol Fugard was immediate in his willingness to take part (he couldn't resist playing the racist General Smuts in the early scenes in South Africa, where Gandhi decides to devote his life to peaceful protest.)

As for Sir Richard, the actor turned director and son of a radical British upbringing, the post-filming depression has not yet set in. He still has to promote the work around the world - including a trip to South Africa, which will be interesting to monitor. But *Gandhi* will almost certainly be his major life's work, and one which he is well pleased with.

[24.1.1983]

ANTHONY PERKINS

RETURN TO HELL HOUSE ON THE HILL

The dusty Gothic-style Victorian house still stands on the hilltop. Below, a broken neon sign flashes on, announcing vacancies in the run-down motel. After 22 years Norman Bates is back in business - and so is one of Hollywood's greatest legends, *Psycho*.

'It was just like coming home,' says Anthony Perkins, who played Hitchcock's crazed killer in that celebrated film of the 60s, and now returns to star in a package directed by Hitchcock buff, Richard Franklin. *Psycho II* is already a hit in sequel-mad America and looks like blowing the mind of the box office when it reaches Britain next month.

It's already well-known that Perkins didn't even wield the knife in the famous shower scene of the original, when Janet Leigh is hacked to death. That shot was acted out by an unknown name on the film lot.Nevertheless, that scene and the role of Bates, has overshadowed Anthony Perkins' entire career, distinguished though it has been in other movies and on Broadway.

'As for *Psycho III*, well I don't know about that,' he says, as we meet up at London's plush Inn on the Park. 'I don't think it would invite a further sequel. This time, with Norman having been released from the asylum, it would seem the natural conclusion. Hitchcock himself never made sequels. He did remakes, some of which he was very proud of.

It's a melancholy tale, and a tragedy. Perhaps it's best now left alone. I mean, nobody ever doubted that there would be follow ups to *Superman*, and even when the industry did its first great follow up to the *Three Musketeers*, one had an inkling that it was inevitable. So I don't know. Do you think *Psycho II* is sufficiently open ended to carry on?' he asks, throwing the question back at me.

Certainly, it's ingenious in plot, and I wouldn't be such a heel as to give it away, except to say that Norman is still obsessed by the influence of his mother, there are more odd goings on down in the coal cellar, and that blood squelches - what's more, the new *Psycho* is in colour, which may not please the purists of black and white Gothic drama, but it certainly ensures a churning of the stomach muscles.

There are even some humorous moments, and the fact that they work well pleases Perkins. 'Hitchcock always called the first *Psycho* a comedy, you know; so if you find it funny, it's the ultimate compliment. Another thing that elicited most comment about the original was how preposterous it was at times. I remember asking Hitchcock why Vera Miles (who also reappears) runs out of the house and stops to look into the cellar. Why didn't she just beat it? He said: "That's what women do in films."

What he was, in fact, doing was showing respect for the story's Gothic traditions, where the place and the setting are all-important. It was pleasure and a treasure to work with him, and he was more accommodating than some people would have you believe. I would only be 28 or 29 at the time, and he adopted most of my suggestions. He was more open to ideas than any other director I have worked with.'

Perkins is glad that it's taken all this time to revive *Psycho*. 'It makes sense. Norman has been institutionalised for more than 20 years. I suppose it could have been rushed earlier by setting the sequel in the asylum, or allowing for a plot line whereby Norman escaped, but I think it works well this way. Not only that, the latest movie is really new territory. It's much more Norman's story, whereas originally, you could argue that the character was there to provide colour. All acting is a risk, of course, but I was convinced that the part was well written. It is a job honourably done. At one stage, there was another script and when people heard about it, I was being got out of bed at 3 o'clock in the morning. In fact, I've still got that other script at home.'

Also at home is Perkins' family: his wife, New York photographer, Berry Berenson, whom he married when he was 42, and their two sons, Osgood, 9, and Elvis, 7. Osgood even pops up in *Psycho II* as the young Norman Bates. His name's not difficult to find amongst the credits, because, as with the first *Psycho*, the cast is small. Hitchcock had wanted to prove to Hollywood that he didn't have to spend a lot of money to make a good movie. He used his TV crew and shot it on a very low budget with a short working schedule.

That famous old house, by the way, had been moved from its original location when Universal Studios' back lot had been redesigned. So this time, it appears on a different site, but with the old setting duplicated. It still has its secrets, and this time - even more so - its lessons. For it could be argued that *Psycho II* is very much wrapped up in the issue of rehabilitation.

'But you cannot make generalisations about mental illness. Knowledge doesn't accumulate in this respect. It only stands good by each individual. So the legislative arguments are not what it's about. More money and attention should be paid to individual cases,' he says, getting into fairly philosophical mood. 'The film is also about the corrosive influence of the revenge motive.'

But don't expect to walk along the streets of London or New York and bump into Norman Bates. Rarely has an actor in real life looked less like the character he plays. In the film, Perkins appears gaunt, his hair drawn forward, his eyes haunted. In reality he is jovial, beaming from behind large-framed spectacles and the hair is pulled back in a 50s look. It gives him a useful anonymity, which he'll be wanting now as he takes a break from the promotional circuit.

'Actually, I'm looking for a couple of tickets to the beach somewhere,' he admits. For being typecast isn't always fun, although it happens less now. 'At one time you'd find an actor, put him in a few films until the public picked up on what they liked about him and then offer him a career doing it. Today the choice is much wider and your life's not planned five years in advance.'

But time gives maturity. 'Only a grown man can do a grown man's job,' says Perkins. 'Acting is all about knowledge of other human beings. If you want to break the mould, then you have to go to another continent to work, which is precisely what I did after *Psycho I*.'

That said, he's more than happy with the Mark II version. 'One of the best things I've heard said is that you don't get to the end of the story before the end of the film.'

[8.8.1983]

BARBRA STREISAND

BARBRA'S *YENTL* TOUCH

Suddenly, after all the anxious glances and petty flusterings of her minders had filled the air with leaden expectation, she was there: a slip of a girl, long crimped hair flowing over cheeks without make-up, long fingernails caressing the wide-brimmed black felt hat, which she places on the table. A quarter of an hour late maybe, but Miss Barbra Streisand had made it for our lunchtime date. For what I was about to receive, may the Lord make me truly thankful...

The eyes smiled behind the rounded spectacles, the imperfect but sensuous lips parted, the quiet voice emerged: 'I don't want to have sour grapes.' They were not on the menu. For *hors d'oeuvres*, the world's number one female box office attraction was putting the record straight over those rumours about her being a tyrant on the studio lot.

'It started the day I came to Hollywood in 1967. The truth is, I am shy. In those days, Marlon Brandon and John Wayne were the stars, not me. I was scared and sat over in a corner. Next day, in the paper, I read that I was arrogant and aloof. So what more can I tell you? It's hard for me to say negative things about people...when I worked with really good directors, there was never a hard time. My role has always been to serve the director, and more recently to serve the actors.'

Miss Streisand understates her case, perhaps. She has just made movie history by being the first woman to star in, co-write, direct and produce a film. It's called *Yentl*, and its sunny seascape finale, with our star in full voice, was filmed aboard the *Manxman* in Liverpool Bay. 'I enjoyed Liverpool, just as I enjoyed filming the other location work in Czechoslovakia. My hotel room looked out over the water. What I didn't know until later was that we'd chosen to be on the Irish Sea for the worst two weeks of the year, when the tides are highest and the winds changing. Half of the 400 cast on board were seasick. Even the nurse got seasick and one of the cameramen got a gash on the head. But it was really exciting battling with nature. As an actress I like the controlled location of the studio, but as a director, I liked the open.'

In the film, which opens here next month, Miss Streisand plays a Jewish girl so determined to learn in a male-dominated society, that she dons the guise of a young boy. We are moving on to the main course: no other project in her multi-million dollar superstar existence has absorbed her so much. She first read Isaac Singer's short story of *Yentl* 16 years ago; she wrote the film outline five years ago and for the last three years it has occupied her totally.

Encouragement for the idea came ever so slowly. 'At first, I was terrified. I work from a very personal side of myself. I am not a student of film and have never been to film school, so I don't know the rules. I went on hunch, using an almost symphonic approach - a legato section here, a staccato one there. It was like delivering a child. At the time, you think you will never go through it again. But now I am through the pain and proud of the child. I kept changing things for a long time. They had to prise it out of my hands in the end...' But even after shooting was completed on October 3, 1982, she remained objective: 'You think I am going to tell you the flaws so you can write about it? No way.'

In fact, it is a smashing movie, with Streisand giving vent to 12 new songs; a musical without the falseness of the stage musical, and not without humour either. However, it has not produced the Oscar nominations you feel she might have wished for. A plaintive smile, and then: 'The comments of my peers whom I respect and the letters I've received are the things that warm you,' she says.

The film is dedicated to her scholar father, an English literature teacher, who died when she was 15 months old. 'It was a way of making him live a little longer.' But now *Yentl* is on screen, Miss Streisand, who once waited five weeks for her dole money in between quitting her first job as a telephonist-clerk and stardom, admits: 'I'm out of work.' She would like, she says, to play some classic roles, like Hedda Gabler, for television. 'I would like to be just a person for a while, to just walk through the streets. I haven't been shopping for a long while.'

[31. 3. 1984]

VANESSA REDGRAVE

Vanessa Redgrave looks down on me. Even without her high heels she would be doing the same. She's a tall lady - nearly 6ft by my reckoning - and with an equally lofty reputation. We stand around eating sausages on sticks, and considering that she can be seen devouring a plate of baked beans in her latest film, perhaps we've all gone up in the world. The movie is called *Wetherby*, named after the town, not the racecourse. In it, Miss Redgrave plays a Yorkshire school teacher forced to come to terms with her emotional past, after a young student visiting her suitably stone-clad house commits suicide before her eyes.

'I'm looking forward to seeing how much you enjoyed it,' she says. More about that later.

As far as the star is concerned it's 'a very exceptional piece of writing…certainly not just another assignment.' A look down the credits gives a clue: here's David Hare, already with stage and television plays like *Fanshen, Teeth 'n' Smiles, Plenty* and *Licking Hitler* under his belt, making his feature film debut as writer and director.

The producer is Simon Relph and the cast includes Judi Dench, albeit in a minor role, making her comeback to the big screen after a gap of 15 years. But there's also Joely Richardson, daughter of Vanessa and director Tony Richardson, still studying at RADA, but notching up her first major film role. She plays her mother as a young woman in the film, the looks of the Redgrave lineage firmly implanted. She joins Mum at the London Press launch. Both are suitably independent. 'I neither encouraged her nor discouraged her from going into the business,' says Vanessa... 'You can learn a lot from children who are no longer children any more.'

'It's the younger version of my mother's character which I play, not my mother,' says Joely.

And so the family business goes on, from grandfather knight to aspiring student. At 48, Vanessa Redgrave, fresh from the triumphs of her film, *The Bostonians*, says that the learning and the teaching never stop. Today, there is no talk of politics and picketing (for which she has stolen quite as many headlines as for her acting). Today it is all theatre and film: Redgrave the actress.

'I always try to place myself in the situation of the character. I have to put myself into the shoes of the job,' she says. 'When I first did Shakespeare, I used to listen to old 78 records of Dame Edith Evans. I used them as a sign-post, a sort of A to Z. You benefit from it, and it's true of all artists. Even Picasso studied the great Renaissance painters before founding his own techniques.'

And so to *Wetherby*. She sees its final doleful toast: 'To all our escapes' as a dedication of the film to the young.

'It is about a group of very lonely people. Like a lot of people, Jean (her character) is a person who has worked hard in life, but not got a lot out of it. She is well-read and conscientious, but she hasn't got very much experience to deal with her problems.'

The film is one of the hall-of-funny-mirrors time-warp pieces, which may not become the darling of the commercial circuits. But it's superbly put together - all the inter-linking atmospheres and tensions are there - and it's remarkable, in my view, for the filming of faces. The focal point is that lofty Redgrave head, with its classic flaxen hair and remarkably expressive eyes.

[6.3.1985]

ALAN BLEASDALE

ON A GRAND SCALE

Yosser's back in town. So is Chrissie. Along with a charabanc of other actors, they are booked into the Adelphi Hotel for the next five weeks, making the average man wonder whatever happened to your average theatrical digs.

There are 70 bedrooms worth of Equity card holders, most of them locals, give or take the odd visitor, like ex-*Z Cars* hero James Ellis, who's nurtured a beer belly and had the sides of his head shaved down to the canvas. Punky!

And just passing through is the man responsible for it all - Alan Bleasdale. He's written his first feature film, *No Surrender*, about a New Year's Eve party in a rundown Liverpool social club. Hence the top people's hotel, crammed with top names on their way to a shoot. But the writer seems ill at ease. 'I was 32 before I ever came in the Adelphi...here, and George Henry Lee's.'

'The characters from the *Blackstuff* are dead, but the actors are back,' he says, referring to Bernard Hill, Michael Angelis and co. And letting us know, right from the start, that his film is not the offspring of his phenomenally successful TV series, which brought in all those awards and led to Melvyn Bragg searching for superlatives on a *South Bank Show* special.

Perhaps the only thing special about Bleasdale is his writing. Which is why he shuns the limelight and didn't bother to go down to London to hand out one of the BAFTA awards last week. And he will not be appearing on the telly advertising *The Guardian*. He appears to be in a constant state of shock. 'A woman showed me a thesis on my work which she's doing for a masters degree. Some people do make a lot out of it. Sometimes absurdly so.'

The producer of the new film, Mamoun Hassan, calls it 'one of the most serious works to come out of Britain in two decades...a tumultuous comedy, but with a most serious intent. Alan's opinions of the world take second place to this experience of it. All the characters are driven by the irrational.'

And the director, Peter Smith, says Bleasdale 'writes from the heart rather than from the head.'

It's a first feature-length movie for all three. Smith is perhaps best known for his work on Channel 4's series, *The Price*, set amidst the Irish troubles, and still servicing the Irish press with letters.

Hassan is former manager-director of the National Film Finance

Corporation, now working for Dumbarton Films, whose backers include Michael Peacock, Tony Jay, Huw Weldon and John Cleese. This little bit of Bleasdale industry is providing work for a cast of 300, including 80 speaking parts. Bernard Hill is a broken-nosed bouncer; Michael Angelis the man in charge of the clubhouse; James Ellis an ex-boxer, and somewhere along the line, pop singer Elvis Costello gets a look-in as a conjurer who can't conjure. 'But he spent a week with a real conjurer,' says Bleasdale, by way of inside info.

The size of the piece, which should be on the commercial circuit by the autumn, gives Bleasdale a chance to work on the grand scale. Yet Hassan, who vaguely mentions a £2 million budget, says he does not wante to get bogged down in the money question. 'In film terms, it's still an epic being made for twopence. In 45 days of shooting, there are only four days when we are dealing with two-handers. The rest have people everywhere.'

The club setting - finding it is a tribute to locations manager John Bernard - is a former Canadian services depot in Warrington. The designers have turned it into something resembling a pink Stalag Luft. It is an arena setting for tribal rites between Irish Catholics and King Billies. The old Orange and Green syndrome. Most of the characters are getting on. And Bleasdale, whose original working title was 'Good Night' (based on the Dylan Thomas line: 'Do not go gently into that good night') says it's about 'the mortality of man'.

'The thing is,' enthuses Hassan, 'they do not go gently. They are volatile. They come ready armed. They only have to speak two lines and they tell you who they are. If you set this in London, it would be totally unbelievable. But here, it works.'

Certainly, Bleasdale believes that it had to be made here, although the themes are universal. '*The Last Place on Earth* had to be set at the South Pole, but that doesn't mean it's a South Pole play,' he says by way of explanation. So Liverpool, complete with an opening shot that includes the Liver Buildings, maybe. But new. 'I wasn't interested in doing "Girls from the Pinkstuff of Scully Revisited".'

Are the 120 pages of script bursting with fresh dimensions?

'Oh, there are times when you can see that Alan has seen other movies,' says Hassan, 'but that doesn't matter. He's the most generous writer I have ever dealt with. It remains totally original, an ensemble piece, a major piece of action.'

What's more it will be getting the big launch treatment. It is not, insists the producer, ' a project for the benefits of the friends, families and lovers of the film makers.'

[14.3.1985]

HARRISON FORD

DESERT ISLAND RISKS

I was tempted to ask Harrison Ford for a loan. Not just because he's filthy rich, having starred in five of the ten most successful films of all time, but also because, meeting up with him in a posh hotel on the Thames embankment, he looked like a rejuvenated version of Michael Heseltine. It was the slashed back Tarzan hair and the pin-stripe suit that did it. From my seat in the cinema, he had more usually been sporting half a week's chin stubble and looked like an advert for the Army and Navy Stores. But the voice was much the same: a tobacco-chewing drawl, well capable in everyday conversation of verging on the monotonous. 'I am sick of production stories and the celebrity interviews. I don't enjoy those sort of pressures when I'm working.'

It was fair warning that reporters would not be welcome when he starts the shoot on his third *Indiana Jones* movie shortly, with Steven Spielberg again in the director's chair. With too much advance hype, a film can become dissipated. By the time it comes up, you feel as if you have already seen it. But Mr Ford, the former space pirate hero, Han Solo of *Star Wars,* and veteran of *Raiders of the Lost Ark, Indiana Jones and the Temple of Doom* and *Witness* (his last big movie hit), is more than willing to talk about his latest screen role.

The Mosquito Coast is the story of an All-American family, who one day leave the supper dishes in the sink and set off for a new life far away from the madding crowd. Yep, Mr Ford is back in the jungle, playing an idealistic chauvinist called Allie Fox, who subjects his wife and kids to a *Robinson Crusoe* survival course in the belief that the high-tec vitamin-consuming U.S.A. is about to disappear up its own alimentary canal. It's a crazy and far fetched story. Not once, but thrice, they try to make a go of it. But I'm not giving too much away, save to say that the weirdest notion is that the Fox father invents an ice machine as tall as the Statue of Liberty in the hope of dispensing deep freeze facilities to the natives.

Americans, it seems, either love it or hate it as a critique of their phony "Have a Nice Day" existence, not least the blind and fundamental evangelism - what Mr Ford calls "a certain type of religious practice which accumulates souls like a string of scalps."

However, a British audience, I suspect, will wish for nothing more than the ghost of Roy Plomley to rear up from behind a rubber plant and play eight records of Mr Ford's choice. Our star had sat around for 18 months before deciding that this was the next step in his glittering career. He says he's pleased with the result. 'I was looking for something to contrast with what I had done in *Witness* (another Peter Weir film, in which he played a detective), something with some ambition and aspect of uniqueness. I get offered a lot of scripts, but I don't read them unless the subject matter appeals to me. I knew this was going to be controversial. Allie Fox is not a comfortable person to be with. But there are lot of positive aspects to him. He has great energy and determination.

In some ways it's easier to play a character who has so much complexity. It's like the choice of trying to fill a large room with an accordion or a full symphony orchestra. Besides, I have quite a lot of experience in common with him, as a son, a father, a husband and a working man.' Perhaps not everyone yet knows that Harrison Ford was a carpenter before becoming multi-million dollar box office. 'And I still am,' he insists.

Now he's about to become a father again after a gap of 18 years. His second wife Melissa Mathison - she wrote the film script for *E.T.* - is expecting a baby next month. It's an arrival which may mean Mr Ford missing out on *Mosquito Coast's* Royal premiere in London, but he doesn't seem too bothered. 'It's going to be a whole new experience. I've started adding up the years and working out how old I'll be when the child is 18 years old (he already has two sons, aged 20 and 17, from a previous marriage). But I am ready for it...'

He divides his time between L.A. and a ranch-style home in Wyoming, where he helps to maintain a wildlife refuge. That's the gentle giant reality behind the macho screen hero. 'Look, I nearly got drafted for the Vietnam War, but I registered as a conscientious objector. I don't think they believed me at first, except that I had been a philosophy student at college. But seriously, I would not involve myself in the taking of human life.'

Nor would Mr Ford, healthy specimen though he is, involve himself in the jogging boom. He prefers to ski, rock climb, deep-sea dive and ride horses. 'The financial success I have had has certainly given me a degree of freedom. That is what I have used my money for. And that is what Wyoming is all about: a way of refreshing yourself and facing up to other simpler issues.'

You certainly won't find him basking in the glory of his own image on screen. 'I see the daily rushes all the time, and I may see a film once or twice when it's over. But once it comes out, I probably would never see it again. I like other films if they are successful on their own terms. There are a lot of good people producing good work. But I don't think I need to see another virgin deflowering, loss-of-innocence film in my life....and I don't like car-chases in a movie for the sake of them.'

He believes in the director's omnipotent rights on set, and says he would never produce or direct his own material. Neither is there any hankering after a parallel stage career. 'It's a different culture. I would have to go to some place like New York to do that, and I just don't get the time. My private life is important to me. I am only ambitious to do what I am doing.'

Just before we met, a girl had asked him what it was like to be at the summit of his career. Amused, he had said 'Perhaps I have nowhere to go but back down. Perhaps we should call it a plateau. My ambition was only ever to be a working actor. I never thought I would have the opportunity to do the sort of roles I have.'

[15.1.1987]

TERENCE DAVIES

VOICES FROM A DISTANT PAST (REVIEW)

Something sensational happens in Liverpool tonight. Terence Davies *est arrivé*. Not that members of his family will be cracking open bottles of the Beaujolais still quite Nouveau, as they see themselves plastered all over the big screen.

Davies, now 43, has spent four years putting together two autobiographical sequences under the idyllic sounding title of *Distant Voices, Still Lives*. The trouble is, the voices are distanced by a generation; the lives are about as still as those of ferrets into Acid House. Most of his family remain on Merseyside. When they see the film, some cry, some are displeased, although all gave permission to proceed. The film depicts Davies' father as a psychotic brute. We see him beating one of his daughters as she scrubs the cellar floor. All she has done is ask to go to a dance. If the story were no more than a brave new interpretation of *Cinderella*, it would scarcely matter. But Davies uses it as a mere incident in the catalogue of a physically abused childhood. 'He died when I was seven. There are still some things I can't believe really happened. Like being kicked all the way up the stairs just because I didn't do something he wanted at exactly the time he wanted it.'

The real-life legacy is Davies' hatred of unpleasantness : 'I only have to go into a room to sense there has been a row' - a feeling of guilt if he's late, and an almost obsessive pre-occupation with the truth: 'I just cannot tell a lie.' But the suffering and the scars have brought their reward artistically. His film has been fêted all over the world, from Cannes to Canada, and tonight it comes home.

And what a truly remarkable work it is: Terence Davies, rescued from the barbs of establishment movie makers by the foresight and generosity of the British Film Institute, has, inadvertently perhaps, become the chronicler of an age. What he shows is the Liverpool of the 40s and 50s, endowed with the sort of bleached tint used for Orwell's *1984*, and presented as a celebration of photographic detail and love of imagery. Not that it's sentimental: 'That's the sort of cosy stuff you want to remember.'

Here the scenario is one of war, warts and all. Life is an abysmal round of births, marriages and deaths, held together by the Roman Catholic Church, the pub and the parlour. Davies is still angry with institutionalised religion. 'To think I once really believed.' He lost his faith somewhere between 17 and 22, and has replaced it with a devotion to film, poetry and music. 'You can achieve a lot through anger, but never through bitterness. Bitterness corrodes you from within.'

Yet there is much left to savour: the cosy voice of the *BBC Home Service Shipping Forecast*, a million miles away from the glowing coals of a terraced house fireside, but providing a sort of assurance that civilisation was intact; even the remembrance that 1959 was a hot summer, when people sat out on doorsteps in polka dot frocks. But what about all the things we have forgotten? Stripy flannel pyjamas; billowing net curtains; hanging out on sills to clean sash-cord windows; chopping firewood with an axe; *Two-Way Family Favourites*; hospital wards lined with cold white tiles; scarlatina, once the scourge of healthy childhood. And, of course, the war and the air-raid shelters.

And songs about barefoot days. Indeed, Terence Davies' film is almost the documentation of an era through songs. There are more than 30 of them, sung with gusto or melancholy, mentioning things like the Harrison Shipping Line and all manner of local detail. But the result is not parochial. 'They really go for it in downtown Osaka,' says Davies, now enjoying global recognition, and prepared to chastise films like Frank Clarke's *Letter to Breznev* and Alan Bleasdale's *No Surrender* as no more than 'filmed plays.' He prefers movies which extol silences and promote picture content. 'When you recall a film, you recall what you've seen, not what was said.'

Certainly, in *Distant Voices, Still Lives*, Liverpool's post-war years are captured as never before. I couldn't help thinking that somewhere just off screen, four little Beatles were growing up. And what happened after that, the world already knows anyway.

[2.12.1988]

THE DRESSMAKER

THE 'LIVERPOOL' WAY WE WERE (REVIEW)

Once upon a time, when film-makers wanted to get away from Oxford plum-in-the-mouth characters, and set real people in real situations, they were partial to setting up shop in Yorkshire. Very ee-bah-gum and hecky thump. And if they were looking for a little aggression, Glasgow, with its Gorbals still intact was a popular stopping off place. Watch it, Jimmy! Nowadays they come to Liverpool - and get the lot.

A whole new industry has sprung up in the streets where barrow boys and girls once chorused: 'Buy me last lettuce, and I'll give ya two.' Much has been home made: *Letter to Brezhnev, The Fruit Machine* and *Distant Voices, Still Lives,* to name but three. But when American producer Ronald Sheldo decided to take up the option on Beryl Bainbridge's novel *The Dressmaker,* runnerup for the Booker Prize back in '73, he was not just doing his bit for provincial England. He knew he was on to a winner. He got another Liverpudlian, John McGrath (founder of the 7:84 theatre company) to rework the book for screen; Jim O'Brien (of *Jewel in the Crown* and *Monocled Mutineer* fame), to direct; peppered the cast with local talent, and headed up the credits with the names of Joan Plowright and Billie Whitelaw.

The scene is Liverpool at the end of the war. The Yanks are at Burtonwood, with their money and their habit of driving into town to seduce the local wenches. You could be swept off your feet, or just left pregnant in a shop doorway; there are two sides to every romance....

Miss Plowright (Mrs Laurence Olivier to you!) plays Auntie Nellie, a woman who presides over a sewing machine with the power of a road drill, and makes party frocks for the neighbours. Parties in 1944 consisted of a sing-song around the piano, or a quick fling around the front parlour to the sounds of Glen Miller on the wind-up gramophone. That, in turn, wound up the Auntie Nellies of the world, matriarchal moral arbiters, always burning the midnight oil on behalf of others - just in case a randy American left his chewing gum on the bedpost overnight. Thus her sister, Margo (Billie Whitelaw) and her teenage niece, Rita (Jane Horrocks), fall under the dowdy spell of stern Victorian morals. Peter Postlethwaite, ex-Everyman and Playhouse, is once again cast as a wayward father figure. Not violent, as in Terence Davies' *Distant Voices*, but never the less bankrupt of the usual parental duties.

Nellie, it seems, has neutered everyone. Her floral pinnie merges with the floral wallpaper. She floats around the house like a ghost in hair curlers. After all, being beautiful in the Blitz consisted of putting curling tongs on a gas ring. You could produce kiss curls, provided kissing was all you did. Every older generation thinks, as this film reminds us, that they are presiding over the downfall of civilisation. It's been like that since the Romans lay on their backs to eat a bunch of grapes.

But with clever camera work, Jim O'Brien has uncovered the lost civilisation that was Liverpool city centre - despite the work of the Luftwaffe. There are cobbled streets, old trams and vintage cars. When they film at the Cathedral, they are careful to shoot only the parts which were built by the end of the war. The shops and offices are beautifully in period (Margi Clarke makes a brief appearance from behind a counter), and the banks of the Mersey are fenced off with warnings of land mines. There are some things which even authentic movie makers cannot achieve, however - like a soot-stained Liver Building. The grey granite gleams in the light of hoped-for victory.

Even so, *The Dressmaker* fully measures up to the hopes of its backers. I can assure you of that.

[16.12.1988]

PAULINE COLLINS

SHIRLEY IS HER DARLING

The once saucy maid from *Upstairs, Downstairs* was very much on the right end of the bell-push as we met for afternoon tea at London's Mayfair Hotel. Life above stairs, amidst the plushest real estate in the land, seemed to suit the scenario of the out-of-town journalist getting the exclusive interview from the new-born movie star.

But some things are basic and cannot be swept like crumbs beneath the silver service. 'It would have been wonderful to have a magnificent body to show off,' says Pauline Collins, the Wallasey actress, who at the age of 48 consented to a romp in the nuddie with Tom Conti, as explicit lovers in the film version of Willy Russell's *Shirley Valentine*. Seemingly eager to get the matter off her chest once and for all, Ms Collins, the real-life Mrs John Alderton, was emphatic: 'I have never had long legs, even when I was in my twenties.'

That's nature for you. I take a sip of tea and contemplate the situation. It probably helped that she and Mr Conti are neighbours in London and that their respective children go to school together? Definitely yes. ''I was surrounded by friends,' says Pauline, who cast caution to the winds for the sake of her art on a motor boat off the Greek Island of Mykonos. She, playing a Liverpool spouse on the loose, and Tom Conti, a taverna owner who serves up more than kebabs, swim, caress and eventually move the earth to the accompaniment of a full symphony orchestra. Not bad, eh?

She had gone topless before: in public, in a TV film called *Knock Back*, and in private on European beaches. 'I suppose I could have had a film career in the sixties, but I didn't look like you were meant to look then, so it never happened.' It has now, however, with our star being chosen from a shortlist of eight for the big screen treatment of Liverpool writer Russell's story of a housewife and mother's bid for freedom and fulfilment. She did, of course, possess immaculate professional qualifications, having won the Olivier Award for Actress of the Year in the West End theatre production, and carted off a Tony for the Broadway show. In both cases, as with Noreen Kershaw's world premier of *Shirley Valentine* at the Liverpool Everyman, she did the stage version solo.

Now, in the expanded film treatment, with a cast of more than 30, there's talk of an Oscar nomination. If she pulls that one off, it will be the first time that the three top prizes will have gone to one person for one role. Understandably, perhaps, she doesn't discuss it. That would be tempting fate. But fêted she has been: 'I'm not a person who goes into anything in order to win a prize. This has probably been my favourite part, which is a prize in itself.'

So back to Shirley. She is much more than a representation of middle-class crisis. She is the embodiment of what happens to a person when they underestimate themselves or are taken for granted by others. And her plight is equally applicable to men, many of whom have written to Pauline Collins, saying just that: 'They said they were the real Shirley Valentines, although most related to being trapped by a work situation.' More disturbing were letters from people who said the play had so liberated them that they intended to get divorced. 'Those were mostly in England, and although I replied to every letter, I would not presume to give any advice. As always, I would suggest people followed their instincts.'

Anyway, Pauline, who says that there were a lot of genuine Shirley Valentines on Mykonos, says that the script is Willy Russell's and not hers. 'I don't see it as a feminist film or a romantic film. If you want to put a label on it, then I think it's a humanist film. You can always understand the feeling of wanting to break free. It's a rare person who doesn't feel unfulfilled in some way. So it's about using all sorts of areas of yourself. I always feel that I would like to knock off a deathless novel ....but I am very lazy.'

Nevertheless, in a career of almost 30 years, Ms Collins has never given that impression. Best remembered for her TV work, including comedy roles with her husband, Pauline got her first job at Windsor Rep. in 1962 playing an Arabian slave girl. Liverpool appearances included John Mortimer plays at the Royal Court with Glynis Johns, Denholm Elliot and Joss Ackland. And in *Shirley Valentine*, some of which was shot locally, she is in company with a whole lot of Liverpool-related talent including Alison Steadman, Bernard Hill and George Costigan. 'I still have relations on Merseyside, mainly cousins and aunts, some of Shirley's generation.'

One of the joys of *Shirley Valentine* is that she spends so much time talking to herself. 'We all do it. I do it all the time,' says Pauline Collins, who for the next few months has promised herself just that: a nice rest away from the madding crowd. And the next role? 'It would be nice to play a hooker,' she jokes. 'That would be a challenge.'

[8.9.1989]

RICHARD GERE

NO MORE MR NICE GUY...

Richard Gere had just returned from visiting his friend, the Dalai Lama, on the other side of the world. So taking afternoon tea, sitting on Regency chairs beneath the cut glass chandeliers and gilded friezes of the Hyde Park Hotel must have been something of a culture shock. A mature lady in a peach-coloured wide-brimmed hat did a double take at the denim-clad idol sitting in the midst of a trinity - completed by a gent in casually crushed attire, and another in a Next suit. They were, respectively, the Director and Producer of Gere's latest movie, *Internal Affairs*. They spoke if spoken to.

Internal Affairs, in which Gere plays an LA cop at the centre of a corruption investigation, is released hot on the heels of *Pretty Woman*, which has Our Hero as a Wall Street mogul. Getting two films launched at once, says Gere, takes care of his career for a while, and leaves space for him to get on with other things - like campaigning for human rights in Central America, and his love of all things Tibetan.

But one movie is enough for one day's conversation. *Internal Affairs* contains both sex and violence. Relentlessly. Gere, one of the nice guys of the big screen, is first seen as a trusty law enforcement officer. As the frames unfold, he is transformed into a lurid, calculating, homicidal maniac. And, as some of the tabloids like to put it, a Sex Beast. All of which makes me doubt if the Dalai Lama will be seeing it.

Gere says the two lives are necessary for him - that of acting, and of inner contemplation. 'Buddhism gives you a way of dealing with anger and negativity when it comes up. There are specific techniques,' he explains. 'To be in the presence of someone (the Dalai Lama) so developed within themselves certainly helps you to look after your own life.' But no. He's not going to become a monk. He had, however, majored in philosophy at the University of Massachusetts before setting out on a dramatic career. Perhaps that's why his perceptions of art tend to be intellectual and historical.

His street cop, Dennis Peck, is invested - or should that be infested?- with Shakespearean delusions of grandeur. 'He is obviously a monster, but you can't just play that for its own sake. You have to find a quality. The nearest is that of jungle cats. The first animal kids want to see in a zoo is a tiger. A charismatic killing machine. But whereas animals only kill for food, human beings are full of malice.' Gere takes a civilising sip of his tea. 'We even tried a script version of the film without the violence,' he says. 'But it lost its motor. It didn't drive.'

And he recalls: 'When I first saw the script, through agents, I found it disturbing. I didn't really want to do it. But when I distilled it in my mind, I realised it was really about control, manipulation and power, with the psychological aspect being the most important.' He did his homework, which included a lot of time with the real Force. On the streets, Gere saw a man so badly beaten that the flesh of his face was detached from the skull. 'I just couldn't believe you could put someone like that back together, but they did. But the experience was extremely shocking to me.'

Now heading up to forty this year, Gere, it seems is more shocked by the notions of his image. I ask him if he regards himself as a sex symbol. The man in the Next suit twitches. 'I have no interest in responding to that,' says Gere, still smiling. The man in the casually crushed attire says that while he agrees with Richard, he sees my point, as 'an undeniable facet of the way people look.' OK, OK. So does he regard himself as a sex symbol in the way he is packaged? 'I have never felt packaged. I am a free agent.' I think he is still smiling. Obviously, this line of enquiry is extinct.

The movie's the thing. 'I have always been on the good side of things, but here I am, as a villain. However, I am initially perceived as good and that's important.' Someone from a foreign paper asks about romance in real life. And in a wine, women and song sort of way. 'I was never particularly a womaniser. It was all reputation,' comes the reply. At this point I opt out, leaving Mr Gere to his reputation as a serious actor - sex symbol and all.

[5.4.1990]

DANIEL DAY-LEWIS

SUSSEX MAN IN THE WILDERNESS

The case of the man seen running around the Sussex Downs with a long rifle can now be closed. It was merely Daniel Day-Lewis, pretending to be Hawkeye.

'I think I alarmed a few people,' admits the star of the new movie, *The Last of the Mohicans*, which opens nationwide tomorrow. But being mistaken for Sussex Man was only the start of things. Day-Lewis was then whisked off to the Blue Mountains of North Carolina for weeks of rigorous wilderness training in thickets of 500-years-old hemlock bushes. He had to learn how to kindle a fire in 25 seconds, how to hunt and skin game, and to use period weapons such as tomahawks and flintlock rifles. In fact, no-one knows *exactly* how Indians fought with tomahawks and knives during the English-French frontier wars of the 1750s.

Back home, Europe was in the midst of Baroque elegance. But in the vast open spaces of America, the laws of nature still ruled over the skill of man. Day-Lewis insists that getting this feel for time and place is essential - 'a luxury that every actor must fight for. This period of intensity leading up to a movie is very important to the work that is eventually seen on screen. And the offer came at the right time. I needed some fresh air and to stretch my legs.'

As he recalls the mood, his gangly frame is stretched out on a low-backed chair at Warner Brothers offices in London. 'Yes, some of it was fun and a lot of it was hellish.'

And some - according to his co-star Madeleine Stowe, who joins us for a chat - was self-imposed. 'He used to sit in a car in 100 degrees of heat, with the windows wound up, saying "I love misery",' giggles Madeleine. Daniel giggles back.

'It's not an easy thing running around with a long rifle. Especially one that's longer than any other recorded in the history of arms,' he says. 'In fact, the first rifles I was training with were not as long as the ones I finally used. Although I did do a lot of running to get used to it, there was a limit because I had to gain weight, whereas, in reality, I lose weight very quickly.'

Day-Lewis, who counts General Wolfe of the Quebec campaign amongst his ancestors - 'the family only mentioned it when we drove past his statue on the way to my grandfather's house' - says he was attracted to the role of Hawkeye because 'we were dealing with the physicality of a frontier that was relatively untouched by man. You never knew from day to day what would be required of you in terms of energy. I really had to set my mind on avoiding little conveniences - such as people offering cups of tea. Those types of comfort were distracting on this movie. The environment was hard - and you had to stay with that.'

Which may explain sitting in the car with the windows up? Whatever, come the wind-up of the production, he suffered considerable culture shock. 'When we finished the last session, which went on for something like 27 hours, I found myself, in a very short space of time, suddenly away from the mountains of North Carolina, and on the streets of Paris. I remember standing on the street corners and watching cars, and wondering how they worked. Then I did indulge myself - lots of coffee and chocolate.'

The winner of an Oscar for his portrayal of the writer Christy Brown in *My Left Foot*, Day-Lewis says his next project is a film for Jim Sheridan about the Guildford Four. 'It's difficult not to be overwhelmed and not to feel rage on behalf of those who went through it. It's a very shocking story. But it's important for me to remain objective.'

Day-Lewis, who made his screen debut with a brief appearance in *Sunday, Bloody Sunday*, at the tender age of 12, had been playing Hamlet in the West End prior to being cast as Hawkeye. And despite his success in cinema, he says it's hard to judge how his Oscar truly affected the course of his career. 'I am in a slightly innocuous situation. Of course, I've been involved in films that have been successful, but they haven't made money.'

For all the fame Day-Lewis remains essentially a shy person. 'The most ludicrous paradox of film making - despite the presence of all the crews and the extras - is that it remains a private experience,' he insists. Dressed in cravat, tweed jacket and black jeans, he looks like a well-to-do student from 20 years ago. He doesn't like interviews, but he does them, punctuated by much laughter and goodwill.

'Yes, my surname does have a hyphen in it. My father started using it because he was fed up of being called Mr Lewis.'

[5.11.1992]

SYLVESTER STALLONE

DEMOLITION MAN

Sylvester Stallone - who bursts onto the cinema screen this weekend, in his new action guise as 21st century cop *Demolition Man* - has the ideal cure for the Hollywood blues. A Scouse minder. Although, as Sly points out, 32 year-old Kevin King from Croxteth - who's worked for him for the last eight years - is much more.

'He lives at my house, he cooks well, he's part my secretary, part security. He keeps the girls away.... and he introduces them to me. I tell you, if Kevin had a fatal accident, I would jump into the grave after him.' And he jokes: 'He's the guy I should have married.'

But after the break-up of his second marriage to Danish model and singer Brigitte Nielsen in 1987, Stallone, the tough guy raised in New York's Hell's Kitchen, really was in a mess. Getting back on track was an uphill struggle that would have daunted even his most macho creations - Rocky and Rambo.

'It had got to the stage when they loved Rocky, but couldn't stand Stallone. I had 10 to 15 bodyguards around me and I became so insulated. I didn't know whether the sun was coming up or going down, so I cleaned out. I started dating again, without having to go out and see 17 guys in a truck. But I have never learned anything through being successful. I learned through failure. I mean, who can revel in their mistakes? Luckily, I have had a second and a third chance. The strongest drug in the world is success because it leads to more and more greed. It's why people go to war. You end up walking around in your sunglasses at midnight.'

Not that the Press in America had spared him. In a now oft-quoted swipe, the *Dallas Morning News* said he had got rich 'producing one of the most reprehensibly manipulative, intellectually bankrupt bodies of work in recent history.' No wonder he wanted to do a life of the opera composer Puccini - a project put on ice before Stallone unsuccessfully dabbled in comedy with *Oscar* and *Stop or My Mom Will Shoot*. The former was originally meant for Danny DeVito. 'Sure...to me films are like sets of clothes. Unless they are tailored to your body, then they look shoddy.'

So he went back to the rippling muscles. Not only did he appear nude on the cover of *Vanity Fair*, in a pose modelled on Rodin's statue of *The Thinker* - 'that was a stunt body' - he also filmed the nail-biting Alpine thriller *Cliff-hanger*. 'If that hadn't worked, I would have jumped off the cliff.' he admits. But it did work, putting Stallone back on the movie making map he had dominated above all others during the 80s.

But the new film - his first in partnership with ace action producer Joel Silver (*Lethal Weapon, Die Hard* etc.) combines both action and comedy. Sly, as a dinosaur figure from the 20th century, is defrosted in the year 2032 AD to do battle in a new politically correct age with Wesley Snipes and Nigel Hawthorne. Smoking, swearing - even sex - are among the things banned! 'If it were really like that, I would want to go out here and become a dog and walk on all fours,' admits Stallone. But the movie was good from an acting point of view: 'They said to me: "Let's try something really unique. Be yourself." So that's it. if you want to see how I really am, this is it.'

Certainly, the sparks and the bullets fly. The speciality this time appears to be breaking as much glass as possible - and there's a joke about Arnie Schwarzenegger having been President. 'The fact that any actor can hold political office frightens me,' says Sly with a grin. 'I have so many skeletons in the cupboard, I would like to spare civilisation that.'

But he gets annoyed when civilisation slams the action movie.. 'I think there is a great disservice done to many action directors, actors and producers, as if we were bottom of the food chain. In fact, more energy, money, preparation and danger goes into this kind of film than any other. They are the bedrock, and yet we are scoffed at and dismissed. The top 15 of the all-time box office record breakers have been action or fantasy movies. There are also the (type of) films that started our business out. They have always been the vanguard. I find it insane that people like Spielberg still get ignored.'

But at 47, surely the time will come for a personal change? 'Well, I've acted, written, produced and choreographed,' says Stallone. 'And I suppose the running, bumping, setting yourself on fire syndrome is eventually going to come to an end. But you can see through people like Clint Eastwood and Sean Connery that action doesn't have to be pedal-on-the-floor stuff. It's also suspense. Inside you are shaking. So I will have to follow that particular route to be faithful to the people who follow me.'

[12.11.1993]

SIR ANTHONY HOPKINS
AND EMMA THOMPSON

A CLASS ACT!

First the footsteps on the creaky staircase. Then the familiar face - with those piercing blue eyes. Sir Anthony Hopkins seemed to be bringing his latest screen role as archetypal British butler to life: he is coming upstairs for breakfast - to the top floor of a restaurant in a London Georgian terrace. But the hour is civilised. It's 11.30am, time for croissants and smoked salmon.

'Good morning, Stevens,' I say - alluding to the movie. 'You may sit here.' The genial knight breaks into a cackle full of his native Welshness. 'Yes, there's a fair likeness to running up and down stairs in the film,' he concedes. Joining him is his co-star Emma Thompson, the housekeeper in an English stately home who becomes the subject of Steven's unconsummated love.

Together, they are a class act. Not just because of the master and servant format of this pre-war '30s saga, but by direct film pedigree. He, the winner of an Oscar for the flesh-eating Hannibal Lecter in *The Silence of the Lambs*; she the owner of an identical statuette for *Howards End* (in which Hopkins also appeared). So the combination is both tried and tested. And here they are on the brink of another triumph. For as dawn breaks on a new year, the duo are tipped for Academy Awards in the spring. The performances are so stupendous that perhaps not incredibly, *The Remains of the Day* - the latest showpiece from Ismail Merchant and James Ivory - is already being spoken about as the film of 1994.

'It's just acting,' insists Hopkins, who can say more with the merest twitch of a face muscle than most of his peers can achieve with a page of text. 'Actually, I think it is much easier to play these parts because you don't have to eat the scenery,' he says. 'I enjoy this minimalist way of working. There's no busting a gut. Stevens is a very simple part - very easy to play, very enjoyable.'

Not so much false modesty, as the reflections of an actor fully in charge of his craft. The astounding thing about the story, which includes the treachery of James Fox as an ennobled Nazi sympathiser, is what is not said and not done. It is the epitome of sexual repression: British reserve at its most trenchant. Says Emma Thompson: 'Underneath it all, my character is screaming: "Notice Me". But a lot of people talk in code. It is an important side of human nature.'

A brilliant aspect of the chemistry between Hopkins and Thompson results from tiny episodes of ad-lib. 'You read the script, you learn it,' notes Hopkins. 'You go over and over it. But for those special moments, you improvise. Okay, if it gets out of hand, you cut it. But if you are relaxed, then you can relax a little on set. And if you don't have people screaming and shouting - like you do on some movies - then it begins to work.'

In the original novel, Stevens has a mental breakdown. He realises his life has been a sham. In the film, however, he retains his dignity, his sense of order. 'I was in the army,' recalls Hopkins, now 55. 'A Lance Corporal during National Service. It was just something I had to do. I hated it, but if you fight the system in the army, they will crush you.' He speaks with the same quiet authority and assurance as Stevens ..... some things are obviously not up for discussion.

Both Sir Anthony and Emma Thompson are cautious about the hype for *The Remains Of The Day*. Despite unbridled success in America, and the clamour of approval which greeted its showing at the London Film Festival, mention of Oscars can be all too premature. Says Emma Thompson: 'In America, certainly, you become "that Academy Award winner" and because of that, there is something highly exciting about you.' She says the central appeal of *The Remains Of The Day* is the tension of the story itself: 'Much more sensual than a fully-fledged hump.'

But adds Ms Thompson, life is not always lived in the closet. 'When I was seven, I was deeply in love with a boy called Matthew Fox. I used to wrestle with him to the floor. He was half my size.' One feels sure that Stevens would not approve. But what the hell?

[31.12.1993]

ROBIN WILLIAMS

IN THE LINE OF *DOUBTFIRE*

Robin Williams is never off duty. He starts by impersonating an auctioneer, switches to what sounds like a cartoon mouse, lapses into the rhetoric of a laid-back Hollywood greaseball, and then he says - in the gentlest of Scottish accents: 'She's a sweet lady.'

The eagle-eyed comic has finally landed - at full revs - to introduce me at first hand to his new creation, *Mrs Doubtfire*. I doubt if anyone else watching this impromptu performance in the Grand Mirror Room of London's Claridges Hotel could have failed to reflect on Williams' enthusiasm for a character set to dominate cinema screens across the UK.

A newly-acquired goatee beard, and a waistcoat which gave him the appearance of a dummy being used by several ventriloquists at once, did not detract from the star of the show - a 60-year-old Scottish matron who turns nanny in San Francisco. According to the plot, taking on the disguise of *Mrs Doubtfire* is Williams' way of seeing his children during a divorce wrangle with Sally Field. But this Celtic amalgam of wig, face mask, spectacles, rubber boobs and tweedy cardigans - off-set by regulation no-nonsense handbag - is much more than some cinematic pantomime dame.

'She gets recognition,' boasts Williams. 'People say "that's Auntie Phyllis" - or they do after a couple of Glenfiddichs.' To prove the point, Our Hero marched around his home town of 'Cisco in full drag. 'I even went into a sex shop. They didn't seem to guess. It was also interesting to see how older people were treated. Sometimes, there was a strange sense of neglect. You'd wonder if people would come to your help.' On occasions his enthusiasm knew no bounds: 'One day, I asked whether I should wear panties. The director (Chris Columbus of *Home Alone* fame) said no. That would be way beyond method acting.' The studio crew responded by blowing hot air up Wiliams' skirt.

But *Mrs Doubtfire* was not assembled overnight: 'Even in San Francisco, they'd say: "You still need working on, sweetheart." In the end, it was a 12-piece transformation, that four-and-a-half hours in make-up,' reveals Williams, whose big screen comedy career took off with *Good Morning, Vietnam* seven years ago. 'And coming out if it all is like decompressing from the bends.

I got advice on the accent from the Scottish director Bill Forsyth. At one point it was so far north that I was at John O'Groats heading into the sea. *Mrs Doubtfire* needed strength and authority. Imagine Margaret Thatcher on steroids, and then sweeten it up. The false teeth helped there. It's like adjusting the tone on a stereo, but not until it's goo. I enjoy trying different things. Just as a musician would take a bass line in jazz and turn it blue. So, at one point, Mrs Doubtfire starts talking about seafood and then mentions crabs (and I don't mean the Dungeness variety.)

Another thing was learning to relax, to let gravity work on you. We had to give the old girl a glow which made it look like she was lit from within.'

Williams insists that it's all very different from Dustin Hoffman's *Tootsie*: 'Cross-dressing goes back to Rome......to Greece....to the caves. Let's face it, we could all do with a good frock now and again. I also enjoy a good cashmere, but we are shooting in the summer, so the tartan had to go first.' But all great fun: 'I'm a comic. Unless you laugh it's a hard day,' says Williams. 'Now let's see, a stretch for me would be playing Ella Fitzgerald....' He stops in his tracks. For once he's being serious - I think. 'Yes, the time has come for me to play some villains,' he announces. We shall see...

[27.1.1994]

MARTIN SCORSESE

TURNING THE CLOCK BACK IN STYLE

Martin Scorsese was putting the finishing touches to *Cape Fear* - continuing his long-established collaboration with Robert De Niro - when he started picking costumes and designs for a film that would be a milestone in his career. After a day dealing with the lewd and psychotic twists of thrillerdom, he would sit down to study Pre-Raphaelite paintings, lush fabrics and haute cuisine. He chose the decor and the dishes as if they were prize exhibits. They were. He was cooking up something really special... The cult movie director - one of a handful of behind-the-camera moguls as famous as the actors they sign - made his name with a tough, streetwise catalogue running from *Taxi Driver* to *Goodfellas*. Well, he's still in New York, but he's turned the corner - and turned the clock back.

The Age of Innocence - starring Daniel Day-Lewis, torn between love for mistress Michelle Pfeiffer and duty to wife Winona Ryder - marks Scorsese's true initiation into filmic high society. Set in the 1870s - and based on Edith Wharton's Pulitzer Prize-winning novel - the movie is set to hang onto the coat tails of Merchant-Ivory's *The Remains of the Day*. The parallels are remarkable: both movies are about passion suppressed by the social etiquette of the monied classes. Just as Anthony Hopkins and Emma Thompson never managed to possess each other within the strictures of pre-war, upper-crust British reserve, so Daniel and Michelle are denied a life together.

And it's a far more British than American denial: 'There is no aristocracy in the U.S.,' admits Scorsese, who was brought up in New York's Little Italy. 'But these people so wanted to be aristocrats, they ended up being more English than the English. I was interested in the way they were capable of strong emotional violence, but by subtle strategies and the supported courtesies of their nature. They did it so politely.'

For the ultra-versatile Day-Lewis - about to be seen in the excellent Guildford Four movie, *In The Name Of The Father* - it wasn't a case of compromise. He joins us after a lunch in London: 'I didn't have to think of playing things as an Englishman playing an American. After all, most of the people in that world were instructed by English or French governesses. They mimicked the European aristocracy wholesale.' Meanwhile, Scorsese, who says he 'always knew Daniel was a great actor since I saw him in *My Left Foot*,' enjoyed working with a pedigree list of Brits on the project, including Alec McCowen, Richard W Grant, Miriam Margolyes, Michael Gough and Sian Phillips. 'I always wanted to work with British actors,' he says. 'They have always formed such a strong part of my own film viewing. Coming from a working class family, there were no books in my house, but we would get TV and great actors like Alec Guiness, John Gielgud and John Mills.'

Scorsese, now 51 and entering a new personal career phase (it hasn't all been roses: remember *King of Comedy*, which undeservedly bombed at the box office, and Paramount's early panic over *The Last Temptation of Christ*?) is passionate about preserving film footage. But he adds that he no longer has as much time as he'd like to catch up on the classics of old. Perhaps that's why he's opted for a classic of its own: a costume and era classic (it ends up in Paris), with food as art, and the air at times thick with cigar smoke. 'We ate these marvellous meals in front of the camera crew,' jokes Daniel. 'Just to make them jealous. But then everyone took home doggy bags.'

In more serious mode, Martin Scorsese adds: 'I worked on the choice of plates and cuisine while doing *Cape Fear*, so that by the time we got together, we didn't mess about. That way we were able to spend the money where it was most useful.' Yet the decorative elements only serve the core issue. Says Scorsese: 'What really attracted me to the book was the sense of poignancy - the sense of loss. After all, this is a love story, and a love between two people, whether successful or unsuccessful, is common to everybody. There's a passion and and an erotic tension which may appear to be inactive, but it's actually very active with that sense of bitter-sweet romance. This is a movie of restraint . It may give the appearance of a lot of freedom, but people opt for the social obligations.'

And the talked-of Oscar hopes - at last? 'Look, when I was a kid the Oscar ceremony was in black and white. No prize can give you self-worth. You have to feel good about what you do.' And certainly, Martin Scorsese is pleased enough with *The Age of Innocence.*

[4.2.1994]

BEN KINGSLEY

OSKAR'S WINNER

Ben Kingsley says a day should be set aside in the calendar to honour the 11 million victims of the Holocaust. 'I personally think that Europe missed an opportunity,' says the actor best remembered for portraying Ghandi - and now one of three British players heading the cast of Steven Spielberg's harrowing holocaust movie, *Schindler's List.*

The film, also starring Liam Neeson and Ralph Fiennes, has won an incredible 12 Oscars and 13 BAFTA nominations. According to Kingsley, the lost chance was for 'a great ritualistic grieving process - as the Australians still do for those lost at Gallipoli, and as we do for one particular Jew who died 2,000 years ago. There is not one single day in the calendar when all the traffic in Europe stops for two minutes to remember these people. I believe that if an individual doesn't grieve, then the healing process will not take place. That's why I think this is a tremendously healing film.'

Kingsley was responding to my question of whether *Schindler's List* - the story of Jews rescued from extermination by German Industrialist

Oskar Schindler - was a warning against to-day's ugly resurgence of nationalism in Europe, South Africa and the former Soviet Union. It was a question that triggered a welter of reactions: Kingsley remains deeply affected by the 10 weeks of location work in Poland. While there, he had witnessed still active anti-semitism first-hand. A German tourist asked one of the actors - Londoner Michael Schneider - if he was a Jew. When told 'yes', the man mimed putting a noose around Schneider's neck.

The incident revolted Kingsley: 'I said some very un-Mahatma-like things,' he recalls. 'I am pleased to say the tourist was not only thrown out of the hotel, but also out of the country.' Certainly, Ben Kingsley, joining me in London with Ralph Fiennes, who plays S.S. work camp commandant Amon Goeth, is in no doubt when he says: 'I think this is a film that should be seen in every continent. Even when the world has rid itself of the terrible spasm it again seems to be going through, this film will still be seen as a hymn to courage.'

Oskar Schindler drew up the now famous 'list' of workers he wanted for his factories as a way of saving Jews from the gas chambers. Today - Schindler, who died in 1974, lies buried with full honours on Mount Zion, Jerusalem. But he was not a saint. He loved wine, women and song - and joined the Nazi Party in order to make money. Yet what he saw shocked him to the core. Schindler soon dedicated himself to saving the persecuted by bribing Nazi officials. In doing so he risked his own life. Played in Spielberg's film by Liam Neeson, Schindler became the link between good and evil, the latter epitomised by the racist thug Goeth (who was hanged after the War). Yet former Theatr Clwyd actor Ralph Fiennes says Spielberg wished to avoid stereotypes.

'With such a long list of Nazis played by English actors, Steven said he wanted to keep away from the cliché and to deal with Goeth as a human being. Although these were obscene characters, they are still human flesh and blood. They came out of their mothers' wombs , they went into nappies, and they ate digestive biscuits. So you must come to these roles in a totally open way and try to open them up. Obviously, sometimes I felt depressed. Everyone was, by the proximity of events which actually happened in locations we were using.'

The film's reward is the response: those who hugged the cast while filming. Or the man from New Jersey, who was overwhelmed to see a random execution he had actually witnessed brought back to reality. Ben Kingsley summed up the particular rigours of this epic three-hour black and white movie: 'It was not an easy landscape in which to work. It did undoubtedly bruise the psyche. Filming was like going to

Auschwitz everyday - being confronted with the terrible sight of those shoes and spectacles and the sacks of human hair.

We are told that we have made a film which is relevant....but I wish to God it wasn't.'

[18.2.1994]

TOM HANKS

STRAIGHT TALKING

'I think I am better in this than I was in *Bonfire of the Vanities* - and that's with the wisdom of hindsight!' Tom Hanks is the master of understatement. Despite struggling against the odds, he will always be associated with one of the most expensive cinematic turkeys of all time. But things have changed. He took a chance with a very controversial role....and when the glittering Oscar ceremony comes round in March, he will be there with the other Best Actor hopefuls, fingers crossed.

And the likeable Hanks even plays down the biggest star-studded night of the year which is seen by millions around the world. 'It's always a good night. I hope that if I get to speak, I won't say something so stupid that it will haunt me for the rest of my career.'

But on the subject of AIDs and the way it has been portrayed on film, he is very straightforward. 'Rock Hudson is dead of AIDS and he doesn't have to pretend to be married to his publicist's secretary any more,' he says. And therein lies the truth about the double standards which have plagued Tinsel Town since way before Rhett Butler kissed Scarlet O'Hara. Leading men were meant to be straight. And not just straight acting.

'But you tell me a movie star who is openly gay even now,' adds Hanks, star of last year's romantic weepy, *Sleepless in Seattle*, opposite Meg Ryan. He may be a Hollywood heart-throb of the distinctly heterosexual variety, but Hanks is still proud to have taken on the mantle of attorney Andrew Beckett, who loses his job after being diagnosed HIV- positive and who takes his battle against bigotry to the courts. UK audiences are about to see him - having shed more than two stones - in the first big budget AIDS drama, *Philadelphia*, set in America's 'city of brotherly love'. Directed by Jonathan (*Silence of the Lambs)* Demme, Hanks find himself the talk of the broad-beamed US.

Says Tom: 'As a white, heterosexual American, I thought I knew everything there was to know about AIDS. But the film opened up my mind up to the vast amount of information I didn't know.' Although there were people from High School and a distant cousin who had died of the disease, Tom Hanks readily admits: 'I had never had the experience of seeing someone waste away in front of my eyes.'

For Hollywood's finest light comedian since Cary Grant, this story marks a drastic change of direction. Hanks, who is married to actress Rita Wilson and a father of three children, told me: 'I consider myself more as an actor than a comedian - and I fully understand the type of movie I am in. The film shows how we are; it's a serious record of how we live in 1994.'

In that sense, *Philadelphia* is not a gay love story. There is no screen kiss. Nor will Hanks become a poster boy for the gay movement. 'I am very comfortable with my image,' he assures me. "I am a Jeffersonian type of Democrat, I suppose. Once, I would preach at a dinner party and still go home and tell jokes about gay people. But I wouldn't do that now.' He says he has no plans to leap into the political fray on behalf of gay rights activists. 'But I am open to the fund-raising part of things that can actually put money into people's pockets.'

Ironically, some people were worried about the effect of the film on Middle America, but they were the ones who embraced it. 'To be stopped at an airport by someone and be told "my son dies of AIDS" is very humbling.' He pays tributes to the real-life HIV patients who helped with the film. 'I felt like a mercenary. Really, they should have thrown me out of the room. But they never flinched from some of the most blatant questions I asked - and I asked questions that were ignorant as well. I was genuinely surprised by the realisation that I had much more in common with these people than I thought.'

[21.2.1994]

JACK LEMMON

JACK THE LAD

Jack Lemmon caught the acting bug at the age of four, when he appeared on stage with his father, a Boston baker. It was 1929, and despite the Depression, the show was called *Gold In Them Thar Hills*. Lemmon, who in early career was forced to shelter in the squats of New York's squalid Devil's Kitchen quarter - often just one night's sleep ahead of the demolition gangs - luckily made it big. But the fun-loving young man who found gold on Broadway and in cinema has moved on.

Now - just a few months short of his 70th birthday - he has been officially cast as both elderly and ill-tempered. Jack the Lad's still loving it - especially as it renews a working pertnership with one of his closest friends. In *Grumpy Old Men*, Lemmon and Walter Matthau play battling neighbours in love with the same woman (the Swedish-born Ann-Margaret - a chick at just 53 years of age). Thus the two Oscar winning veterans fall ever more in hate with each other. Both are great survivors - both in terms of the movie and their overall careers. Lemmon and Matthau have been sparring on screen since they made *The Fortune Cookie* almost 30 years ago. Since then - most notably - there have been *The Odd Couple, The Front Page, Buddy Buddy* and *Kotch*, for which Lemmon directed Matthau.

Jack Lemmon, who was in London this week, loves the story of how the Hollywood tyrant Harry 'King' Cohn, one time head of Columbia Pictures, unsuccessfully tried to change the name of his 'tame Harvard man'. 'How do you do, Mr Cohn. I'm Jack Lemmon.' Cohn brought up his right hand and sent the riding crop he was holding crashing down on the desk. 'Nobody,' he growled, 'can be in films with a name like that. The critics will use it like a baseball bat. They'll crucify you. They'll say Lemmon is a lemon, and that the picture is a lemon and they'll go ha! ha! ha!' However, this particular Lemmon was on the threshold of a career that would silence not only Cohn, but any other doubters. How will we ever forget him with Monroe in *Some Like It Hot* - or with Matthau in *The Odd Couple*.

In reflective mood, he says: 'I don't know anyone who has been more fortunate than I have - not luck. There's a difference. In other words, I'm a terrible gambler. But I'm not self-effacing. If I had not done a good enough job in playing some of these wonderful parts, I would not be around any more.' But he conceded: 'There is, beyond any talent one may have, an element of luck or good fortune, and this has happened to me a number of times ... I can only hope that it continues.'

What does continue is Lemmon's sheer professionalism - both on stage and screen. Five years ago (it seems like five minutes), he was in Manchester playing a cheerful piano playing ex-serviceman in Donald Freed's gripping drama, *Veteran's Day*. Many Merseysiders made the pilgrimage to pay homage to a man who had become a performance hero, be it in comic vein, or more latterly, as a 'serious' actor.

Even today, Lemmon continues to astonish and delight. Most notably, perhaps in the art of transferring an original stage play like *Glengarry Glen Ross* to the screen. In David Mamet's wonderfully-written scenario, Lemmon plays a salesman in a Chicago real estate office, who faces the sack because his returns are down. The result was a remarkable blend of dread, nervous tension, tenacity, self-preservation and humour. And only weeks ago, Lemmon turned up in glorious form, turning his hand to a cameo role in *Short Cuts*, Robert Altman's epic splicing together eight stories from American suburban life. The still great master of casual nuance, Lemmon was superb as a tragi-comic floundering father figure.

He does not see much difference between comedy and dramatic acting, except in technique. 'That comes in timing and delivery - and most of the time you cannot explain it,' he says. 'If you are fortunate you are born with it - but you cannot just learn how to play comedy. A sense of humour is knowing what is funny, knowing how to make it funny.' And he concludes: 'The trick is not necessarily to believe it yourself but to make an audience believe. An audience will be disappointed if the actor himself thinks it is funny.'

Lemmon likes all kinds of humour. But he says he will settle for Walter Matthau - with his world map of a face - turning up for breakfast and saying: 'Hullo Jack!' There we are ... I told you they were friends really.

[14.5.1994]

JACK NICHOLSON

JACK THE BAD

I don't argue - I just work with people who agree with me

'Play the piano Jack,' I say - pointing at the baby grand in the corner of the hotel suite. 'I don't play the piano.' 'Jack Lemmon did when he was here.' 'He's got to.'

Breaking the ice with Jack Nicholson is important. Otherwise, he may just choose to stare you out with those chameleon's eyes of his. Off come the shades. Surely not the same pair he turned up in after *One Flew Over The Cuckoo's Nest* and *Terms Of Endearment*? They just could be. Jack hasn't changed that much in 20 years. So why should the effects? The only real transformation takes place in his latest movie, *Wolf*, which requires him to howl, grow hairy, frighten horses ... and make love to Michelle Pfeiffer. It's as much a rethink of *Beauty And The Beast* as a throwback to gothic horror. And it's funny too. 'There's something of the wolf in us all,' says Jack in that dry drawl that's made the voice as famous as the face. 'Wolves have the same expressions. They smile, they frown. They have that baleful gaze. That's why I don't have to act.' Nicholson is quite capable of taking himself down a peg - provided everyone else moves down one further.

Of course he'd done research: 'I read a lot of books, watched a lot of films. One of my neighbours actually had a young she-wolf and I watched it. I watched my dog teach it to swim. But eventually they had to get rid of it. They're still wild animals. In fact, I have always felt a bit of an endangered species myself.'

He's smiling now, relaxing, looking me straight in the eye over the top of a floral display that's more suited as a tribute to a werewolf's victim. Quite apart from the movie, he's back in the news, having just fathered a daughter to a 20 year old waitress. Nicholson is 57. Such is life. 'I don't seem to have stepped out of a door for a week without being followed by photographers. At this moment, I don't have anything much to lose, but the attentions of the Press have cost me in the past. They pay tremendous amounts of money to people for stories - whether they are true or not. But the papers have been kinda 60/40 kind to me. I like what I do. I like my job. I chose it.' There are benefits. He's been seen around London town with some of the most beautiful women on the planet: 'I am on top form at the moment,' he enthuses.

I was beginning to notice. Jack was getting into overdrive. 'I'm easy to talk to and easy to direct. It's just that not many people have ideas which are better than my own.' And *Wolf* director Mike Nichols can live with that. This is his fourth collaboration with Nicholson, who came in from the Hollywood fringe of playing teenage rebels and horror roles to work with Nichols on *Carnal Knowledge* in 1971. Two years earlier, the world knew it had a new star when Jack made *Easy Rider*. 'I always act a character as if the film is about them, no matter how large or small the actual part is.'

The time comes - and it has - when Nicholson can afford to sit back. 'I haven't had time off for nine years, but now I'm going to take 12 months out. It's not as if I'm retiring. What I shall be doing is looking at life - and that's the material of movies. The upside of being a successful actor is that I can afford to take a year off. I had to do something this extreme because I had worked harder than I ever thought I would over the past few years. One of the ways to start this year off is not to read a script.

I'm not joking. I have actually been asked to read a script by my own ex-wife. So I have to be not just "off" - but "off-off". Yet it's hard to be "off-off" in my position, because a couple of thousand people go to work when I decide I am going to do something. On every movie, a member of someone's family dies and yet they still have to turn up at 8am the next day. It's one of those jobs when your time is not your own.'

Playing a werewolf is something that has fascinated Nicholson for a decade. He has chosen to take a leaf out of Spencer Tracy's 40s version of *Dr Jekyll and Mr Hyde* by using minimal make-up. 'My idea about all these kinds of parts is that they are the character film parts for modern actors, and it's always interesting to find a way they have not been done before. The unpredictability of the scenes in *Wolf* is one of the strong things of the story. You have to make people engage their belief in it.'

And what about evil? Does it exist in any old-fashioned, romanticised sense? 'I don't believe that if you are not nice, then you come back with one eye. But I do believe that if you follow the other path, then eventually there's justice.' But Nicholson says for *Wolf*, don't just read werewolf. There's comedy and romance and adventure all rolled into one. 'It's a creative challenge. But people like me don't argue. I just work with people who agree with me.'

[22.8.1994]

STAR TREK

DOUBLE TROUBLE FOR PICARD AND KIRK

What a great double act they make - on and off the screen. The captains of the *Enterprise* beam down *together*.

'It's like being in church,' says Patrick Stewart, the British Shakespearian actor, who took over the hottest command seat in the galaxy from Canadian William Shatner. Stewart immediately defers to his time-served predecessor, who first boldly went out into the universe when *Star Trek* was launched on television in 1966. 'He is definitely the high priest. I am merely an acolyte.'

Meanwhile, the world waits with bated breath for Friday, when both men star in the latest big screen epic, *Star Trek Generations*. Trouble is, old Bill finally snuffs it. Indeed, he had to film his death scene twice in three weeks, as the producers threw a few million extra bucks in the air and demanded a 'new' ending. So, instead of being shot, Captain Kirk dies with dignity beneath a mass of twisted metal on the planet Meridian III. 'There is no life after the *Enterprise*,' says William Shatner with mock seriousness. 'Only darkness I see before me...'

But right now, nostalgia rules: 'There's a joy to making a *Star Trek* film which a lot of other movies do not have,' insists Shatner, veteran of seven big screen adventures. '*Star Trek* has had some influence on most of the things I have done over the past 25 years. I have been able to do things that many other actors would have killed for, including writing, directing and producing.'

Patrick Stewart, who's 'quite proud' of the 178-hours of TV mileage his Captain Jean-Luc Picard has notched up so far, readily admits, 'there's no doubt that the role has opened doors for me. But I was very mindful that this incredible piece of good fortune could also become an albatross around my neck. A series like this eats up great chunks of your life. So, away from *Star Trek*, I concentrated on theatre work and, so far, the experience of being a freelance actor has been good to me.'

He recalls Stratford with the Royal Shakespeare Company 'catching a glimpse of myself in a mirror wearing chainmail or a false beard and thinking: Is this a career for a grown man?' But now that his career spans several centuries - *Generations* is set in the 24th - things don't look so bad. Two TV series are running in America, with up to 40%

of sets tuned in. No wonder there's already talk of *another* movie.

'I think there should be a gap of 18 months or so,' says Stewart. 'Paramount, please note. Anything less would be almost indecent.'

William Shatner, however, is philosophical about his own demise. 'When we started with the TV shows, the ideas were quite forward thinking for the time. But this is definitely the era of the new generation, and they are far more popular in their series than our show ever was.'

Back at Captain's Log, February 1995, Captain Picard has invited Captain Kirk to sample the delights of the moors near his home in Wharfedale.

'You know Yorkshire?' I ask Shatner.

'Not yet, but I've ate the pudding.'

Only one problem to shatter the tranquillity, apparently: RAF training flights. 'I think we should go and see that local squadron leader together.' says Bill to Pat.

That certainly shows enterprise. And there's certainly one RAF officer in for a shock when his office door opens...

[6.2.1995]

AN AWFULLY BIG ADVENTURE

ADVENTURE PLAYGROUND (REVIEW)

Post-war Liverpool. The Overhead Railway, luxury liners at the Pier Head, trams, fog, the Liver Building stained by soot, buying coffee at Coopers, tea-cakes at the Kardomah, shopping at the Bon Marché. But still no Beatles. Yet there was one great institution that's still going…the Playhouse.

Now time and place combine with box office opportunism to bring us Britain's number one film star - Hugh Grant - in the everyday story of being stage-struck in 40s Liverpool, ration book in one hand and a script in the other.

An Awfully Big Adventure, which flickers across UK cinema screens from tonight, is actually Merseyside writer Beryl Bainbridge's semi-autobiographical tale of life at the Playhouse at a time when you had to kick the plumbing to make the taps work. For true authenticity, the movie even boasts Liverpool actress Rita Tushingham (as Bainbridge's aunt), who was so initiated, treading the Playhouse boards in the wake of such luminaries as Michael Redgrave, Rachel Kempson, Cyril Luckham, Michael Dennison, Dulcie Gray et al.

During this halcyon era, Britain's senior repertory theatre - then fronting on to a cobbled and self-contained Williamson Square - was ruled with a rod of iron by legendary general manager Maud Carpenter (the role model for Prunella Scales in the film). If two shows lost money, the next one had to at least break even (so what changes?). Thus we join the Bainbridge fantasy with a company of grandly inflated egos being fed on a diet of J.B. Priestley and Shakespeare. But there was only one thing to balance the books for Christmas - the magic of *Peter Pan*. Riding into town on a motorbike comes Alan Rickman - 'the best Captain Hook there has ever been.' Hugh Grant, meanwhile, is squaring up as the director of a company of neurotic thespians.

Bainbridge's view may be a romanticised one, but it's certainly not glamorous. An actor's life was a constant round between overcrowded dressing rooms and dingy digs. In both, there was a risk of being exterminated by faulty gas rings. It was a case of a little heat or perish - in rooms so cold and damp that, if Rickman's character is to be believed, you left your vest on to have sex.

The object of his affections is none other than the Bainbridge alter ego, Stella - an awfully impressive debut by Georgina Cates. The young girl, who joins the Playhouse as a dogsbody assistant stage manager, moves from adolescence to womanhood in a single night's offstage performance. Her days are spent daydreaming over Grant, whose character uses actors as pawns in some grand emotional tragedy. No star status for Stella. More a case of making tea, running messages, painting scenery and polishing dressing room mirrors. The reflected glory was that of a bunch of trained actors - as glitzy and bitchy a profession then as it is now - to whom being anyone other than themselves was a meal ticket.

Like Beryl Bainbridge, Hilary Heath, co-producer of *An Awfully Big Adventure*, was a student at the Playhouse. She recalls: 'During my school holidays, I begged for - and got - a job, and was paid the princely sum of £1 a week. You had to be quick on your feet to get away from some of the older male actors.'

Although the Playhouse takes centre stage in theory, the film was shot in Dublin. It wasn't just that the Victorian surroundings of the Playhouse had been wrecked in the madcap 60s rush to modernise the city centre. Director Mike Newell, who made *Four Weddings And A Funeral* with Hugh Grant, offers another damning reason: 'The Irish Government simply made the financing of the film so much easier. The reason why Liverpool lost the contract belongs in Whitehall.'

In critical terms, the end result is not as good as Terence Davies's Liverpool-set movies. But it was shot on a shoestring budget. And it does capture the essence of the repertory theatre work of yesteryear when a full company was resident in town, performing a new play every three weeks.

You've read the book, you've seen the play, now see the movie. If nothing else, it's a luvvies love-in.

[7.4.1995]

124

CLINT EASTWOOD

BEAU BRIDGES

Go on, Clint. Make my day...

What's it like, looking back, seeing yourself in the saddle as Rowdy Yates, that square-chinned son-of-a-bitch, still kept alive by Channel 4 on Sunday mornings?

-'I just think, "Tom Cruise, eat your heart out",' comes the quietly spoken answer. 'Sure, my hair wasn't grey then, but I know more now - and maybe I have more fun knowing more,' says the guy who, 40 years on, reinvented the Western and brought us *Unforgiven*.

There's a whole lot of chewing going on. Is it gum? Is it a candy. It's Eastwood in relaxed mood at any rate, sizing up the latest project. *The Bridges of Madison County* - a great film based on a badly-written novel - may sound like a mixed blessing. Until that is, Meryl Streep comes on board and turns it into the ideal night out for 40something romantics. After *Dirty Harry*, it's difficult to imagine Clint with a glint of tearful regret as he bids farewell to the woman he's lost after a whirlwind affair. From mush to masterpiece in a lingering kiss. They didn't rehearse the kiss either. They just went for it, good professionals that they are.

'The most important thing an actor can do is make something look like it's happening for the first time. If a mechanical attitude takes over, then it always shows on film.'

Bridges is Eastwood's 39th film as a Hollywood leading man. And it may just win him the prize which has always eluded him - the Best Actor Oscar. Certainly, Streep must expect a nomination in the Tinseltown ladies' stakes.

'She didn't do anything to make herself more glamorous. None of us wore make-up. In fact, we deglamorised from the book.'

And just in case you didn't read through the world's unlikeliest best-seller, Eastwood plays a National Geographic photographer who encounters Streep home alone amid Madison's sweeping countryside. This is Small Town America, where a woman can invite a stranger into the house for an iced tea.

The two great issues are middle-aged love and the acceptance that children's glossy, time-honoured view of their parents may be the wrong one. 'People think the sun rises and sets over them. That their parents didn't have a life before. But that's not necessarily the case.'

Interesting. Clint's 31-year marriage to Maggie Johnson ended in 1984. His son, Kyle, 26, is a musician; his daughter, Alison, a Paris model. His second long-term relationship, to Sandra Locke, ended in still ongoing lawsuits. Since then, he has become a father again. At 65, he's Pensioner Pop to a baby daughter.

'As an older parent, you can devote more time,' he says, gently tapping the table with the sort of weather-beaten fingers Moses would have pawned his chisel for.

'My father died suddenly when I was 40, and I had tremendous guilt feelings over why I hadn't asked him to play golf more often.'

He says that *Bridges* marks 'the culmination of a lifetime.'

'I have played rogue cops and killers and cowboys, and maybe I am actually more of a romantic than some of those guys. I wanted this film to be a love story, not a sex story. He's not looking for anything. Neither is she. It just happens. I am sick of seeing people faking and groaning about on screen. Maybe I am telling it from a point of view I wouldn't have done 30 years ago, but in a middle-aged romance, you have to start with the friendship,' insists Clint, who can do just that - because he also directs. In fact, he is making a habit of starring/directing, plus writing the theme music.

'I have never spoken to anybody about this before.' Can this be? 'Although there's so much precedent for it, going right back to Chaplin. There again, the only way I could get the job of starring in *Play Misty For Me* was to be the director. There is a trick to it,' says your man, the voice trailing to a whisper, 'and that's just being able to throw a switch in the brain between one job and the other. A bit like writing left-handed. I remember years ago, in *Josey Wales*, somebody was having trouble with dialogue. The camera assistant leant over to me and said: " Excuse me, you're moving your lips, when *he's* talking." And, of course, it does get you tired, directing particularly. Concentrating all day long without the breaks that actors take. So I make sure I rest. I don't go out much.'

Eastwood has nothing but praise for his leading lady, complete with one of her famous accents - in this case, Italian.

'I have lived in an area where I was one of the few non-Italians. I have seen this woman many times. I didn't like the fact that in the early planning stages, people were talking about women in their 30s. Some of the best actresses in the world are between 40 and 60.'

Meryl Streep is 45. Between them, Clint and Meryl venture into new territory.'You try to do different things. Anyway, you shouldn't be playing the same roles you were 30 years ago. And from a selfish point of view, you don't want to repeat yourself. I have had a strong image in the past of a certain type of film. I have tried busting it over the years, sometimes successfully, sometimes not. They said to me after *Every Which Way But Loose*, "you lose the girl, you don't shoot anyone, you work with an orang-utan"…but it's obviously entertaining to some people out there.'

And once more, the actor moves on - and becomes the philosopher. He strokes his chin and ponders the moral of the tale. 'Maybe there's room for several great loves in life…but certainly not more than several.'

[8.9.1995]

SEAN CONNERY

KING CONNERY'S COURT

At the Court of King Connery, the chandeliers sparkle and light up the red hessian-covered walls. A profusion of blue, yellow and white summer flowers cascade from plinths either side of the throne. Rows of chairs are neatly arranged in front of the dais. There is enough microphone cable to circumvent the earth.

Without ceremony, King Sean 1 (for there has been no other by that name) appears in an open-necked shirt and jacket. His Queen - a true English rose named Julia Ormond - sports a red cardy over a navy blue dress with rounded white collar.

In attendance is Mr Jerry Zucker, court jester, film producer and magician. Jester, because he cracks reassuring jokes as and when required. Film producer and magician, because he alone is responsible for whisking King Sean and Queeen Julia back 14 centuries in the twinkling of a broadsword. Suddenly, we are in many-towered Camelot, King Sean refers to an earlier life - when he was King Arthur and Julia, Queen Guinevere.

But a single disappointment: Lancelot (so called because he lances a lot) is missing. He is produced on film overtaking malcontents on horseback and striking them to the ground. One of the very earliest examples of road rage. He's also wearing Levis and is a dead ringer for Richard Gere. Lancelot is 'First Knight', a title by which Arthur and Guinevere now hope to re-establish their Empire by having it projected on to cinema screens throughout the land, starting this very eventide.

But hush...the flunkies are flunkying. Tea is served and a voice booms down from the throne: 'It's good to be king and tell everybody what to do. I like it.' The King is smiling and appears to be chewing gum. The court jester has a go: ' I wanted the movie to be successful, so I wanted the best possible people. In the case of King Arthur, it's hard to imagine anybody else.'

Indeed. With a Scottish accent. Novel. The jester continues: 'As for Guinevere, what was needed was a woman of great strength. And a woman you could genuinely believe two men would also desire.'

The Queen, whom I can reveal has a flat in Hackney, breaks her silence. It was a case of 'just getting on with the job'. (For novices in Arthurian legend, this involves being dutiful to the King and lusting over Lancelot). But Guinevere, once hailed by Prince Steven Spielberg as 'the best thing since Audrey Hepburn', is picking up screen suitors a-plenty. Apart from Gere, there have been Harrison Ford, Tim Roth and Brad Pitt, recently named 'Sexiest Man on the Planet'.

'What! Brad Pitt! Are you serious?' roars the King, who himself held the title from the same magazine, but a year earlier. Brad Pitt is 31, the King, 64. In August, he gets his bus pass, a joke one is allowed to make without one's head ending up on a pikestaff. 'I'll have to see my lawyers,' says King Sean, arms firmly folded, 'The bus pass could inhibit my earning capacity...getting older is a double-edged sword, but I am probably busier now than I've ever been.'

A project on the back burner for 20 years is the golfing equivalent of baseball's *Field of Dreams*. In this case, King Sean would come back as a ghost to haunt his long-time pal, referred to in conversation only as Clint (Royal watchers, however, know this to be the even older Lord Eastwood of California, formerly *Dirty Harry*). The thing is finding the right script, admits the King.

There wasn't that problem with the Camelot story: 'There have been so many versions. Had it been written the other way, with Merlin and all that stuff, then I'm sure it would also have worked. But I like the way it's told here so that everybody can easily understand it. The simplicity of the triangle.'

However, the weather in Wales (at Trawsfynydd Lake, Snowdonia - now the official site of Camelot) had been atrocious, the experience only lightened by good beer; and the generosity of a passing shepherd who offered King Sean a collie dog. But a dog is for life and not for Christmas, so the King had declined.

A peasant asks how the Royal couple warded off the chill winds. 'Don't tell,' muses the King, pleased at his own wit. The Queen defers: 'You try to keep warm between takes. You kind of forget about it.'

Another peasant, surely risking the gibbet, demands to know why the King sometimes has hair upon his head and sometimes not. 'In this case, I was after a certain look. There are cases when it's not so important.'

An audible sigh of relief passes through the court. The King is in a good mood. The Queen is also generous of spirit. She had especially asked for scenes where Guinevere was 'having fun and mucking in with the people.'

Future engagements for the King include playing the voice of a dragon: 'It's next generation *Jurassic Park*. I've just been in LA seeing some of the stuff.'

Meanwhle, the Queen is deciding whether to get an American pad: 'I am keeping my options open,' she says, ' I may get a place in Los Angeles or New York, but I would still keep a base in London.'

But, Your Majesty, please choose between the King and Lancelot. 'This is my favourite James Bond,' she says, smiling radiantly. Until then, nobody had dared mention the King's pseudonym from his days as a commoner.

'She's got good taste,' he says. 'She's very good, too. And I'm not just saying that because she's here and because I own 10%...'

The crowd bay for him to renounce his title and challenge John Major. There is much laughter. He thinks not...Zest ruleth the day. 'I'll see how it feels when I get my bus pass, but I don't feel in the mood for retiring at the moment,' says King Sean, dismissing the court.

[30.6.1995]

PIERCE BROSNAN

EYEING UP THE BOND CROWN

Heard the one about the Scotsman, the Englishman, the Welshman and the Irishman? Answer: they're all called James Bond.

'I only hesitated after I accepted the role,' says Pierce Brosnan - proof, he says of being the Irishman in question. And there's the trace of a County Meath accent to match - which you won't be hearing as he dons the mantle of the British Secret Service's most famous agent. Brosnan, now 40, takes over the licence to kill from Sean Connery, Roger Moore and Timothy Dalton. There was also an Australian called George Lazenby in *On Her Majesty's Secret Service*, and dear old David Niven in the spoof, *Casino Royale*. But there's only been one first among equals - and that's Sean Connery. 'He's created such an icon,' says Brosnan. 'There was no-one who stood beside him. That's why I still say that my aim is to be up there with Connery.'

There's every chance he could be - with two more contracts secured and the option on a fourth. After a six-year gap caused by turmoil at MGM Studios, Bond is back in business, and the producers are well pleased with their choice. Pierce Brosnan, too, looks relaxed as we meet in London.'I am very pleased with the picture,' he announces unprompted. Could he have said that 10 years ago, when originally offered the role of Bond (he had to turn it down because of a TV contract)? 'The first time I was rather nervous. If the truth be known, I was secretly relieved that it didn't happen. And I could still be known as the chap who could have been, even should have been - and got away with it. This time, however, there was a sense of elation - but I knew there was hard work ahead.' Lucky to get a second chance?

'I mean I had a career before (*Remington Steele* on TV; *The Fourth Protocol; Lawnmower Man* etc on screen) and it was going along very nicely. But once Timothy jumped ship, that was a nod, really.'

Dalton sent a letter of support to his successor, and there was further backing from the top. 'Sean was just really generous in print. He said some wonderful things in a *Time Out* interview. Whereas Roger, who I have known for a number of years, sent me a note saying: "Kill 'em sport!"'

But making the 17th Bond film brought its own challenges, not least continuity. 'I rented *Dr No, From Russia With Love* and *Goldfinger*. I was secure in my own belief that I could play the role - and I had even bought a compilation of the Bond books back in '86 - but I wanted to remind myself how it all started. I watched them casually while I was painting in my studio.'

Brosnan admits that finally landing the role of Bond 'gives me a certain power...now, there's a certain clout.' But he adds: 'I would also like to produce or direct. I may even want to give up acting, and I would like to have another string to my bow. I see this as another stepping stone in my career, I don't have ultimate goals. But from where I am sitting right now, there's a sense of achievement.'

We are actually sitting in the Hyde Park Hotel in Knightsbridge. Brosnan's Perrier water is neither shaken nor stirred. He is drawing in pencil on a note pad. What would this 'doodle' sell for - as James Bond, artist? 'Oh, well,' says Your Man with a smile. 'I have sold a couple of paintings for charity. Gene Hackman and I have the same publicist who persuaded us to offer work for an auction. One of the paintings is hanging in public in Sussex House, New York. That sold for five grand. The other is in a producer's house. I left school at 15 and started out as a commercial artist. But once acting came into my life, it was salvation.'

Yet the boy who first saw *Goldfinger* as a 10-year-old in Ireland was not an 007 fanatic. 'No, I never wanted to be James Bond,' he admits, 'Batman was my hero. We used to put our raincoats around our necks and hang off the bicycle sheds.'

But Bond he is. Charming. Sophisticated. Tough. Humorous. 'Yes, all of those things,' he jests, 'You can't separate them out.'

So any changes? 'Well, the Aston Martin should come back in a big way - but I don't know whether they will listen to me or not. As it's a revival, then it's almost like doing a period piece. And that means it's still got to be M16 against the Russians - to lay the foundations for those who are going to grow up with Brosnan as James Bond.'

There speaks a man who wants to go the distance. The actor who will take James Bond into the 21st century.

[24.11.1995]

131

MICHAEL DOUGLAS

THE WORLD'S TOP JOB

Michael Douglas admits he relished being President of the United States. 'I was very sad to leave work at night,' he says of his time inhabiting Hollywood's replica of the White House. The result - *The American President*, with Douglas running the world and falling for Annette Bening at the same time - hits UK cinema screens tonight. Such is the stuff of fantasy.

'I think it's everyone's dream to play the President,' reflects Douglas. 'And yes, it did give me fantasies about doing the job.'

Power, politics and sex is a potent combination - and here's a movie with all three.

'There's certainly a sense of power,' says the actor who's spent the last decade up to his thighs in such raunchy outings as *Fatal Attraction, Basic Instinct* and *Disclosure*.

'I used to arrive at work half an hour early, just to walk around the set and get the atmosphere. It took a little while, but after we had been into make-up and we looked okay, you could get into it.'

Certainly, as leader of the Free World, Douglas cuts quite a dash. But gone now are the sharp suits with the inch of cuff below the sleeve. Douglas turns up in navy sports shirt, dark tweed jacket and casual trousers. He's grown a straggly beard.

'I've just come in from France. .. in two days, I'm going to South Africa.'

The disguise almost works as we meet in London's Dorchester Hotel. Except that with him is his director, the larger-than-life and twice-as-loud Rob Reiner, whose credits include *When Harry Met Sally*. Trouble is, when you meet President Douglas, it's chief-of-staff Reiner who appears to want to do most of the talking.

The Clinton administration had been most co-operative in the making of the movie. Douglas, who had met Clinton formally three times - the first when his father, Kirk Douglas, received the Kennedy Honors Award - was later invited into the Oval Office while the President prepared a radio address to the nation.

'I was allowed to follow him around,' adds Reiner, who - in what must be a 1,000-word discourse - describes Clinton as his favourite-ever American President.

'He's by far the most decisive President we have had out of the last nine…the only problem is that he has broken the cardinal rule of doing his thinking in public.'

It's something Reiner himself might ponder as I try to interview the star of the show.

Michael Douglas says he particularly liked Jimmy Carter 'for the way he conducted himself after his Presidency.'

What isn't in dispute is that Douglas and Reiner are Democrats and that the movie has a Democratic President fighting it out with a reactionary old Republican. Yes, it could be Bob Dole, but it comes in the form of Richard Dreyfuss going on about family values (Douglas plays a widower President who beds Bening while his daughter is sleeping down the corridor). But, says Reiner, no way - as has been suggested in the British Press this week - was the movie done as a campaign aid for Clinton. To be fair, when filming started, Republicans were enjoying a new wave of support. It seemed for a while that the project might turn into a counter-culture movie.

As it happens, Douglas was once approached to go into politics as a career. 'There was a time when the Democrats asked me to run for governor in California. They said they wanted someone with a recognisable face who would pay for his own campaign. That was the end of that.'

So much for the power and the politics…er, what about the sex?

'Sex in films is difficult unless followed by humour or fear,' pronounces Douglas, whose seduction techniques here are a little more subtle than in some of his other on-screen escapades. And just for the record, he adds whimsically: 'I have decided I will *not* be dropping my pants any more in the near future!'

The American President is Michael's 21st movie, while his legendary father - whom he refers to as Kirk rather than Dad - has made 80 pictures.

'It just means we are all getting older. Coming up as second generation in that way teaches you a real humility. I have a 17-year-old son, and if his career as a disc jockey doesn't work out, he may have a go at acting. Who knows?'

And who knows what a *real* President Douglas would do, except, as he volunteers, 're-decorate the White House.' Would he agree with

America acting as world policeman, sending troops to Bosnia, for instance?

'I support the US upholding its NATO commitments,' comes the cautious reply...followed like lightening by another voice.

'I don't think the US wants to be the policeman of the world.'

It's your man Reiner again. The only thing is, I don't recall asking him the question.

[8.12.1995]

SIR IAN McKELLEN
THE GREAT DICTATOR

Sir Ian McKellen is in no doubt about his new Fascist version of *Richard III*. 'I didn't invent it. It's all in the text,' he says, adding that Shakespeare's evil king has been the true model for generations of despots. He and director Richard Loncraine studied footage of Stalin, Mussolini, Franco and Saddam, as well as material from China and South America. So the fact that McKellen turned out looking more like a doppelganger for Adolph Hitler is purely coincidental. A sort of composite dictator. The pencil-line moustache is a nod in the direction of Clark Gable or Ronald Coleman, he insists, as we chat over coffee.

'Of course, it's not the *real* Richard III, who as we know, was a splendid chap. Instead, it's the monster Shakespeare created.'

All to do with Tudor political correctness. Shakespeare was an 'umble subject of Elizabeth I. As her grandfather had murdered Richard, the Bard was inclined to look askew at history.

'Even so, many actors tend to play Richard as a psychopath. He wasn't,' insists Sir Ian. 'He never actually murdered anybody. He got others to do it.'

So we are talking manipulating. Public relations. Ultimately, fear.

'Stalin's butler used to keep a spare pair of trousers for people who were going in to see Stalin,' notes Sir Ian, proving that his research has been nothing if not thorough. Nor was it always a case of battling your way to the top.

'Richard didn't lead a military coup. It was the same with Hitler. He got elected. What the story also teaches us is that we can no longer say that any individual is evil without wanting to enquire what made them like that.'

Although McKellen's Richard is totally different from Oliviers' 1955 film, there was a feeling, until recently, that the late Lord's version was sacrosanct.

Says Sir Ian, 'at one time, I would not have dreamed of repeating a film that Olivier had made. It was really Kenneth Branagh's *Henry V* which opened my eyes to what I had already instinctively known: that no role belongs to any actor - not even Sgt Bilko any more.'

But some things do last. McKellen's *Macbeth* (with Judi Dench) is still available on video. Yet film stardom has come late. His debut was supposed to be with Gregory Peck in a 60s venture called *The Bells of Hell Go Tinga-Linga-Ling*. They did. The movie was cancelled because of snow. A later effort saw him being air-lifted out of Betwys-y-Coed 'for a rest' on a Channel 4 project that never reached cinema audiences. It was playing disgraced War Minister John Profumo in *Scandal* (with a scandalous haircut to match!) that finally clinched a movie future for McKellen.

Prior to *Richard III*, he did all sorts of cameo roles to feel part of the industry. 'By the time we came to do this, the camera was a friend,' says Sir Ian. 'It wasn't that different to do things in the 'wrong' order. Stage actors do it all the time in rehearsal.'

Richard Loncraine was chuffed when he managed to do a four-and-a-half minute single take of McKellen and Co in full flow.

'I told him that was nothing - in the theatre we do three-and-a-half hours takes!' says Sir Ian.

The result is enigmatic. A 30s London riddled by civil war. 'The Royal Family live in St Pancras Station. Bosworth Field is outside Battersea Power Station. The style is art deco. The use of red is the only true reference to the Third Reich. Indeed, 50 styles of Army headgear are used. There's a lot of cigarette smoking, but no scene on a telephone. Says Sir Ian: 'As David Hockney had already noted, it all looks so familiar, but where actually is it?'

Our Star is pleased: 'I could watch the opening over and over again.'

Meanwhile, McKellen now moves on to play Czar Nicholas II to Alan

Rickman's Rasputin. The slain Nicholas was 'a confused man in the wrong place at the wrong time.' Sir Ian wasn't. 'I had to make some money. I didn't come out of Richard exactly rich.'

The project almost went bust: Americans like Robert Downey and Annette Bening appeared almost for nothing. But it has been worth it. I say how dare McKellen have missed an Oscar nomination by two votes. The BBC also has egg on its face for refusing to put in money. But the truth will out: it's a triumph.

[26.4.1996]

ARNOLD SCHWARZENEGGER

SHOOTING TO THRILL

Sch...it's You Know Who...

The smoke clears and Arnold Schwarzenegger proffers his right hand. The world's biggest action star looms genially out of the gloom caused by igniting a mammoth cigar. A personal special effect costing less than a tenner.

A big handshake, a broad smile, a tease. 'You want an exclusive? I'll give you an exclusive!' he promises. He then breaks into German - his native tongue - adding that there's no satisfactory German phrase for 'Witness Protection Programme'. Mark that down. It's Arnie's new territory. His latest movie, *Eraser*, sees him as an elite U.S. marshall arranging new identities for those whose courtroom testimonies put their lives in danger. Cue the usual suspects - and the usual explosions. Plus what will become the Big Man's new catchphrase.'YOU'RE LUGGAGE!' - a line delivered with consummate calmness as Arnie dispatches a bunch of snap-happy crocodiles sent to kill himself and leading lady, Vanessa Williams. He laughs: 'I always try to inject an "Arnoldism". That's what they call them on the set now, you know.'

Alas, no more '*Hasta la vista*, baby!' or the promise of 'I'll be back!' 'Of course, you can overdo it,' he concedes. 'It needs to be very subtle.' Subtlety hardly seems the first rule when you're back in the frame as a killing machine - but Arnie insists that he's self-censoring. 'There's a scene when I jump out of a plane and land on a car. I was going to say "This job's killing me", but it spoiled the effect of what followed, so I took it out.'

Schwarzenegger also takes out the villains. 'People love spectacle and that James Bond sort of stuff in the summer. However, if you're taken on nothing more than a ride of madness, people get immune to it. No matter how dramatic life is, there's always a funny side to things.'

Which explains why Arnie - two years on from *True Lies* and having-a-baby comedy, *Junior*, intents to stick with both action and comedy - despite the rumours. 'There was a quote by Stallone in which he said he was finished with action movies - but not from me, as some people said. I can assure you that I'll continue doing action movies - and also do comedy. For summer, always action pictures, and for Christmas, always comedy. It's quite simply because I love doing both. Having said that, action movies are very tedious. You have to do extraordinary stunts at three in the morning. That's when they always seem to want you to walk through fire or hang out of an aeroplane.'

That's the downside of earning $20m, I guess. 'I hear complaints around me on the set - like a bunch of babies whining.' And the worth of it? 'With comedy, you feel guilty taking a salary,' says Arnie, disappearing once more behind a smokescreen in the mirrored suite at London's Dorchester Hotel. 'Comedy should not be a budget of more than $35m. But with an action movie, there is no limit - $100m or whatever…'

Although Warner Bros never disclose budgets, that figure isn't being disputed for an incredibly long 130-day shoot, which included one scene change (because it was too like a sequence from *Mission Impossible*) and one legally required name change (which cost $1m in itself).

Arnie had been handed the script - on a ski lift - by Warner's head of production. 'I took it home and read it that night and was fascinated by the Witness Protection Programme - something few people know much about (despite 16,000 cases in the U.S.)' The end result called for stamina all-round.

Arnie is unstinting in his praise of Vanessa Williams: 'My wife (Maria Schriver, niece of the late J.F.K.) suggested her in the first place. Vanessa did a great job. This stuff is tough for women. She was hanging in harnesses and all that. She's a great mother, too, and had her three children on the set. I always judge people by things like that. I think it's nice to have your family there. However, when my first daughter, Kathrine, came on the set of *Terminator II*, she saw me with half a face and freaked out. My wife had to calm her down and explain that Daddy was all right and his face wasn't really melting.'

But all change. Next up for Arnie is playing the evil Mr Freeze in *Batman and Robin*, with *ER* star George Clooney, Chris O'Donnell and Elle Macpherson: six weeks work for a supposed $16m...obviously no pay freeze yet.

[16.8.1996]

MICHELLE PFEIFFER
MOTHER LOVE

It's the big four-0 for Michelle Pfeiffer. Time enough to reflect and say: 'I suddenly realised that the modern definition of heroism was surviving the day as a working mother.'

Not only because the still sexy star of vintage *Dangerous Liaisons* is a mum off set, but also because it reflects her latest role as a harassed, working single parent on the edge of another love affair. In *One Fine Day*, which opens next week, she is paired with cinema's Man Of The Moment, George Clooney, this time minus Batman hood and cape, and in a similarly fraught part as a lone journalist dad coping with offspring.

What's more challenging - the plot or reality? Feisty Pfeiffer has cause to contemplate. Only the other day, she was on an American TV show - crowned with breakfast cereal.

'I was wearing this superb Armani suit in pink satin. I *thought* I looked great. Nobody told me I had a lump of oatmeal stuck in my hair. The kids just throw the stuff at you.'

Oops. Was it adopted Claudia Rose, aged four, or John Henry, aged two? That's for Michelle and TV producer husband David Kelley to know and me to guess.

Ms Pfeiffer is also a movie producer these days. Her company, Via Rosa, put together the latest project. After a life of acting - resulting in three Oscar nominations - she moves on as a Tinsel Town mover and shaker: 'I do like my own way,' she concedes. 'I may be a little less tough on myself now, so I may, in turn, be a little less tough on other people. They don't usually tell me what my reputation was, or is, but I guess I could be pretty stubborn. I think I gave myself a hard time. I'd berate myself, lay awake worrying about stuff, like whether I was liked. I was pretty neurotic. Now I just crash out. I don't have the energy.'

Producing is a whole new ballgame. 'The benefits outweigh the added stress,' she concludes. And, as regards women in the Hollywood machine, she has interesting views. 'Women largely don't "open" movies. They don't have that clout. It's still Jack Nicholson, Arnold Schwarzenegger and Sylvester Stallone. The great stories aren't there for women.'

That said, *One Fine Day* is every bit (if not more) her movie as it is Clooney's. In an industry where everything has to be new - or at least, dusted down - they have been likened to Katherine Hepburn and Spencer Tracey - something which causes a wry smile to cross the Pfeiffer features. 'The comparison is very flattering. In fact, George went out with my younger sister, Dedee, years ago. They stayed friends and she is still crazy about him. We joke now that she road tested him for me. Actually, George is a really funny man. When you are in his company as a woman, he makes you feel good. We certainly laughed a lot. You just know when people are enjoying themselves on screen. I wouldn't rule out us working together again soon.'

That said, I can reveal that Ms Pfeiffer will be taking some time out to be with her family. A question of priorities.

'I couldn't give my children up for six months for the greatest screen role in the world, ' she insists. ' I want to be there for them. I came to this the wrong way, really. I had a career, and then I was a mother. Being a parent happened at the right time, however, for me. I was ready. I wanted it badly.'

Like her latest character, Melanie Parker, she says she once wanted to be perfect. 'I strove for perfection in every sense,' she says. 'I know now that you can't achieve that, but I give everything my best shot.'

That includes the little things of everyday life: 'I know people think that "Michelle Pfeiffer couldn't boil an egg." And they'd be wrong. I can cook well when I choose to. Once I have the recipe in my hands, and the kids are busy, I'm OK. Actually, I'm so lucky because I'm happily married and my husband is there for me and our children. When he's tied up, I get help. There's no other choice. But most women aren't in that situation.'

[27.6.1997]

MEL GIBSON

TAKES IT TO THE MAX

What's star quality? When you can get a crowd to stand on the shoulders of another crowd in the sultriest heat of the decade, just to catch a glimpse of you. When you're 41, still pass for 31, and the glint in your eye is as shiny as the gel on your ungreying hair, that's also star quality. Witness Mel Gibson exiting from limo outside the Empire, Leicester Square, for the charity premiere of his new movie with Julia Roberts, *Conspiracy Theory*.

And I have a theory that Mel is still loving every moment of it: the glamour, the buzz, the being centre stage. It's one I put to the test the next day, when - glitz gear replaced by purple sweat shirt and decidedly dogeared blue jeans - he joins me to mull over the game that last year gave him a clutch of Oscars for *Braveheart*.

'Yes, I'm still in love with the process. I really enjoy being in the action,' he confirms. 'As you get a little longer in the tooth, you have a little less patience with some things. I think I will probably end up moving on towards directing more, and pull out of the front.'

But Mel is still very much out front. For 20 years, he has been the world's most consistent male box office draw. But all is not in vogue. Unfashionably, Mel still lights up a cigarette with the relish of his silver screen forebears.

The latest screen manifestation has Gibson as a New York cabbie - a man with no identity and a hidden past, and a fear for the future. His character is a mass of suspicions about government conspiracies. But

Joe Riley

*Enjoying the high life:
testing the technology
for a Royal Court
production of
Peter Pan*

Lunch with Dustin Hoffman at the London launch of his film, Tootsie

Pipes of peace: with Prime Minister Harold Wilson at a fund-raising event for the Everyman Theatre

At the Matterhorn

*What do you want
for Christmas?
A chat with
Father Christmas
at Lewis's*

Receiving a national award for campaigning arts journalism from Sir Richard Attenborou

The woman who brought down a government: Christine Keeler on a visit to Liverpool's Cavern Club

With
Hannah Gordon
and Bill Kenwright

Joe interviewing
the singer
Paul Weller

*With the BBC's
John Humphreys,
at the Echo Arts Awards*

*Joe and Co:
with a group of
Liverpool's finest -
Wally Scott,
Brian Labone,
Johnny Kennedy,
Billy Butler,
Mike McCartney,
Ken Dodd,
Bill Dean
and Tommy Smith*

Game for a laugh:
a celebrity interview
with Sooty

& Miss Piggy

*Chatting with
Norman Wisdom*

*On the record -
an interview with
Liverpool's most famous son,
Paul McCartney,
at the Philharmonic Hall*

could they be true? Only Ms Roberts can help sort it out. It calls for charm, wit, self-doubt, action, romance, you name it.

As for New York, there's havoc in the streets, bridges closed, subways flooded. They even land a helicopter in Union Square, leading director Richard Donner to conclude that the city should get equal star billing.

Mel has no doubt: 'Cab rides are the best fun you can have in New York. You get every variety of creature driving. Some of them want to be your best buddy and tell you their life story. Then you get the Neanderthal guys with no teeth and you wonder who gave them their licence. They have food and gravy stains all over their clothes, and you have to wear a peg on your nose while they give you the white knuckle ride through the city and scare the hell out of you - and all for five dollars. It's better than Disneyland.'

Our star has the hell scared out of him in the new movie: a terrible form of torture, where his eyes are held open with transparent tape while he's half drowned in a ducking stool.

'It looks more menacing that it really was,' says Mel, drawing on a fresh cigarette. 'Apparently, you have to be able to blink or you don't get the necessary changes of neurological mood.'

The things you learn in this job...

'You get a miserable headache out of it.' he adds.

Sounds awful. And talking of weird brain patterns, Mel - the veteran of *Lethal Weapon, Mad Max* and *Hamlet* - insists that 'every character in a movie should be off-centre in some way. It's just a quest to find it. You give it a lot of thought. Then you hit all around it until you hit the right level.'

But he assures me his days of combining acting with directing - as in *Braveheart* - are over.

'There's nothing more irritating than doing both,' he now admits. 'You actually end up bumping into yourself. It's an odd out-of-body sort of thing.'

And what of the reviews?

'I don't think it matters one jot. When I look at some of these critics, I say thank God that they're there to tell us where we make mistakes.'

It's called ironic humour - and there's more. 'You know, if these guys would make the supreme sacrifice and make a movie, then we'd all witness perfection and learn by example. But I guess that's too much to ask.'

Controlled tirade over (inspired by mixed reviews for *Conspiracy Theory* back home), he turns his scorn to journalists who purvey scare stories. 'First you get an idea that's on everyone's mind. Then people are left scratching their heads. No wonder we're so paranoid. These (conspiracy) theories get put about by people wanting a satisfactory answer. They come up with some really hairbrained stories, but some of them are plausible. They're all over the internet.'

So finally, Mel, how about my own flier about a return to *Mad Max* and *Lethal Weapon*?

'There is no *Mad Max 4*. That's someone leading you up the garden path. However, *Lethal Weapon 4* is a good idea. It's evolved to a point where it's right. Enough time has elapsed for us to have a fresh crack and not be over-influenced by what's gone before. There are some good ideas in the pot,' says Mel, failing to resolve a question on everybody's mind...

[22.8.1997]

MRS BROWN

A REAL CROWN JEWEL (REVIEW)

When this momentous movie was shown to the Press just eight days ago, I remember wondering what Princess Diana might make of it. Forever the Royal revolutionary, she would doubtless have been amused. Alas, a week is a long time - not only in politics.

Perhaps surprisingly, distributors have gone ahead with today's UK release of a film which shows how scandal and intrigue are not new skeletons in the Royal cupboard. Queen Victoria's relationship with her highland ghillie, John Brown, was the gossip of the age. The magazine *Punch* - then a force in the land - parodied Victoria as 'Mrs Brown'. A newspaper cartoon also asked 'Where is Britannia?' - a reference to the Queen's self-imposed highland exile following the death of her husband, Prince Albert.

The Queen was angry that the Government had not conferred the title King on Albert, petulant about her own supremacy and inconsolable at the loss of her consort. She became a recluse - for years. There were calls in Parliament for the abolition of the monarchy. Eventually, the Prime Minister, Disraeli, had to insist personally on the Queen's return to public life. If the reformist legacy of Diana will now haunt the Royals for eternity, one may reasonably conclude from director John Madden's illuminating drama, that they were lucky to escape extinction a century ago.

No-one need ask why Judi Dench (Victoria) is Dame Judi. Her acting talents are stupendous, and never better displayed than here. You can fully expect Oscar nominations for both her and Billy Connolly as John Brown. His performance is disarmingly forthright, full of magical nuances, flashes of brilliance and unequivocal humour.

Fencing between the chief protagonists is equally commendable: portrayals from Antony Sher, as a particularly oily and cunning Disraeli, and Geoffrey Palmer as the scheming chief Royal aide, Henry Ponsonby. When it becomes apparent that Victoria and Brown had been carousing, and there is a hint of sexual indiscretion, Ponsonby advises: 'Don't even think of it.' And that is where the politicians, civil servants, public and paparazzi (here spying with telescopes at Balmoral) draw the line (as do the film-makers). How different from today. And how far less tragic the outcome.

[5.9.1997]

RALPH FIENNES

MAKING HIS BIG SCREEN DEBUT AS HEATHCLIFF

Heathcliff had come down from the moors at long last - and opted for an off-the-collar haircut. Being cast as mad, bad and dangerous had given the actor Ralph Fiennes - pronounced Raif Fines - a feel for the sort of big screen heroics which many leading men never get a shot at in the whole of their careers. Yet playing Emily Brontë's villain in *Wuthering Heights* - opposite the French actress Juliette Binoche - marks his first movie. Prior to that, he had swiftly made his mark on stage - first at the National Theatre and then, for three years, with the Royal Shakespeare Company, where he tackled the classical canon to great effect.

But when playing himself, Fiennes is quite retiring, almost shy. And being interviewed is, apparently, not one of his favourite pastimes.

'Most of my experience is in the theatre, so all this is fairly new,' he admits about the promotional trail around for the film. ' In the theatre, you rehearse for six or seven weeks, and then do the show for two or three hours. But with film, you do scenes in the wrong order and have to maintain the concentration for up to 10 weeks. For me, it was a whole new ball game.'

Yet *Wuthering Heights* is no ordinary film. First, there is the epic novel, which Fiennes readily admits deserves top billing. Then there is the Laurence Olivier/Merle Oberon 1939 cinema classic - a hard act to follow. But Fiennes was perhaps helped by only a passing acquaintance with both: 'I didn't know the book very well, and the screen version hadn't played a very great part in my cinema education.'

This means that his view of the role was uncluttered - 'but I know people have their own expectations of it.' he adds.

So the actors came first, and everything else, from accents to hairdos, second. As it happens, Fiennes - who as Heathcliff bears an uncanny resemblance to Irish pop singer Bono - opted for designer stubble and the long locks of a man who has long since pensioned off his barber. The result, in terms of image, is what they are still wont to call 'mean, moody and magnificent'. Which is more ideal for a baddie.

'And to think that most of my roles in the theatre have been those of honourable men,' reflects Fiennes. 'Heathcliff had a pretty rough childhood, and he's turned in on himself. When he meets Cathy, he shares an understanding with her and they are in harmony. But when she denies her true self and marries Edgar Linton (the part Fiennes was originally destined for), Heathcliff senses it is wrong. Something in him goes bad which could have been rather wonderful if they'd been together.'

Character analysis is second nature to an actor, although Ralph Fiennes says that playing T.E. Lawrence in David Puttnam's TV film, *A Dangerous Man*, presented a different sort of challenge to Heathcliff.

'It's sometimes harder to play a real person because they are infinitely more complicated than fictional characters, which you can mould to your purpose.'

Emily Brontë's spurned villain has been moulded by Fiennes in such a way that it will stick in the mind for its smouldering revenge.

So will he have to carry on being the bad guy?

'Oh, I suppose I could try to be as sweet as pie,' he jokes.

This *Wuthering Heights* - made in England with a budget of just nine million - does at least tell the entire story of the book. And although not the sort of package its American studio backers would normally go for, they are hoping to cash in on the universal popularity of the novel, and that particular sort of wild, above the tree-line Englishness which America still holds dear.

'I don't think Heathcliff had great sartorial priorities,' admits Ralph Fiennes.

Now he's off to an even more remote place - to mid-Wales, to film for BBC2. Quite fitting, surely, for a distant relation of the explorer, Sir Ranulph Fiennes?

[20.10.1997]

STEVEN SPIELBERG

SPOILS OF WAR

The King of the Movies doesn't look like a guy who earns £100m a year. The stone-coloured jeans, the open-necked black shirt framing a tapering silver-grey beard, and the geeky spectacles that have finally come into fashion, are not the trappings of stardom. There again, Steven Spielberg, the most successful producer/director in film history - is the one pulling the strings. He's paid three times more than any Hollywood actor, his nearest rival for the record, being Harrison Ford. Spielberg has masterminded seven out of the 20 top selling films of all time. And now he's at it again.

Prepare for a veritable shower of Oscars for *Saving Private Ryan* - quite simply the most harrowing war picture ever made. 5,000 American troops - average age 19 - advanced on Omaha Beach, Normandy, on D-Day - June 6, 1944. Such was the carnage, only 18 of them made the shingle. Spielberg's three-hour evocation of that event, plus the 'hedgerow' and 'bridge' battles which followed, spares none of the senses. If you can't look in a butcher's window without contemplating the very same human filleting, don't bother to buy a ticket.

But Spielberg is adamant in self-defence: 'I worked hard not to sensationalise it at all,' he assures me. 'I put my scissors as close to the fine point as I could, so as not to try and stick it in people's faces.'

But, of course, he has. And how. Yet those people for whom Spielberg made the £65m heart-wrenching epic, the veterans, have nothing but praise for the result. One sergeant at Omaha, now 75, collapsed, sobbing with the words: 'Thank you. Now they know, now they really, really, know what happened.'

'I only wish the vets were here,' says Steven. 'I feel I'm bragging about my own picture, and I hate doing that. But their reaction has made everything worthwhile. They see the film as an authentic acquittal of their experiences. It wasn't Hollywood-ised or sanitised. A lot of veterans were cynical about how the industry had treated their war over the past 50 years. They asked me if it was going to be another *Indiana Jones*-type forum, with World War II as a stand-in for something much more entertaining.

What people come to see is not the carnage, but valuing what those teenagers did for us. And it's surely worth a little pain to honour their memory. However, I never thought I went too far. I think I raised my personal limit of tolerance, but not enough to presume that everyone would reject the experience. I did have an imaginary line in the sand I never crossed. You can only use your imagination about how I might have done that. I think human decency will stop people from escalating the violence. I think we are clearly in an historical context that justifies the reality. But if you wanted to do a science-fiction movie and wanted to achieve this level of violence, then to me it would be indecent.'

There was a time - four weeks into the shoot - when Spielberg thought he might have overdone things.

'I said to Tom Hanks that I'd taken the movie from the black into the red. That his audience - typically, older women - would stick for 11 or 12 minutes and then be out of the theatre. So I was amazed when it took off in the States - and held on every weekend in the ratings.'

The main actors, including Tom Hanks (Spielberg's friend for 14 years) were sent to a Boot Camp and put through their paces by a former Vietnam veteran.

'It was a requirement,' says Steven. 'It was a cold, wet, horrible week and there was a true mutiny. But it was Tom who rallied the troops and kept them there. The whole idea was to get a respect for soldiering. You can't be a solder in the USA unless you have had 120 days basic training. These guys only had seven - but better that than basing their knowledge on John Wayne movies.'

Spielberg insists that although he had 'been circling the bait of a World War II movie for several years' this is not a sequel to his already Oscar-feted *Schindler's List.*

'The Holocaust is a separate event from any other since Moses and the Hebrews, and stands alone as man's most cruel inhumanity to man. I'm convinced it would have happened without World War II, although that war may have eventually been declared to stop it.'

Spielberg's wish to make *Private Ryan* in France - 'but not on the hallowed killing field - was thwarted by a 57% tax on each actor - and he needed thousands of extras. John Major had refused Army co-operation in the UK, but Ireland - on the advice of Mel Gibson, who had made *Braveheart* there - came up trumps, providing hundreds of soldiers.

'They were marvellous,' says Spielberg. 'All they wanted to do was to be treated with dignity and talk with the cast and myself between takes. We gave them a stipend and provided their meals.'

And he tells me with a smile: 'When I talked to Prime Minister Blair, he assured me that if he had been in office, we could have shot the entire film in the UK.'

Does nothing go wrong for the man with the Midas touch?

'I do get bored easily,' he admits. '*Lost World* was the mind-numbing experience of my life. It was as if I had come back to the same hamburger stall and they didn't even want extra pepper. But what could I do? I had spent 15 years denying people *ET II*, which I shall never make. So how could I say "No" to another *Jurassic Park*?'

But that's in the past. The present mission is well accomplished. A modern classic, no less.

[11.9.1998]

STAGE

CHARLIE CHAPLIN

CLOG DANCING AT SCHOOL IN LIVERPOOL

'Probably nobody in the history of mankind has acquired such a universal name in so short a time,' said an article in the *Echo* in 1918. It referred to Charlie Chaplin - now requesting to be known as Charles - who had made millions laugh through an era of international crisis, and made fashionable the toothbrush moustache. The *Echo* was quick to point out that in real life Chaplin was clean shaven, but nobody could deny the popularity of his latest films, *Shoulder Arms* and *A Dog's Life*.

As 'Chaplin fever' spread, each city lay claim to its associations with the 'prince of clowns'. Chaplin, it was later reported, had been discovered by two Liverpool men, Dan Lipton and Will Murray. Lipton, who had a flat in Charlie's native Kennington, London, featured the 'quaint, ragged little figure' in a sketch he wrote called *Casey's Circus*, which was produced by Murray. Lipton, a songwriter, also had the distinction of penning George Formby's first song with William Hargraves, a son of the proprietor of the Roscommon Music Hall, Liverpool. And it was Lipton who wrote the parody on *Finiculi, Finicula*, with which the Lancashire comedian had such success.

Having been 'discovered', Chaplin was to tour in a group of child clog dancers called 'The Eight Lancashire Lads', and during this time he came to Liverpool and Birkenhead, where he played the Argyle Theatre. He is recorded as having attended St. Francis Xavier's Elementary School, Haigh Street, for a short period in 1900. His address was 9 Salisbury Street, where he stayed with a Mr William Jackson. Chaplin also went on to appear in Liverpool with Fred Karno's Company. But his associations with Merseyside apparently go back even further. According to a Wallasey journal, he 'kicked and frolicked' on the beach at New Brighton at the tender age of two, 'playing around the Red Noses and slinging mud pies on the Prom.'

However, in 1918, it was a more mature Chaplin that journalists were writing about, and the *Echo* carried a 'sketch' of his first wife, Mildred Harris, whom he had just married in Los Angeles.

[9.7.1976]

KEN DODD

THE SHOW GOES ON

The relaunching of Kenneth Arthur Dodd upon home waters was something akin to the refitting of an old warship. There were butties a-plenty, but none made of jam from the mines of Knotty Ash. As it happens, Mr Dodd's charity maiden voyage will be at Southport Theatre on September 3 - 'the day war broke out'.

That catchphrase in itself, evokes memories of one of his boyhood heroes, Robb Wilton, a man Doddy served down-bill to, back in 1958, on the occasion of Wilton's last appearance at the old Shakespeare Theatre, then known temporarily as the Pigalle. 'Just look at the list of people I had to look up to: Arthur Askey, Ted Ray, Frankie Howerd, and, of course, Sandy Powell. I was brought up listening to his records. They cost sixpence each from Woolworths.' On the actual day war broke out, the teenager Doddy was glued to the radio: 'War was declared at around 11 o'clock. Ten minutes later, the sirens went off. In the end we got used to the raids, and we'd sit through them in the Curzon cinema. Sometimes, when we did go down the shelters, a group of us used to do shows. We were choirboys and we'd sing for them.'

Ken Dodd has been entertaining ever since. Once, when he was at the London Palladium, John Osborne, the playwright, took the entire cast of the National Theatre along to watch him so that they could study the art of timing. Osborne wrote *Look Back in Anger*, but looking back at his own recent life, Doddy is without anger or harsh words. 'It's been five years of torture, 12 months of agony, five weeks of hell, and two weeks of heaven,' he says in his own summing up. 'But today, we are here to talk about a celebration.'

This latter remark is his reply to a gentleman from *The Guardian*, who, in Doddy's words is trying 'to bowl a googley'. How's your health, Ken? 'Standing up fine at the moment, because I'm not doing anything.' Will George Carmen be at the show? 'I don't think so, but we'll be having dinner with him in London shortly.' What are your immediate plans? 'I'm going to go around some shows, starting with *Shirley Valentine* at the Playhouse and then the summer show at Llandudno.'

A woman of 60-plus plants a kiss on his cheek. 'Hello young lady ....that's the best offer I've had all day,' he says waving a tickling stick of red, blue, white, orange and brown hue. To Doddy, everyone is 'young.' He is, after all, approaching pensionable age himself. But the act goes on. And that includes the four protruding teeth, a hair-do that is the perfection of the non-blowing-drying, and a tie with a Windsor knot the size of a tennis ball. Your service, Mr Dodd....

'I am at the moment, as they say in showbusiness, very hot," he says, taking a swig from his half pint of lager. 'I have had some ludicrous and wonderful offers. Indeed, I am expecting a call any moment now, and if it's the one I want, then that will be a story.' No further details are forthcoming on that one. But there is talk of a book: 'There's no title yet, but I have a very original concept - perhaps using the twin masks of comedy and tragedy. Even in the bleakest moments, you can find things which are hilarious.' Someone suggests the title *You Can't Take It With You.* Are you going to write it yourself? 'Maybe, maybe not. There could be a job there for you, Sir Joe.' I remember that back in the early 70s, Doddy had conferred a knighthood on me. 'The things I had to do in those days to get the attention of the Press - like breaking the world non-stop joke telling record at the Royal Court.'

Now the steadfast fans of two generations are urging him to continue: 'I've had about 5,000 letters, and support from some people in the business whom I have never met. And in all those, I have had not one cranky letter.' So once more into the fray, with his fingers covered in biro stains. 'They're key words. I always try out about six new gags a night, just to see how they go.'

Doddy knows literally thousands of jokes. They form together in chunks, and can stretch a show on until nearly midnight. Once during a Rolling Stones riot in Manchester, the theatre management actually implored him to go on until the early hours, so that the streets outside the Opera House Theatre could be cleared of crowds. And, of course, he did.

There is just the hint, perhaps, of a slower pace for the future. As Doddy puts it, he's going to take more time 'to smell the flowers.' Meanwhile, apart from shows, there are personal appearances. 'England is an island surrounded by garden fêtes,' he says. It sounds to me as if the Squire of Knotty Ash has matured into quite a sage.

[4.8.1989]

NORMAN WISDOM

One of my ambitions when I took this job was to see all the great acts live on stage before TV technology took such a grip that the art of 'working an audience' would depend on how many re-takes could be afforded. One man who knows all about timing, whether he is rolling on the floor or sitting behind a drum kit, is the incredible Mr Norman Wisdom.

Norman, now rumoured to be in his early 70s (not even *Who's Who* records his date of birth) is still a cult figure - among the young. Is it because he is young in heart, or simply because even a new generation is becoming disenchanted with plastic stereotypes? For Mr Wisdom does it all: sings, tells jokes, throws his torso from one side of the stage to the other, and then plays a host of instruments. Last night's show included solos on trumpet, piano, saxophone, clarinet and even hunting horn.

The drums were incorporated into the sort of knockabout slapstick routine that used to be reserved for the silent movies. So did the tripping, falling over, and apparently forgetful clumsiness, which go towards making Mr Wisdom the sort of natural clown for which there seems to be no mould left.

I did notice, for the first time, how this time-served practitioner has influenced Michael Crawford, one of the few artists who has brought the old stage crafts through into the New Age. It is not just the physicality. Even the little-boy-lost expressions and the voice show a remarkable similarity. Believe it or not, Mr Wisdom still looks quite boyish: a full head of hair, a cheek to cheek grin, and the agility of someone more than half his years.

To be able to look at a stage and say: 'Eeh, son, that's Norman Wisdom you're seeing out there' is the stuff of legend. What's more, this master of slapstick still does a six-day week, five of them twice-nightly, as they used to call it in the great days of variety.

[25.9.1989]

EMLYN WILLIAMS

VARIETY IS THE SECRET

Once upon a time, there was a boy who lived in the Flintshire countryside near Mostyn. The son of an innkeeper, he walked several miles to school each day and spoke no English until he was eight. Later, he won scholarships to Geneva and Oxford University, and the locals knew he would do well for himself.

Emlyn Williams did better than most. In fact, by the age of thirty he'd established himself as one of the leading actors and playwrights of the day with a new thriller, *Night Must Fall*. The play still appears regularly in repertory seasons throughout the world, as do many of his other works. And Mr Williams, who'll be 70 in November, does a fair bit of globetrotting himself. For during the past twenty-odd years - only half of his actual stage and writing career - he's been pulling in capacity audiences with readings of excerpts from Charles Dickens. The Americans loved it as much as the Russians, and next year Mr Williams is hoping to take the Dickensian magic to Peking. Not surprising therefore, that today the people of Ffynnongroew, Mostyn and Holywell call him 'our Mr Dickens'.

And this week, Emlyn Williams is at the Chester Gateway Theatre doing some of those solo Dickens readings. 'I've been touring for six weeks now and there are another six to go. Then I'll take a holiday before going to New York again. I've introduced two new pieces during the past fortnight. I never do it long enough to go stale,' he told me.

Mr Williams isn't too keen on his show being referred to as a solo recital. 'That sounds as if I'm going to sing madrigals or something. They are dramatic presentations. The secret is finding enough variety of material to last a whole evening and hold and involve an audience. It is the realisation of the readings Dickens himself gave. I have a great affinity with him, although I'm quite pleased to be living in my own times,' he says.

'The readings started by chance really, I was asked to take part in a charity show, and so I read a ten minute extract from *Bleak House*. It worked so well that the whole idea snowballed from there.' Dressed as Dickens and standing at a reading desk, the magic of the stories soon began to capture the imaginations of audiences everywhere. *Bleak House* is still one of the all time favourites and Mr Williams has just recorded a four part reading to be broadcast on Radio Four later this summer.

Another of his solo performances, *A Boy Growing Up*, is based on the works of fellow Welshman Dylan Thomas. Mr Williams's Welsh background has greatly influenced his own writing. The schoolmistress played by Dame Sybil Thorndike in *The Corn Is Green*, was based on Miss Sarah Cooke, one of his teachers at Holywell Grammar School. And his boyhood in Flintshire is reflected in a comedy, *The Druid's Rest*, while his miracle play, *The Wind of Heaven*, draws on a wider, inherent, Welsh background. Mr Williams hopes to find time to go to Flintshire during his Chester visit. 'The area around Mostyn has changed very little,' he says. 'The inner parts of the country are the same as ever. I'm going to try and do some driving and walking over there this week.'

Wales has showered honours on him over the years. He's adjudicated at eisteddfodau and been made a member of the Gorsedd of Bards. But his family also had some Liverpool connections. His mother was at one time in service in Walton, and his father once sailed from the Pier Head as a stoker on the *Luciana*. Later, two of Mr Williams's plays - the thriller, *Someone Waiting*, and the war play, *The Morning Star* - were premiered in Liverpool.

Over the years, he has combined the tasks of producer, actor, writer and film star. His three books during the past 10 years have included the best-selling *Beyond Belief* about the Moors Murders. 'In fact, the last time I was in Chester was to attend the trial. Writing that book was different to anything else I have done. It was a chilling experience,' he says.

But writing, of course, has always been his first love.'Just now, I'm working on a musical version of *Spring 1600*, a play I wrote 40 years ago. It's about Elizabethan theatre and Shakespeare's company at the Globe. Mind you, I haven't got a composer for it yet,' he says with a chuckle.

[11.6.1975]

ALAN AYCKBOURN

JUST BETWEEN OURSELVES -
THE MASTER OF COMEDY CAUGHT AT THE DRAWING BOARD

Meeting Alan Ayckbourn is always unnerving: he has a merciless eye for observation, and one twichily imagines a journalist with a pipe turning up in his next comedy ... Indeed, he himself could be a character from one of the plays. Now 43, with brown hair thinning and waistline expanding, he even dresses in the check shirt and cord trousers of laid-back suburban Mr Jones.

The definition seems important when assessing the people in the 30 or so Ayckbourn plays which have been filling our theatres for the past 15 years, making him our most successful British comedy writer since Noel Coward. 'Alan Bleasdale and Willy Russell, for instance are urban writers,' he says, 'whereas I am suburban, even rural ... I spent years of my life in villages. I am deeply unhappy in big cities. My idea of hell is a week in New York.'

He's been there, of course, to see his work on Broadway, but he doesn't think American casts can capture the droll British manner. 'They tend to tee-off with what they see as big laugh lines. They read it as buffo farce.' It helps to explain why he doesn't like being labelled as the British Neil Simon. For there is another side to the Ayckbourn style - that of the acid tragicomic creator, as seen in *Just Between Ourselves*, which opened last night at Liverpool's Everyman Theatre.

Bob Eaton, the Everyman's artistic director, is a former member of Ayckbourn's resident acting company at Scarborough, and maintains that his old boss is one of the few writers to have crashed the culture barrier. With that, he dismisses the idea put about by intellectual trendies that the popularist Ayckbourn has no place in a radical playhouse like the Everyman.

Just Between Ourselves is a serious play with a bleak ending. It's about selfishness and non-communication between a husband and wife. 'It started as a play about Dennis, the husband,' says Ayckbourn. 'He's a terribly nice chap, but nobody likes him. I think we've all met someone like that. If you see them coming, you run for it. But suddenly I saw Vera through the corner of my eye. She's being destroyed by this man, although, ironically, he wants to help her.'

And with that we learn how Ayckbourn's people actually develop on the drawing board, so to speak. They always have, and they continue to do so. One of his latest ventures is a script called *Intimate*

Exchanges, due into the West End next year. It's really six plays, comprising 30 scenes, which can be played in various orders. In its complexity, it is typical Ayckbourn and follows on the theatrical 'tricks' of plays like *How the Other Half Loves, The Norman Conquests* and *Sisterly Feelings.*

'But this time, I'm going for broke,' he says. 'It's a play about decisions and how small decisions lead to bigger ones. And we're actually performing the first parts while I'm writing the last scenes, I've got about five to go and I'll finish it off by February, I hope. The canvas is enormous and quite frightening. It must be one of the biggest two-hander plays in the world. I just hope that if other theatres take it up, they perform it all and not just bits of it, for it's possible to do the scenes in 16 permutations. You could call it the ultimate lunacy.'

As we talk, he underlines his love of making life difficult for himself by playing with a Rubik Cube. 'I can't do this one yet, but the ones with days and dates on are a doddle.' As it was, he was counting the days to his Christmas show, a re-write of Sheridan's *A Trip to Scarborough.* 'It's as much like the original as *Rosencrantz* is like *Hamlet* ...' Then there was his latest musical, written with Paul Todd, and called *Making Tracks*, which was opening that very night at the seaside theatre in the round where he has been director of production since 1969.

But still uppermost in his mind are those closing scenes of *Intimate Exchanges*: 'It's rather like an ancient monument. You keep coming back to it and finding new aspects. By now, both the actors and myself are dealing with people we all know very well. Anyway, this puzzle and game thing is very much to do with a live theatre. It's not a TV idea or filmic. The best thing that can happen to a theatre is for it to take itself by surprise.'

They say that had Alan Ayckbourn gone in for film writing, he would have been a millionaire. As it is, he has remained a theatre person, and a close friend says you would probably 'have difficulty getting to half a million' in assessing his wealth. Still, not bad. And he has known what it's like to have five of his plays in the West End at the same time.

Yet it's in Scarborough where he stays put, living in a converted Georgian vicarage overlooking the harbour. 'I'm always struck by the idea that the regional theatre was the place I belonged, and I'm glad. I don't find much difference between Scarborough and the places down south where I spent my childhood. I suppose my writing process is quicker now. I always think it's a bit like driving a car: there's a lot of technique to be learned, but eventually one doesn't consciously think about changing gear. You simply continue your journey. Similarly, I no longer worry about lengths and masses of stage instructions about getting people on and off here and there. I don't even know how many plays I've written. In the early days I used to write my head off. There are probably about 10 totally unproduced, totally forgotten plays, not including five one-acts done by amateurs.'

Ayckbourn writes his plays working all night for usually two or three weeks. It used to be in the winter, but now he says he's going to return to the spring, because he feels very bouncy then, just like a rabbit. But what about a holiday? 'My idea of the perfect break is to stay at home. I am very happy with my own things. I like to potter.'

Now that really does sound like one of his characters - pottering about in everyday situations, yet growing to be larger than life.

[12.11.1982]

JIMMY McGOVERN

UPSTAGING THE DYNAMIC DUO?

Jimmy McGovern apologised for being late. He'd been at home bathing the kids before his wife, Eileen, got home from Oxford Street Maternity, where she works as an auxiliary nurse. A day earlier Jimmy had given up his own job as an English teacher at Quarry Bank to pursue the dream of becoming a full-time playwright.

It's just that at 33, he finds it rather twee to be labelled as 'a new young writer'. New, well almost. Young, not really. What's more, he's had a list of jobs as long as your arm. And if the playwriting thing doesn't work out, he can always go back to being 'Sir' in front of a blackboard. The bigwigs in the Education Offices have told him so. Hopefully (in the nicest sense) it won't come to that, and the initial omens would appear to be good. Certainly, he's achieved a scoop which would make many a tried and tested writer, let alone an almost new one, pop a cork: he has new plays coming up in both of his home town repertory theatres.

A comedy, *City Echoes*, the story of a Liverpool family's struggle for a better life over five decades, opens at the Playhouse (and on the main stage at that) this Saturday. Then, in mid-June, a musical play, *A*

True Romance, which explodes the myths about teenage love, is set for the Everyman. The rapid follow-on is said to have ruffled a few feathers high up in the rookeries of the theatre planning departments, but as McGovern says: 'All that every writer wants is to get his work performed.'

Nevertheless, the sudden emergence of McGovern as the man who will virtually have the Liverpool stage to himself this summer, has given rise to all sorts of speculation. Will he (again in the nicest sense) break the monopoly which Willy Russell and Alan Bleasdale have come to hold over local audiences? Will he make it a trinity of talent? There are those who reckon he's in with a chance, while there are others, taking into account what they've already seen of his work, who are still unwilling to commit themselves.

There are certain strategic points in McGovern's favour. Like Bleasdale and Russell, he's a genuine Scouser. He didn't have to go and live among them to take the pulse of the city. And like them he's also been a teacher, so he's in touch with the audience of tomorrow. His style also fits into what appears to be now compulsory formula for box office success: that is local, humorous and with a community (not to say Leftist) tilt. The Everyman show will even have the bonus of music. Say no more. Finally, again in the mould of the Dynamic Duo, there is something of the quiet aggressor in McGovern. In his case, it's the rejection of a strict Roman Catholic upbringing - 'I think the whole family is lapsed now' - the fundamental reaction to a spartan childhood - 'We were always skint, never had holidays, and wore pumps instead of shoes' - and a personal restlessness - 'I've never stayed in any job more than three years."

He was one of nine children, and he left St Francis Xavier's with six O-levels, including English, French, Latin and Chemistry. The only one he went down on was Greek. 'I was quite bright, I suppose. They put me in the fast stream, which meant I got out a year earlier.' He went to work as a clerk in an insurance office. Then there was more clerking down at the Crown Court 'where I saw some tremendous cases.' There followed a period in a car factory before he went to Butlin's at Bognor Regis as a waiter and kitchen porter. He did the same job at the Prince of Wales Hotel in Grasmere, the only difference being that Wordsworth's famous village also produced his wife.

McGovern was 26 before he considered teaching. 'I thought the gates were closed because I didn't have A-levels. But I went along to Scotland Road Writers' Workshop and found out how to better myself. I expanded my horizons, so to speak.' Back at college, he met other mature students, including an amateur actress called Kathy Sturgeon, for whom he wrote a half-hour husband and wife duologue called *Lost City Echo*.

It was the beginnings of the new and retitled show for the Playhouse. He remembers Bill Morrison who'd just had his Ulster play, *Flying Blind*, done at the Everyman, being dragged along to see it by a tutor called Harry Pepp. 'He said some kind things, although at that time, it didn't really work as a stage piece.' Pedr James, then Everyman Artistic Director, also saw McGovern's work and asked him to adapt Dario Fo's play *Can't Pay, Won't Pay* for Hope Street. Not all the critics liked it, and McGovern says the response 'taught me never to be as easily hurt again.'

Chris Bond, by then in charge at the neighbouring Playhouse, saw potential in another McGovern script, *Home Truths*, about a marriage falling apart, and offered him a £1,000 commission 'to write the play you've always wanted to.' It was *City Echoes*. 'I wrote my heart out. After all, people can give you pats on the back, but to come up with the money like that was a great act of faith. I handed in the first act at half-three on a Friday afternoon, and by six, they were back to me praising it. I put the phone down in tears.'

That first act also brought McGovern extra fortune. He sent it as a sample of his work to Channel 4's *Brookside* team, and he's now written ten episodes of the local soap opera. Meanwhile, *City Echoes* continued to emerge, in three drafts, handwritten over 18 months. 'It cost me over £100 just to have it typed.' *A True Romance*, however, was an altogether quicker piece, completed in just six weeks. McGovern didn't write the music, but he did the song lyrics. Both *City Echoes* and the musical don't have to be set in Liverpool, he notes. They could belong further afield, if necessary. 'On the other hand, why should they? Nobody asked Sean O'Casey why he wrote all those Dublin plays.'

People keep telling Jimmy that he's an 'angry writer', which somewhat perplexes him. 'If that's true, then I also want to be known as a person who expresses hope.' We'll see. Suffice it to say that these are important days for someone with a family and a mortgage on a terraced house off Smithdown Road. 'It's amazing really. I never even went to the panto as a kid. Until I started writing, I'd only been to the theatre once - on a schools' trip to see Shakespeare's *Henry IV Part 1*. And even then I fell asleep.'

[20.4.1983]

PETER USTINOV

FACE TO FACES: WITH THE MAN WHO HAS MORE THAN MOST

Peter Ustinov sits down to lunch with a civilised thud. I suppose you felt the tremor?' he muses. A gent to fill a restaurant, if ever there was one, with conversation to match the port and stilton. The Good Companion, a self-styled Common Market of ideas and intellects, and certainly someone to whom a slimline tonic would be like garlic to a vampire. Actor, playwright, producer, director, novelist, raconteur and much more. Not least the embodiment of anyone he happens to be talking about at the time.

'My mother did a good Augustus John, even without the beard, and my father was an ace Queen Victoria. I am much more of an animator,' he confides. His impersonation of Ronald Reagan is forgetful, and doesn't have much to say. But that, in itself, is an excellent impression. 'I think we expect too much of the famous,' he says. 'I mean, if Beethoven walked in here and said "Vell, zee weather is picking up nicely", we would be greatly disappointed. We would be expecting him to be humming a new symphony.' Nowadays, says Ustinov, it's all down to image cultivation. 'The test is, when you are looking in the mirror and the person looking back at you is less interesting than the person looking in, then you know you have failed,' he advises.

He, however, takes a global view of things. Not everyone has a flat in Paris, a house in Switzerland. and is a friend of Mikhail Gorbachev. Ustinov's grandfather was exiled from Russia in 1860. The result, two generations on, is a benevolent internationalist and linguist. 'The language business has been exaggerated,' he insists. 'I speak French. My wife is French. I have a bit of German and Italian; can get by in Spanish, and read Dutch or Portuguese papers - so as to get entirely the wrong impression. And in Russian, I can tell whether I am being interpreted correctly.'

That comes in useful when you're invited, in company with the American writer Arthur Miller, to an 11am meeting with the Soviet head of state to discuss cultural exchanges. 'I was in a committee room within the sound of the Kremlin bells,' he explains. 'At 10.45, various slots in the wall began to open, and at 11 on the dot, Gorbachev came in for an hour's talk. He left three hours later. He had become very interested. In the end, one even forgot who he was.'

Right now, his time is taken up with a one-man show, which can been seen at Manchester's Palace Theatre until Saturday. Then the collection of anecdotes moves to London, for 36 performances at the

Haymarket. Apart from that, our man has just written a novel, *The Old Man and Mr Smith*, which is about God and Satan. God even gets the line: 'We may be immortal, but it doesn't halt the ageing process.'

Ustinov goes on: 'I still think writing is the most exciting thing in life: how a blank sheet of paper fills up and becomes a habit. You just have to bear in mind that everything that's ever been written is that teeny bit too long.' He concludes: 'But that's the way it is. This show is the grit of life. I feel as if I've been privatised. I did it in Adelaide in a theatre holding 6,000 people, and I felt like a postage stamp.'

[15.3.1990]

THE REDGRAVE FAMILY PLAYERS

The curtain goes up on a unique performance at Liverpool Playhouse on Sunday, when the theatre's vice-president, Sir Michael Redgrave, and three of his famous theatrical family, present a benefit show for the Croxteth Community Action Centre. With Sir Michael will be his wife (actress Rachel Kempson); daughter Vanessa and son Corin. It will be the first time that all four have appeared on stage together.

For Sir Michael, the one-night show will have a double significance. For it was at the Playhouse that he made his acting debut in 1934 in a play called *Counsellor-at-Law*, by Elmer Rice. It was also at the Playhouse that he met his wife, who joined the company seven months later.

Sunday's entertainment is entitled *Shakespeare and his Players*. The first part is biographical, telling the story of Sir Michael Redgrave's actor parents, Roy Redgrave and Daisy Scudamore, to his own marriage in Liverpool. The second part is devoted to Shakespeare, complete with suitable music.

[29.9.1982]

REX HARRISON

They used to call him 'Sexy Rexie'. He was the immaculate English actor of the black-tie tradition. The fair sex were beguiled by the flair and the style. Today, in his 75th year, he can no longer claim to be a sex symbol - although he is enjoying his sixth marriage to Mercia Tinker, an independently wealthy lady who is three decades his junior. But his style, now tweedy, is still there, and when I met him in Manchester yesterday, he was sporting his first set of real whiskers. 'When I did *Henry VIII* on Broadway, I simply stuck on the beard. I thought that this time we'd have the real thing,' he said.

Harrison is back on the British stage for the first time in six years, playing a vigorous 88 year old in Bernard Shaw's *Heartbreak House* at the Palace Theatre. More, he looks every bit as distinguished as Shaw, to whom he owes the mainstay of his career; after all, *My Fair Lady*, in which he played Professor Higgins in New York, London and on film, is a product of *Pygmalion*.

Rex Harrison was a lad of five, living in Lancaster Avenue, Sefton Park, when Shaw wrote *Pygmalion* in 1913. He then went to Liverpool Playhouse, where as a 16 year old, he got a studentship, doing everything from brushing the stage to bit parts, and earning 30 shillings a week. His first appearance was as the husband in something called *Thirty Minutes in a Street*. His last appearance in his home city - he was born in Tarbock Road, Huyton - was 12 years ago, when he was MC in a Royal Gala show at the Empire, on the night the Queen opened the second Mersey Tunnel.

'I used to like going back, but I have no relatives there now, and I shan't have time to pop over this week,' he said. Indeed, Harrison admits to being a man without a proper home. He's sold his house at Cap Ferrat, on the French Mediterranean coast and his place at Portofino in Italy. 'We have a small two roomed apartment in New York, but that's all,' he says, adding that he hasn't ruled out the possibility of returning to the English countryside. But he has no plans for retirement. 'If I like something, then I'll do it. If not, I certainly won't.'

As a millionaire, you can be that choosy. Way back in '49 he was pulling in £54,000 a year, ahead of folk like Bing Crosby, Bob Hope, Tyrone Power and Edward G. Robinson in the Hollywood earnings league. Quite apart from his Tony Awards and his Oscar, and all the other accolades which the entertainment industry has showered upon him, his private life has always been in the headlines. The other Mrs Harrisons were Marjorie Thomas, Lily Palmer, Kay Kendall (who died of leukaemia), Rachel Roberts, and Elizabeth Harris, the ex-wife of Richard Harris. But he's been wed to Mercia Tinker, a onetime neighbour in Monte Carlo, for the past five years. She'll be joining him in two week's time, when the *Heartbreak House* tour reaches Bath.

Acting has always been in the Harrison blood. Through his mother, he's descended from the famous Edmund Kean, and one of his first Liverpool memories is of being taken to the old Royal Court to see Fred Terry and Julia Neilson in *The Scarlet Pimpernel*. After leaving the Playhouse in 1927 to appear in a London production of *Charley's Aunt*, his career really took off. Since then, it's never really come in to land.

In all those years, he's bumped into the great and famous, including Bernard Shaw himself - 'very strong and very opinionated, but with a marvellous sense of humour' - and Noel Coward - 'a very difficult man to follow in his own plays because he wrote them for himself.' But today Rex Harrison, thanks to the new beard, enjoys walking round the streets unnoticed and indulging in his new hobby, painting. 'They're mainly watercolours of landscapes and seascapes. I must try portraits some time,' he said. 'It's all come about because I travel around so much. I particularly like to paint out of doors.' He hasn't sold any of his art yet, but one suspects there's enough money to go round from his better known activities.

[9.2.1983]

DAME MARIE RAMBERT

AT 90, STILL ON HER TOES

'Pleased to meet you. How are you?' My somewhat pedestrian greeting to Dame Marie Rambert is answered swiftly and with extaordinary agility; her 90 year old frame gives two high kicks to touch the outstretched fingers of her right hand: 'I'm fine, thank you. Still going.'

With a laugh like the tinkling of a miniature jewellery box, she welcomes me to her London home, full of paintings, books amd memories. 'I thought our meeting was this morning,' she says. 'I'm terrible, you must forgive me. I forget many day to day matters now, but the things I learned by heart remain with me. I can still do my 40 Shakespeare sonnets. They really matter.'

Something else that really matters to multilingual Dame Marie is her piano, standing in one corner of the large drawing room. She taught herself to play in her mid 70s, when Ballet Rambert was going through a temporary crisis of numbers. 'I've started to learn when I was young, but I refused to have lessons when my teacher grew ugly and fat - or so I thought. Of course, I didn't realise in those days that she was pregnant.'

When Dame Marie says: 'In those days', she is talking of her native Warsaw, during the 1890s: days when the influence of the Russian Emperor was so great that she and her friends were forbidden to speak Polish at school. But they were allowed to learn their national dances. 'From the moment I started, I loved movement as an expression.' Her introduction to classical ballet was 'an awful Italian production of *Swan Lake*. The Swans didn't so much glide as throw themselves around the stage.'

Then the great dancer Isadora Duncan visited Warsaw in 1904 and young Marie's imagination was captured for life. When she was sent to Paris the following year to stop with relations, she gradually began to give dance recitals in fashionable salons. In 1910, she went on a 10 day summer course to Jacques Dalcroze's school in Geneva, and stayed three years. M. Dalcroze had invented Eurhythmics - the art of interpreting musical rhythms into bodily movements. And it was this skill which brought Marie into contact with another prime influence in her life, the famous Nijinsky. She joined Diaghilev's Ballets Russes to teach them the complicated rhythms of Stravinsky's *Rite of Spring*. Half a century later, she was to learn that the composer considered this production to be the best.

Now we are into more recent history: her 41 year marriage to the playwright Ashley Dukes, which began in 1918, and the opening of her own school of dance two years later. Her first male pupil was one Frederick Ashton, who was to become the genius choreographer of the Royal Ballet. On the bookcase in her home is a prized sculpture of them dancing together in *A Tragedy of Fashion*, a work created by Ashton and which marked the real beginnings of Ballet Rambert back in 1926.

For more than 40 years, Dame Marie nursed her company through rehearsals and performances. In short, no other director, with the exception of Diaghilev, has had a greater influence in the forces of ballet anywhere in the world. New dances were created and new challenges found. The pattern continued up to the present, when Ballet Rambert has just enjoyed its best London season, culminating with a 15 minute ovation for the last night performance of *Cruel Garden*. Dame Marie notes my review comment that it was 'one of the most important dance works of the 70s,' and with a twinkle of the eye, adds: 'I'm a little older. I would say more than the 70s.' Certainly, it is a dazzling full-length spectacle on the life of Frederico Garcia Lorca, the Spanish poet. In its use of mime, song, poetry - and of course dance - it seems to sum up all the multi-media stamina and excitement which has characterised Ballet Rambert's 52 years.

Today, Dame Marie takes a seat at London performances, often seeing works several times. She keeps in touch by telephone during the week but has passed the real mantle of her work to others. She remains, however, at the centre of the company's affection, for they know their success in London, Liverpool or anywhere else, owes itself to the vision of this truly remarkable woman.

[16.5.1978]

JUDI DENCH

BACK WITH US - 'HAND-BAAG' AND ALL

Judi Dench has good reason to remember Liverpool. It was here, as a mere 19 year old in 1957, that she made her stage debut playing Shakespeare's Ophelia with the Old Vic company at the Royal Court. And it was to the Court that the then established classical actress returned to make her debut as a modernist in a play called *A Shot In The Dark*. This time she was wearing a saucy black crepe outfit - the first time she had donned a short dress on stage. Liverpool also gave Judi her husband - actor Michael Williams, educated at St. Edward's College, Sandfield Park, who was later to star with her in the popular TV series, *A Fine Romance*. And next Tuesday she returns here - this time to play Lady Bracknell in Oscar Wilde's *The Importance of Being Earnest* at the Empire.

That calls for wigs, big hats and padded shoulders, transforming the five foot one and three quarter inches Miss Dench normally attains from stocking feet to the top of her own cropped baby-fine hair, into a formidable stage presence. And all the more formidable because of the association which Dame Edith Evans gained with the role of Lady B delivering that immortal line: 'A HAND-BAAG!'

'People will not let me forget it,' says Judi. 'They always end up by asking about that line. It's become so fused with the interpretation of one person, but people should remember that Edith Evans was only in her forties when she first played Lady Bracknell.' Miss Dench is now of that vintage herself, but resents it when people imply that Peter Hall's new production is trying to be different. 'All we are doing is going back to what Wilde wrote, yet some people have got a set view of it. Lady Bracknell doesn't apologise to anyone for having got money or breeding. She's been brought up to think that way. But she's also got a soft spot. I don't think the character should be pigeon-holed. As it is, the play itself is a great classic, an old master. It's the food for the Gods.'

That said, Judi Dench is insistent that the play should flow at the right pace. She sees no mileage in actors standing around like pretty cardboard cut-outs waiting to deliver their own clever pieces of business, as happens in some Wilde productions. That's why you'll always find her in the wings a good eight to ten pages before she's due on - 'to get the measure of the play and the place.'

This has always been her approach. She's convinced that she only got the Old Vic job as a teenager because she'd been to a performance in the building the night before her audition. She has remained most closely associated with the classical Shakespearian roles, as one of the brightest stars in the RSC's galaxy. Very very well known to a theatrically minded public, but lesser known perhaps to the public at large.

She still finds film work slow. There's too much sitting around waiting for the weather. She's been selective with her television work, which means that she remains a special theatre person. Her prize possession right now is a letter from a 12 year old girl who's playing Lady Bracknell in a school production. It asks for a meeting 'as one Lady Bracknell to another.'

'Of course, at my age, I presume that everyone knows the play,' says Judi. 'But that's not true. To many of the kids it's completely new and that's why we want it to look fresh.'

[12.11.1982]

BLOOD BROTHERS

WILLY RUSSELL: WITH A SONG IN HIS ART
LIVERPOOL PLAYHOUSE

For someone who's not a nuts and bolts musician in a crotchet and quaver sort of way, Willy Russell's not doing too badly. Tonight, all those years of guitar strumming and pounding the folk club beat pay off, when Russell's first 'real' musical, *Blood Brothers*, bursts onto the Liverpool Playhouse stage. Back in '75, of course, he received the Best New Musical Award for his Beatles show, *John, Paul, George, Ringo and Bert*, which started life at the Everyman and then ran for a year and a day in the West End. 'I thought of getting up and asking them what they were on about,' he recalls. 'After all, the music and lyrics were by Lennon and McCartney.'

This time it's different. It's all Russell - with a little help from his friends. Out front will be Barbara Dickson, who owes her fame to the Beatles show, this time playing the mother of twin boys, separated at birth, one growing up an urchin, the other a nice middle class Nigel. And fundamental to the whole shebang is Pete Filleul, a 31 year old keyboard player, who's arranged, edited and set Russell's music out on chord charts for the nine strong theatre band.

Willy's regard for Filleul's musicality is evident. He doesn't sing in the show, but Russell hails him as 'the best undiscovered singing talent around.' They met when the Jersey-based Filleul was working with the Climax Blues Band in Stafford. Russell showed him a ballad (which reappears in *Blood Brothers*) called *Dance the Night Away*. The Blues Band did a tape and when their American agent heard it, he insisted they put it in an album. Then, as a single, it went to number one in Pensylvania. So good news again, for the play-by-ear Mr Russell.

Obviously, most people now think of him as a playwright. His comedy *Educating Rita*, written for the Royal Shakespeare Company, has become one of the most successful of modern plays. It's been made into a film with Michael Caine and Julie Walters, while on stage it's still being seen in Denmark, France, Germany, Turkey, Belgium, Israel, Mexico and Australia. Its theme, of an individual striving for self enhancement, is universal, and Russell hopes that there are some universal joints in *Blood Brothers*.

He'd like it to be seen as 'an English musical presented through Merseyside ... and Merseyside is the heart of England, for God's sake.' What he's tried to avoid is having a 'play with music'. Also, the old American musical idea of the plot grinding to a halt for the sake of a song. Stephen Sondheim is the best example of a modern musical writer kicking against the old format, although Russell says he's followed no textbook plans for *Blood Brothers*. The idea of the story came to him eight years ago, and the tunes had been forming up over the years (his first public appearance as a folk singer had been in the old Spinner's Club in West Derby Road, when he was a lad of 17). Singing was only ever an escape, a hobby, although he reached the semi-pro ranks.

He'd thought of doing *Blood Brothers* for his R.S.C. commission instead of *Educating Rita* and also discussed the idea with Chris Bond, now artistic director at the Playhouse, and director of this production. 'He told me he wanted to do the show,' says Russell, 'but when Paul Harman asked for a script for his Merseyside Young People's Theatre, I told Chris I'd do a play version of *Blood Brothers* with just a few songs.' As it is, only one unaccompanied song went before the M.Y.P.T. company's Merseyside schools' audiences. Russell had thought that they were getting in an extra actor-musician for the job, but the budget didn't stretch to it. So tonight really is the premiere, and all hopes are on Russell's local pulling power. The theatre is taking the unusual step of having two preview nights to warm up before the critics go in on Saturday. And if all goes well, they hope to get eleven weeks business out of it - a very long run for provincial rep.

Barbara Dickson, in her first acting role, has already praised the show's guts and emotional appeal. But as Russell says, he wants it to be seen as the complete musical. The benefit of having Pete Filleul around has been to make the mode of the music more accessible, says Russell, whose own leisure tastes extend to Randy Newman, Joni Mitchell, James Taylor and a New York all-women's band, The Roaches. He says his musical appreciation is fairly catholic these days. 'Always at the centre of music for me must be melody. I've been one for these pyrotechnic players. I can watch Harpo Marx if I want that sort of thing.' Further digging reveals a love for the precise mastery of Noel Coward, but sadly, a tribute to Coward called *A Light Romance* is cut from *Blood Brothers*.

There can be no doubt that the venture marks the focus of a lot of hopes. London managements are already preparing their spies to set up a possible transfer. 'For me as a writer it's been a way of moving forward,' says Willy Russell. 'It's definitely not a one-song show. There's an hour of music in two and a half hours of playing time. Hopefully, it could be the start of something, but usually after completing a script, I like to get as far away as possible and into something different for the next thing.'

[6.1.1983]

PETER O'TOOLE

MACBETH

Peter O'Toole strode across the stage of Liverpool's Empire Theatre and stared down into the new orchestra pit: 'Wow, it's huge. Almost makes you nervous to go to the edge. From now on, that's "The Moat".'

Thus spake *Macbeth*, the most controversial *Macbeth* for years ... But the maunderings of the critics who universally slammed his portrayal of Shakespeare's Thane, don't seem to have affected O'Toole's sense of humour prior to the production's sell-out provincial premiere in Liverpool tonight.

'I must have been to Liverpool more than any other place in the country during my 48 years,' he said. 'Literally thousands of times taking boats to and from Ireland, but I've never stayed here before. When I arrived on the train I soon got lost however. It seems to have changed so much. But I did go to the two cathedrals and I'm looking forward to walking around a bit more this week.

I've only acted here once before. I had just two lines in a production of *Twelfth Night* at the old Shakespeare Theatre years ago, but that was only because the boy originally playing the part had a sore throat!'

[14.10.1980]

FAR FROM HORROR CAULDRON
(REVIEW) LIVERPOOL EMPIRE

Last night's regional premiere of Peter O'Toole's *Macbeth* was obviously destined to be something of a curio. There is a voyeuristic trait in every theatregoer, and just as circus patrons secretly wonder whether the high-wire act will plummet into the sawdust ring, I suspect that the Empire was brimming over with the expectation that this ex-Lawrence of Arabia would fall off his Shakespearian horse.

After all, weren't the London critics virtually unanimous in their condemnation? Hadn't we secretly been saving up rotten tomatoes to throw at the stage? Well, I'm sorry to have to disappoint the headhunters among you, for although O'Toole's towering and gaunt frame is more suited to some dramatic portrait of a Paganini rather than a Macbeth, his interpretation is nothing like the cauldron of horrors that it has been painted.

Indeed, there can be no doubt at all in my mind that the Old Vic *Macbeth* works far better than its partner production of *The Merchant of Venice,* at least in terms of the Empire Theatre. Here, the playing needs to be big, and whereas I can imagine that O'Toole's rendering of the lines may have been too declamatory for the company's much smaller London home theatre, there's very little chance of any single human being proving to be overwhelming in the Empire without the aid of a microphone.

Things did start warily, almost urbanely, and there were times when dramatic impact was visually as well as verbally lacking (when Duncan's murdered body is discovered, for instance), but in fairness I felt that Mr O'Toole successfully transmitted the frightened and the frightening aspects of Macbeth's turmoil for, unlike Othello, Hamlet or Lear, he has to face the consequences of his own creation.

And now for the bad news: Frances Tomelty's Lady Macbeth is a wet. If anything or anybody lets O'Toole down, then it's this shadow of a performance of Shakespeare's Iron Lady, who, to my mind, is the chief character of the play. She has to be seen as the instigator of her husband's dilemma, and the *raison d'être* of all the ambition, blood and gore that follows. As it is, Miss Tomelty is for the most part an amorphous 'extra.'

Thank goodness, there's a springboard elsewhere for Macbeth's ruminating neurosis, and that is found in Brian Blessed's excellent Banquo, the friend who returns to haunt the feast.

[15.10.1980]

DODDY

To see Ken Dodd's stage act for the first time is to witness a brilliant barrage of comic material and to be assuredly surrounded by gales of laughter. To see it time and time again, as I have done from the critic's seat, is to begin to understand the very real science and psychology of his comic genius.

Nobody in the theatre business - and I include all those who choose to regard themselves as being on a higher cultural plane - nobody can control or communicate with an audience as directly and as keenly as Doddy. What's more, these are qualities which apply whether he be giving an after-dinner speech, topping the bill at the London Palladium, or as of now, doing a summer season at Southport. I could write a book on the man's technique alone, if the critic Michael Billington hadn't already done the job with great insight.

For my money, Doddy rarely, if ever, comes over well on television and that's because TV is not the medium for a clown and a creator of atmosphere. And that's what Ken Dodd is all about - a latter-day flowering of all that the music hall end-of-the-pier tradition strived for in its heyday, but never achieved with such gusto.

His Southport show is bright and well-dressed. The line-up includes a slick singing trio, *Young Love*, (the kind of act you see on Round the World cruises) and a clever magician, Paul Derek.

[27.7.1980]

THE WOMAN IN BLACK

(REVIEW) THE LIVERPOOL PLAYHOUSE

Richard Todd is of the Old School of acting, for which there is much to be said. In other words, he has range. He can walk out on stage and assume several identities without recourse to plastic surgery.

In this good old-fashioned ghost story, complete with off-stage screams and smoke effects, Todd - veteran of *The Hasty Heart, Dam Busters* etc - plays a man with a dreadful story to tell and a personal exorcism to perform. The real Mr Todd is distinguished, with the air of a church warden. But he can shrink in stature, grow again, switch accent, manner and mood as he fleshes out details of ghoulish goings-on in a remote house, located across a tidal causeway. You can see why Stephen Mallatratt's adaptation of Susan Hill's spooked-up novel was ideal West End material: all those Yanks yearning for a little bit of Old England...

But also, as a play of illusion, it harkens back to the 'Let's pretend' dramatic style more associated with post-war theatre than with the realism instituted by people like John Osborne. It was, you may recall, Osborne's much-heralded sequel to *Look Back in Anger*, with Peter O'Toole, which was meant to be filling this flagship slot in the Playhouse season. Yet what amounts to an 'emergency' production, directed by Ian Kellgren, and co-starring Dominic Letts, is no poor substitute. Very different, admittedly, but beguiling in its period setting and fundamental technique, which incorporates mime and quicksilver character acting. Messrs Todd and Letts, quite apart from entertaining us, offer a workshop to any aspiring thespians in the audience who may mistakenly think that acting is about signing a contract and merely being themselves.

It suddenly dawned on me during the first act, that I once saw a television version of *The Woman in Black*. But technology is no substitute for presence. And I'll guarantee that this high spirited show will have you jumping in your seat.

[15.11.1991]

PETER PAN

ALIVE AND WELL
(REVIEW) THEATR CLWYD

Whether or not it's healthy to have a dog kennel in the bedroom is neither here nor there. Nor should we be at all concerned that most children's idea of the good life doesn't yet run to a nursery with bathroom en suite. J.M.Barrie's *Peter Pan*, the boy who just wouldn't grow up, is not a creature of social realism.

For the past 80 years, ever since he first flew onto the stage of the Duke of York's Theatre, he has remained an enchanting piece of magic. Long may the tradition continue, and if Theatr Clwyd's magnificent production is anything to go by, I am wholly optimistic. It is quite simply the most beguiling piece of fantasy drama, for it will offer refreshing escapism for all the family this Christmas. If you want to keep each and every generation of the gathered clan happy during the holiday period, then I'll lay odds now that this show won't be bettered anywhere in the North West, and possibly further afield.

Mind you, it is the most expensive production in Theatr Clwyd's history. And they have been working on it since June. Everything - except, perhaps, the nursery floor carpet - is sumptuous, as we travel through Never Never Land with its pirates and Indians, take to the high seas by courtesy of some extraordinary stage-craft, and gasp in delight as an amazingly realistic crocodile gets snap-happy with the evil Captain Hook. The man getting all the boos is Alan Gill, in booming, dark-voiced mood as the old seadog himself, having started out as a Ned Sherrin-like Mr Darling, not past giving the dog a bit of stick.

I'm always full of admiration for actors who spend their Christmases on all fours, and this year it's Howard Cooper as Nana (although he does get a stand-up part later on). A bit of the old sex reversal going on beneath the fur here, but it's good to see that Peter Pan is a boy (Ken Sabberton), as there's no longer any real need for this girl- plays- boy stuff that dates from silly old laws about children's performance times. Not that Mr Sabberton is a child Peter; more the mature youth. But then he is leader of the gang, and has a most healthy attitude towards girls (i.e.Wendy, played by Janthea Williams).

I may return to see it all again, such is the lure of the Director Paul Chamberlain's vision in putting the show together. It's time and money well spent. Anybody disapproving of it should be sent to bed early. Besides, they probably made the mistake of growing up.....

[9/12/84]

EDUCATING RITA

WILLY RUSSELL PROBES THE MEANING OF LIFE
(REVIEW) THE LIVERPOOL PLAYHOUSE

Where do you find the true meaning of life? Is it in Yates' Wine Lodge or in the poetry of William Butler Yeats? According to Willy Russell, ex-schoolteacher and now playwright and man-of-the-people, the answer lies in a little of each.

And he's absolutely right, of course, for his award winning comedy, *Educating Rita*, asks us to consider the differences between academic achievement and plain bar-room commonsense. Writers like Chekhov, Beckett and even our own Tom Stoppard have already covered this territory in an overtly scholarly way, a convention which can blunt the very debate it seeks to initiate. But Russell is the sort of communicator who calls a spade a spade until he's in danger of tripping over it.

So, instead, he provides us with basic - and local - terms of reference. There are indeed teachers like Frank (William Gaunt) who commute from Formby and points north to their lecture rostra. And there are indeed girls like his Open University student, Rita (Kate Fitzgerald), who want something better from life than blue-rinsing in city salons.

Russell's excellent two-hander not only exposes the humiliation of a willing learner being mocked by an established thinker, but also champions the idea that education doesn't end with the last failed school examination. There is a cosmopolitan feel - hence the well-earned batch of West End nominations and awards for the RSC production.

But at the Playhouse, with Russell as co-director with Pip Broughton, the message comes home to roost. Differences of chance and confidence are being underlined every day by Merseyside's unemployment figures. Yet this play also teaches us that formal education isn't everything; it can stifle individuality and make people believe they have style, when all they really have are the cast-off thoughts of their mentors.

[6.2.1981]

CHESTER MYSTERY PLAYS

GOD'S IN HIS HEAVEN (REVIEW)

The Chester Mystery Plays are a truly enormous enterprise with a cast of hundreds under the umbrella direction of George Roman, the first artistic director at Theatr Clwyd, and using a translation by Edward Burns of Liverpool University. Heaven, Hell and the Miracles are themselves divided into sub-sections, each part of the main trio taking up to three hours. No wonder a limited company has been set up to handle this gigantic challenge, which is presented every five years.

The setting - in a big top on Cathedral Green - has a circus air to it: the actors, some in cars, enter and depart singly or in multitudes. The modern version of the medieval guild players, criss-crossing the city in their carts. If creation, sin, death and resurrection are the eternal cornerstone of these five-centuries old playlets, man's interpretation, like theology itself, has evolved. Here, Cain and Abel are sharp-suited spivs in a Land-Rover with a personalised number plate; Herod is a despot with the trappings of neo-fascism; Noah's wife looks like she's been to the sales. But, despite an allusion to the Trinity, God as three supposedly unison voices - irritatingly out of sync so the Almighty becomes a Dalek - is the one overbearing annoyance. And yes, you've guessed it, in this newfangled age of women priests, the Deity is one third a girlie.

Elsewhere, despite the myriad of sub-plots, there is a good sense of cohesion and inventive design. On Saturday, Heaven still managed to be quite a fearful place (goodness knows what awaits in Hell!). One felt sorry for Adam and Eve, bemused by Mr and Mrs Noah and somewhat bored by Abraham's plight, which could and should have been sacrificed (sic). Meanwhile, God is in his Heaven and all's fairly well with the Mysteries.

[7.7.1997]

HAMLET

(REVIEW) ST GEORGE'S HALL

First things first: St George's Hall works as a theatre space. High vaulted and majestic, it even bears curious comparison to Manchester's Royal Exchange, which is the best arena in Britain. So let us hope that the experiment of staging lyric theatre there continues, while in the meantime being thankful to Liverpool's Everyman Theatre for grasping the nettle and persuading this touring production to visit.

And now to the production itself, which is high on melancholia and low on motivation. For here is one of the greatest tragedies of all time. Perhaps not - in itself - the personal Shakespearian Everests that are *Macbeth, Lear or* even *Othello*, but nevertheless, the highest continuous range of obstacles for an ensemble company. Alan Rickman's Hamlet, is a knowing beast. The actor's eyes have it. Yet, in reality, Hamlet, as Shakespeare intended, is for ever finding his way. It is a journey of discovery which is halted only by a poisoned sword. His anxiousness arises from his circumstances. Not least his family circumstances, which, today, would be guaranteed to provide a graduation examination for social workers. Mr Rickman's interpretation, within a very physical rendition, is rich in colour of language, but odd in punctuation. It's not what he says, but the way he *doesn't* say it that makes for peaks and troughs of comprehension.

Yet in all this, Mr Rickman is no way primed up by either David Burke's Claudius, which is completely lacking in menace (he would be better suited as a suffragan bishop of some outer diocese), or by Geraldine McEwan's sitcom Gertrude. Between them, they make Punch and Judy appear to be brimming over with self initiative. But there are strengths: Julia Ford's Ophelia has guts, while Adrian Rawlins as her brother Laertes, at least has reason - even for mistaken revenge. But, in this case, the play remains the thing. As does the setting.

[4.11.1992]

RUDOLF NUREYEV

FIRST NIGHT
(REVIEW) EMPIRE THEATRE

After Rudolph Nureyev made his famous 'leap to freedom' in Paris, 30 years ago, he was hailed as the greatest male dancer since Nijinsky. He has since become an even more legendary long-distance runner than Red Rum. And now, the chap who did more to promote ballet as a viable fitness alternative to field and track events, is hanging up his shoes.

But his farewell to the fans consists not so much of the gymnastics of yesteryear - although there is a bit of that - as of sage-like mime delivered by someone who is still a fairly good mover. Nureyev is 53 and dance is a precise and physical thing. Had he been a singer, he could have gone on doing things his way as long as Sinatra. Alas, he will doubtless continue to develop his other career as an actor - something which showed through in the two works he chose. *The Lesson*, choreographed by the Danish dancer Fleming Flindt, is a re-working of Ionesco's Absurdist play of the same name. Nureyev, as a sort of 'Phantom of the Ballet', kills off his star pupil (Evelyne Desutter) in a scenario more suited to Max Wall than high drama.

But Nureyev's facial imagery and body language are astutely worked out. In Moor's *Pavane*, based on the Othello story, the mood is graceful and noble, as befits the suite of Purcell music to which it is danced. But again, it is mainly slow-moving, more reliant on acting prowess than physical feats.

When I last saw Nureyev - in Manchester three years ago - he took on the roles of a faun and a clown. He was already slowing down, becoming characterful. So I wasn't expecting fireworks, like some in last night's audience. Even so, despite the pre-recorded music, which I disliked intensely, the occasion was one of witnessing a piece of theatrical history. And, of course, there will be those one day able to tell their grandchildren that they saw Nureyev's last show in Liverpool.

[29.4.1991]

TOSCA

(REVIEW) EMPIRE THEATRE

The durability of the Tosca story was demonstrated by Glen Walford at the Everyman 10 years ago, when she staged a completely effective chamber version. The large-scale Puccini score merely underlines the treachery of a duped heroine driven to suicide by the malice of a rapist police chief. Add jealousy, republicanism and free-thinking anti-religious fervour, and you've got a hot plot, that a century ago brought realism to an increasingly stuffy opera house.

Welsh National Opera kick-started their Spring season in Liverpool by fielding the very special Suzanne Murphy in the title role. Tosca has been traditionally played as a tigress (Callas etc) but she is as vulnerable as Puccini's Mimi or Butterfly. Michael Blakemore's production emphasises this, only giving full vent to her ruthlessness prior to the murder of the villainous Scarpia (Peter Sidhorn). His slaying has all the trappings of a Roman assassination of old. Although his pivotal character of the despot is ably sung, this Scarpia is somehow lacking in venom. He has the countenance of a country rector from the pages of Trollope.

Nevertheless, an ever-buoyant orchestra does some of the devil's work on his behalf, enhancing three magnificently bold sets. The musical highlight is the duet between Tosca and her true love, Calvaradossi (Carlos Ventre), prior to his death by firing squad. The only thing left is for Tosca to throw herself from the castle battlements - a strange anticlimax after the intensity of the lovers' lament. But it does prove that old ruse about opera: if the characters don't bleed to death, they sing themselves into oblivion.

[1.4.1998]

MOZART'S *SERAGLIO*

(REVIEW) EMPIRE THEATRE

Mozart's opera *Seraglio*, outrageous in its borrowed plot and radical by its musical nature, is the one the Emperor Joseph of Austria complained about as having too many notes. Fans of the film *Amadeus* may recall that little incident from a film which otherwise contains as many popular myths as it does facts.

Welsh National Opera's new production of *Seraglio* is pleasingly atmospheric in terms of its physical presence, conjuring up the steamy decadence of the East and the romantic-comedy of the adventure and rescue. Yet there is the distinct feeling that performance-wise things are still being run-in, with some fairly hit or miss singing and over-stilted dialogue. This is, after all, *singspiel* (literally a 'sing-play') with speaking between the musical content which itself has a leaning towards more formal Italian opera. It may not be the most complex of Mozart's works from the early part of his final great period of composition, but he is striving to achieve an emotional musical whole, rather in the way that Shakespeare had done with plays.

Mozart, therefore, becomes the catalyst for bringing together all that had gone before and laying the ground for the future. It is no coincidence that he had studied Haydn and discovered Bach; nor is it just chance that *Seraglio* was the first exposure to the music of Mozart for a very young Beethoven.

The real beauty lies in the linear qualities of the score, with complementary harmonies working in every direction from a tonal centre. And here Mozart runs the gamut, from jolly major keys (he even incorporates authentic Oriental sounds, particularly in the percussion) through to his own tragic key in G minor. But in no way are we setting out on a journey of academic analysis. *Singspiel* had been specially developed for a much wider audience beyond the realms of the wealthy and musically aware. And therein lies it use of blatant humour, perhaps the best quarried from the WNO setting, in which, without being deliberately sexist, it has to be said that the gentlemen fare somewhat better than the ladies. The production is repeated tomorrow.

[6.4.1989]

LES MISERABLES

(REVIEW) THE LIVERPOOL EMPIRE

The arrival of Les Miz sets a new high water mark by which future spectaculars must be judged. This particular one - the world's most popular musical - is with us for 10 weeks, fully giving the feel of Lime Street as Liverpool's very own West End. The scale and effect of the show is gargantuan. A cast and crew of more than 100 not only create a no-expense spared scenario, but also carry with them the largesse of internationalism.

This isn't the stop-go musical of old, where favourite songs were beacons in a sea of banal dialogue. Rather, it belongs to the realms of opera, being fully sung, and with structured character developments. Jeff Leyton as heroic Jean Valjean, the escaped convict who takes on the Establishment, has an amazing vocal range. The other Himalayan performance comes from Peter Corry, as Javert, the thwarted police inspector. All this puts Les Miz in the same league as *West Side Story* or *Sweeney Todd*. And to confirm that, the comic song, springing up from the show's bedrock of revolutionary Paris, is pure Sondheim.

That's not to detract from the craft of French creative partnership Boubil and Schonberg who, despite the show's global fame (and that of *Miss Saigon*), have yet to become household names. Their songs, which emerge as part of a continuous thread of melody, were never pre-marketed as 'hits' like the Lloyd Webber classics. Nevertheless, you will know them when you hear them. Numbers like the intimate *A Heart Full Of Love*, eventually sung as a wonderful trio, right up to the magnificence of *Do You Hear The People Sing?* which nowadays suffices as a second French national anthem.

The refurbished Empire Theatre comes into its own. In one scene, below the streets, the deepened stage, back-lit and with dry ice effects, creates a sense of infinity. But the true spectacle is the frequent use of the stage revolve, and the emergence of the barricades, like huge Roman battering rams, from the wings.

The oft-quoted message of the show is about 'the human spirit'. It is, of course. But most of all, it's about how people carry on, because and in spite of everything that life's fates can heap upon them.

[21.12.98]

MUSIC

MAHLER'S FIRST SYMPHONY

(REVIEW) PHILHARMONIC HALL

Emerging - minus score - to conduct a Mahler symphony is akin to playing *King Lear* in swimming trunks. That is, you don't make a habit of this sort of exhibitionism, and you hope there won't be any flabby bits.

Libor Pesek, Liverpool's uncrowned King of Charisma, had no need for pre-concert nerves - even though, before his mesmerising feat of memory, he had to get through a dozen of the same composer's folk songs. His allies in this less prepared part of Saturday's proceedings were the Dutch mezzo, Jard Van Nes, and the British baritone, Stephen Roberts. Both singers, heard in duet, made their most telling contributions solo: Ms Van Nes (wearing a hyacinth blue dress, and looking disarmingly like Hyacinth Bucket!) in the subtle *Urlicht*, Mr Roberts, recently here for Faurés Requiem, in *The Prisoner in the Tower*.

The Mahlerian sound-world - as important and varied for songs as for symphonies - is a thing well understood by the RLPO, who were the British pioneers of such performances during the 60s. There are shades of Bruckner, another composer with whom the players are well versed, in the more driving parts of Mahler's final symphony. But Mahler isn't just about massive tonal resources, animation and volume. It is also wonderfully subtle music, and Pesek's approach, full of left-hand expression, was by turns seductive, gentle and teasing, as well as vibrant and grand. A full range of dramatic moods, which ensured a captivated audience from start to finish.

For that's another great concert hall bonus for epic work of this kind. Actually seeing it performed gives that extra dimension which even the best of home video and sound equipment cannot hope to capture. Such music reminds us what a live performance by a great orchestra is all about.

[3.2.1997]

NEW, IMPROVED BEETHOVEN

(REVIEW) PHILHARMONIC HALL

New Beethoven, like New Labour, comes as a shock to dyed-in-the-wool veterans. Stalwarts of the LP era could not be expected to recognise it. But here, for the CD generation, is a fresh look at the master symphonist - one recorded by the Liverpool Phil with that Wizard of Oz, Sir Charles Mackerras, and unanimously praised to the heavens as the box set to end all box sets.

Unfortunately, Mackerras was too indisposed to conduct the concert which completed the cycle - *Symphonies Two* and *Eight* - his place being taken by Roy Goodman, another back-to-basics specialist who has secured his recording reputation with the Hanover Band.

So what is the New Beethoven edition - which scholars assure us, is Beethoven as Beethoven intended, and not overlaid with generations of bluster? Is the transformation more substantial than the claims made for new, improved detergents and shampoos?

Well, it will all come out in the wash - and the answer would seem to be performances which are livelier and more virile (pity the poor string players). There is better sound separation - physically aided, in this case, by the first and second violin sections being on opposite sides of the stage, with violas and cellos in the middle. Mr Goodman spared neither effort nor pace. Things were fast and crisp. But there is a sort of penalty to pay; some of the sinuous, beefy emotion of Beethoven is sacrificed. Last night's two symphonies aren't the greatest in the canon, which is why everyone seemed to try that little bit harder. And, sure enough, the truth did come out in the wash. New Beethoven is like Mozart on steroids.

[29.1.1998]

BRAHMS' SECOND PIANO CONCERTO

(REVIEW) PHILHARMONIC HALL

The largest work of its genre when completed just over a century ago, the concerto is a magnificent beast. Its placing at the start of this week's concert by the Royal Liverpool Philharmonic Orchestra, under their principal conductor, Libor Pesek, was doubtless dictated by its very nature.

The soloist was Ivan Moravec, the chap who played the piano in the cult Mozart film, *Amadeus*. But here he was playing Brahms with the dynamism of Liszt, scooping up the notes with elasticated arms and ringing them through the auditorium with tremendous aplomb. Yet he was not gambling with the product. Brahms' romanticism (and don't forget, this composer provided the bridge between classicism and romanticism in his *Fourth Symphony*) was not sacrificed to effect. Nevertheless, with Pesek's supportive and well-ordered accompaniment, together with a most telling cello contribution from Timothy Walden, I couldn't help agreeing with the person who commented to me in the interval that it is a work worth interrupting between each movement - for the sake of applause.

The other major item was Debussy's *La Mer*. A programme note mentioned that there is no real recapitulation in the first movement, *From Dawn to Midday on the Sea*. I would hardly expect there to be in a scenario that so evolves, with superb orchestral colouring and momentum. This is a score that cannot be taken to bits like a Baroque fugue. It is one great elemental encounter, and Libor Pesek, despite coming from land-locked Czechoslovakia, missed none of the ebb and flow. The scheme of things is so vivid as to challenge the top league Impressionist painters of landscape. Debussy himself believed that music had the edge, and so do I. It is, after all, the purest of art forms.

Ravel's *Pavane for a Dead Infanta* served as a prelude here, and although it is virtually contemporaneous with the Debussy, there is a medieval air to its slow-moving progression of shifting harmonies. The initial laying down of the theme did suffer, however, from harsh annunciation, giving a razor's edge effect where there should be only introspective calm. As for the title, Ravel said he chose it simply because of its pleasant sound upon the ear. So - no hidden messages of grief and despair. What would Mahler have made of that?

[18.11.1988]

VIC HUTSON

PULLING OUT THE STOPS TO MAKE A DREAM COME TRUE

Back home in Malaysia, Vic Hutson runs a zoo, where the star attraction is an orang-utan called Wira who does a nifty bit of break-dancing for more than a million visitors a year. This incredible spectacle is available on video to anyone partaking of a private audience in Vic's suite at the Adelphi - his home from home for the next fortnight.

But the equally incredible Mr Hutson isn't here to publicise the eccentric antics of anthropoids. He is in our midst for Liverpool Cathedral's summer festival, to which he has contributed - for posterity - the largest and most complex piece of musical hardware in the world. It takes the form of five-key-board fully mobile organ console, with enough stops, pistons pedals and dials, you'd swear it was capable of putting the first Britisher on the Moon.

As it happens, Vic gets here, sometimes up to three times a year, by flying British Airways Club Class from Kuala Lumpur. His mission: to hear what he quite rightly describes as 'the most spectacular instrument in all creation.' For the Cathedral organ, installed back in the 1920s, when Britain's largest church was but a third built, is still in mighty voice, generating 120 decibels of sound. Decoded for keyboard enthusiasts of more trendy persuasion, that's louder than Led Zeppelin ever managed at full revs.

The trouble was the organist remained hidden from view. But now, the Victor Hutson Recital Console as it's officially known, brings the player down to earth for concerts. Folk had talked of that possibility for years, but the prophets of gloom always dismissed it as too expensive. Yet Vic, at three score years plus ten, has gone one better than the prophet Moses, and actually reached the Promised Land.

Originally, he had made provision for the console in his will. But by covenanting £40,000 in shares to the Cathedral, the dream has become a reality during his lifetime. 'It's a miracle. I never expected to see the thing,' he says. 'I am not a particularly religious person, but I really do thank God that He has allowed this to happen. I feel extremely humbled, and genuinely count myself as a parishioner of the Cathedral.' Quite apart from the musical specifications, there was one overriding specification of Vic's own: no ivory was to be used in the making of the keys. The man from the zoo was doing his bit for the preservation of elephants.

Vic is an unassuming fellow, despite his elevation in the Malaysian hierarchy, where the composite title of Tan Sri Dato, conferred by the state and Sultan, adds up to the equivalent of a double knighthood. Not bad for a Dubliner by birth, which explains an association with Liverpool Cathedral going back to 1935, when he came to stay with an aunt in New Brighton. 'We went and heard the organ and I was hooked for life.'

Later, the war and Army service and an eventful involvement in the rubber and palm oil plantation business, took him overseas for good. 'I started out as a practical planter with a French Company,' says the Irishman who became so integrated into Malaysian life that the country's then Prime Minister, Tunku Abdul Rahmen (now a close friend), asked him to found the first Outward Bound School to be built outside the UK, and later to chair the Malaysian branch of the Royal Commonwealth Society, the only one outside London with its own premises.

They go by the grand name of Commonwealth House, and it is there, in October, that Vic will entertain the Queen and Duke of Edinburgh to tea. 'I intend to ask Her Majesty to sign the visitors' book with the same pen she used on her last visit,' says Vic. 'It belonged to my dear mother in Ireland, and it's been locked away in a safe ever since.'

But October? Doesn't Vic always come to Liverpool for the Anniversary organ recital then? 'Her Majesty is with us on the Friday morning. On the Friday afternoon, I hope to get on the plane for the Saturday concert.' Even if he doesn't make it here this autumn, Vic has a collection of tapes and videos of the Cathedral's music that could grace the archive. And house guests in Kuala Lumpur, where there is no tradition of organ music, are not spared: 'Every Christmas morning I throw a huge party, and they get the works,' he says. 'They go away mesmerised. Then I phone the Cathedral organist, Ian Tracey, and to prove the point, hold the receiver near to the speakers and say: Here I am 9,000 miles away and still listening to you!'.

As for Ian, now approaching his tenth year as I.C. biggest Mersey Sound of them all, having been appointed Britain's youngest Cathedral organist at 25, he looks like the cat that got the cream as he surveys his new 'toy'. 'It's just fantastic. There are no words I could possibly dream up to thank Vic enough for his kindness and generosity.'

[7.7.1989]

BARBARA DICKSON

'BEATLES' STAR FACES A NEW CHALLENGE

Barbara Dickson is working on her Liverpool accent to replace the inherent Scottish lilt of her Dunfermline childhood for a new musical by Willy Russell. She plays the mother of twins separated at birth, one raised in working class hardship, the other in middle class comfort. The mother works as a cleaner to make ends meet, a Scouser from head to tip of mop and bucket, but not, says Barbara, 'a Hilda Ogden jokey figure.'

Russell's show, *Blood Brothers*, opens at the Playhouse on January 8 and according to Miss Dickson, whisked back to Merseyside as its star, we can expect much more than your average musical. 'There's nothing flimsy about it. It's a full blooded, very human play, something I just couldn't say no to.' Then there's the nostalgia element, of course, for it was Russell's Beatles' musical *John, Paul, George, Ringo and Bert*, which plucked Barbara from the obscurity of the folk-club circuit and turned her into an international pop star.

'The personality cult thing was in full swing by the time the show transferred from the Everyman to London and the critics picked me out for special mention. When I left the show I had the ticket to a new career with a recording contract, radio interviews and television shows. If all that hadn't happened, I suppose things wouldn't have changed much, as there's no real top and bottom billing in folk clubs.'

It was a gamble. She had never played the piano in public before and she feared all sorts of strange and cruel comparisons when it came to doing Beatles' numbers. The strength and bell-like clarity of her voice in those songs caught the imagination. Right after leaving the show, her debut single, *Answer Me*, reached No. 9 in the charts. The hits continued with *Another Suitcase in Another Hall, The Caravan Song* and *January, February*. Soon after, her following ranged from 16 to 60, and in no time she filled the Royal Albert Hall.

The gamble had paid off. She's known Willy Russell from his days running a folk club in Runcorn, but when he showed her the Beatles' script and offered her the singing commentary role, she was terrified. 'But Willy and my agent, Bernard Theobald, just kept insisting,' and Barbara made her stage debut at the Everyman in the winter of 1974. Now to another gamble - her acting debut at the Playhouse in the winter of 1983. If all goes well it could be a long run, as the Playhouse have left their main house schedule wide open for possible extensions.

Barbara has taken a four-bedroomed house in one of the leafier suburbs. She has a stray cat for company and says she survives on salads and Marks and Spencer flans. 'I'm having to learn how to be an actor and I'm not having too much trouble with the accent,' she says. 'After all, my mother is from Liverpool 8 and we used to come down here in the school holidays. And don't forget, I had five months here with the Beatles' show.

Any problems I am having are purely dramatic ones. In one sense, I couldn't have jumped in the deep end more, as I play a very complex character. However, I have applied myself 100 per cent. If it doesn't come off it will be a shame, but it will not be because of lack of effort.'

She enjoys working with Chris Bond as a director and one of the bonuses has been to find herself cast again with George Costigan, who played Bert in the Beatles' show and plays one of the sons in *Blood Brothers*. 'Everyone's been very kind, as this is a new dimension for me. But I enjoy a challenge and I love a live audience. It's the same with my singing. I adore concert tours. Having people out there is more important than anything. I am not a plastic pop star.'

She gets four big songs in *Blood Brothers* - two ballads and two up-tempo, giving her the range she enjoys. 'I like to push my voice, do anything from Brecht to the Beatles,' she says. Barbara hopes for a push in other directions too. 'I spent a week as a D.J. on Radio Tees this summer. That was great. I'd also like to do some more serious journalistic type work for television.'

[22.1.1982]

190

CLIFF RICHARD

THE TIME LORD OF ROCK

Like Walpamur and Hotpoint washing machines, Cliff Richard has been around for as long as most of us can remember. When Quiff Richard (as he then was) burst into our living rooms back in '58, Franz Liszt had only been dead 72 years. And they used to scream at his tight trousers too.

What could all this mean to young Harry Webb, changing his name at 18 and surrounding himself with Shadows on a matt-finished screen, bought only five years previously for the coronation of our own dear Queen? The show was *Oh Boy!* There was an organist called Cherry Wayner and a sax player called Red Price. And this lad in drainpipe leathers just clear of post-pubescent spots.

Now 30 years on, he is in our midst for four nights at the Empire. Ten thousand of you out there are either going or have gone, paying £13.50 a ticket and an extra five quid for a souvenir programme that will be even more valuable one day. While some of Cliff's contemporaries (48, going on 49) now have false teeth and hairpieces of their very own, their hero defies the ravages of time better than Dr Who, who has been around a mere 25 years. He appears, from the back of the theatre, to be as durable as those self-sealing envelopes that still stick down after a lifetime in the desk drawer.

I had forgotten that Cliff played the guitar. But he does so at the Empire as if this was his finest hour. Perhaps it is? Familiarity plays a great part in people's happiness. The bouncers were on duty, but you could tell they were going to have an easy time of it. When did you last see a 16-stone advert for Brut and silver medallions rushed by a nice crowd of middle-class frocks and designer jumpers?

Smoke machine, subtle lighting, white suit, speech: 'Roll 'n' Roll is a middle-aged art form.' Applause. To prove the point, Cliff becomes as animated as Peter Pan without the wires. No wires on the microphones these days either. So you can really bop. 'We did this tour on one condition: we had to go to Liverpool.' More applause. The sort reserved for a man who predated Mersey Beat and had seen the Beatles come and go. He's the very lynch-pin of remembering. An aide memoire from the days when Teddy Boys (and Teddy Girls) had just grown out of skinning cats to make Davy Crockett hats.

In that time, Cliff has had more hits than a dartboard. You can now get the fave raves on compact disc. Rather like getting the whole of the Old Testament written on the back of a postage stamp. Tomorrow, there's the wonder of Cliff at the Empire and simultaneously, on the *Royal Command*, for the pleasure of the Queen Mum.

There could surely be a knighthood or an honorary degree at the end of all this. If it ever ends. The first Rocker Emeritus I remember at the Empire, in 1956, was Guy Mitchell - and he's still going at 60. Now how would that sound? 'Please put your hands together and welcome......Sir Clifford Richard, M.A., ...or Dr Sir Harold Webb.'

[25.11.1988]

LIBOR PESEK

KING OF THE PHIL

'My beloved Liverpudlians,' says Libor Pesek, with the conviction of St Paul writing to the Corinthians. Certainly, faith, hope and charity have played their part. As well as two jugs of sangria. Libor is waxing lyrical.

When he arrived as conductor of the Liverpool Philharmonic in 1987, he knew very little British music and could hardly speak English. Eight years later, he conducts Elgar like a native and discusses his hobbies - physics, Eastern philosophy and literature - with a fluency which suggests that he could casually work them into the plot of *Brookside*. 'What I would love to do even now is be a writer,' he admits. Instead, he's a musician, raised in Prague, the cradle of classical music. In a week's time, Liverpool returns the compliment of Pesek's commitment to his newly-adopted city. The Philharmonic Hall reopens after a £10.3m refit. And as everyone always said...there was only one person who could possibly be centre stage on the night. Maestro Pesek.

'I remember the headline in the *Echo* when I took the Phil to Prague,' says Libor, gearing up on the emotions. 'It called me an "Honorary Scouser". It was the most fantastic moment in my career. When you really are accepted by a city, as I have been here, then it is better than being awarded medals. This is the happiest time of my life.'

The restaurant manager - a friend of Libor's - has been hovering to add his tribute: 'You realise, Libor, how important the Phil is to the local economy. Now you are back in the Hall, the streets will be alive again.'

Libor graciously acknowledges the accolade, picking his way carefully through the mountain of food. At 62, he doesn't eat as much as he used to. He's mainly vegetarian and has stopped smoking. A lot of changes since he first stepped ashore. Not least in Czechoslovakia, which was then still firmly behind the Iron Curtain. Today, the Czech Republic is liberated - run, following the famous 'Velvet Revolution' by Libor's lifelong pal, President Vaclav Havel. 'We go back to college days. He is an artist and a great man. He understands the people.'

Like all good Europeans, Libor turns a meal into a grand social event: 'I enjoy wine and occasionally a good whisky. It's a good way to relax. In my job, your mind is always linked to your music. I often study scores in bed late at night, or even in the morning, although when I get up at 7am, I can feel in a very negative mood. At the moment, I have five symphonies going around in my head.'

About to pop to the fore is *Beethoven's Ninth* - the great choral symphony which will mark the opening of the new Philharmonic Hall.

'We considered a number of monumental pieces. I would have liked Mahler's *Resurrection Symphony* because it is about rebirth, but in the end, we came down to basics. The Beethoven is a work which can never be done without a certain special attention.'

Not that Libor's a musical snob. His favourite music includes the Beatles' *Abbey Road* album, Frank Sinatra songs and Henry Mancini's *Moon River*. 'George Gershwin was one of the most inventive people in music,' he insists, adding with throwaway Liboresque charm: 'I used to play jazz trombone. I had my own big band.' Proof, if it were needed, will come later in the season, when Libor lifts the baton on Sun Valley Serenade. 'That will be the first time I have conducted the Phil as a jazz band,' he says. He was brought up playing a piano and cello. 'I came very late to conducting - at 18. Most people know this at 10 or 12 - look at Simon Rattle.'

Libor conducted his first major concert at 23. Liverpool, he says, will be his last post. 'I will stay until 1997, and after that, return for four guest concerts a season...until I drop, if they so want it. The rest of the time I will freelance.' That will include an increasing amount of work in America. Last year, Libor made his debut at the Hollywood Bowl, which he found 'quite civilised'. But the man who turned down a fortune of millions of dollars to set up home in Dallas and leave Liverpool, has no doubts where his affections lie.

'Liverpool has meant everything to me from the very beginning. Of all the cities I have ever worked in. Okay, some of it is ugly, but so are parts of Paris. What's more, I am becoming sentimental about British music. When that happens to a central European boy, it must tell some stories about the British soul.'

Libor, too, has soul. Yards of it. 'I still love to walk amidst nature. I think if I had not been a musician, I would have made quite a decent cameraman. It's still all to do with composition and balance.'

Ah yes, balance…

Libor and the restaurant manager discover they have both been in earthquakes: Libor in Japan, the manager in Chile.

'You would never want to experience that again,' says Libor, kicking off a new subject. But it's been that sort of evening…

[7.9.1995]

CARL DAVIS

ENLIGHTENING CONDUCTOR

If only going to a concert could be seen as a natural thing to do.

'Not boring, tedious or stuffy,' says Carl Davis, a man so cosmopolitan that refuelling midday with a cheeseburger and Coke also seems par for the course. Born in Brooklyn; lives in London; summer job in Liverpool.

The director of the city's classical pops - now Britain's number one outdoor attraction - knows the challenge: 'A concert is not on the same level of accessibility as the cinema or a pub. For some, it's even easier to go to an art gallery. Punishment, school, church…it belongs to all of that.'

But here's the man who eventually broke the mould: played the tunes everyone knew, and a little more besides: 'This year, I'm introducing Rachmaninov's *Third Piano Concerto* on the back of the movie *Shine*.'

Carl will be shining too: positively shimmering in any one of the job lot of Moschino designer waistcoats he bought for thousands of quid after, by chance, making the crows bray with laughter by donning a British Rail cap. The fave rave is his 'We're in the Money' coat, which catches the lights in the King's Dock big top: the concept of conductor as glitter ball. Could the pops possibly survive without this man?

'Why not? It's not copyright,' notes Carl. 'Anyway, I pinched the basic format. It's from the Boston Pops, and dates right back to the 1890s. The inventor was John Philip Sousa, famous for *Liberty Belle* and *The Stars and Stripes Forever*. The whole thing becomes a relaxed social occasion. You can eat, drink. But I've taken it further than Boston ever did. I make it personality led. I chat to the audience.'

And to think that from 1959, when he quit America for Europe (Stockholm, Vienna, Berlin, then London), Carl Davis was, by his own admission 'a back room boy'.

He wrote music mainly for film and television and conducted only in studios. That was before what he describes as 'the extraordinary event' of his score for the epic silent film, *Napoleon*. Five hours, four acts, three intervals. The British Film Institute predicted an audience of 200. It sold out in 45 event' of his score for the epic silent film, *Napoleon*. Five hours, four acts, three intervals. The British Film Institute predicted an audience of 200. It sold out in 45 minutes. Eleven hundred turned up.

'You can never predict the things that are going to have such enormous influence on your life,' says Carl, who has scarcely stopped waving a baton in public ever since.

From the age of three, he had been immersed in entertainment. He saw Kirsten Flagstad sing Wagner at the New York Met. At the other end of Broadway, the original productions of *Oklahoma, Carousel, On The Town, Guys and Dolls*, and most notably, *West Side Story*.

'It hasn't been as good since. Everything was available in New York. You didn't have to go anywhere else.'

Unless, like Carl, you wanted to forge a new career - in his case, as a composer. Had he stayed, he may have become entrenched, accompanying singers and chamber groups: 'If you are at an opera house, it's totally consuming. Ten in the morning till eleven at night.'

He had started to play the piano at seven; dabbled with painting at 12; gone to three colleges after age 18: 'I think I was deeply mixed up and probably remain so,' he jokes. 'The one thing that was clear was music.'

For a time, he worked with famous choral director Robert Shaw. But then what?

'To a New Yorker, going to LA for a film-music career is like going to the moon. The moon would be more familiar.'

So Europe it was, the first big British break being Ned Sherrin's suggestion that Carl should write songs for the groundbreaking TV satire show *That Was the Week That Was* - 'I have a very good facility for musical parody. It's stood me in good stead over the years.'

That very morning, he had been composing. Pencil on manuscript paper. No computers.

'I am still from a generation that writes things down,' he says.

He has just finished a movie about Gilbert and Sullivan, directed by Mike Leigh and starring Jim Broadbent. And he's been working with Marianne Faithful on *The Seven Deadly Sins*. He's also brought classical music to Radio 2, with his own series of record shows. Biggest job in hand is a ballet based on *Aladdin* - 'the genie is a laser beam' - and the latest in a long line of silent movies, Douglas Fairbanks Snr's *Man In The Iron Mask*.

'For me, a silent movie is a concerto for film and orchestra. In a documentary, music is part of the script - what I call "the war of the mixer". That's why for me, film and television cannot be the only things,' says the man who scored *The French Lieutenant's Woman* and *Pride and Prejudice*, among literally hundreds of projects.

Most hyped, perhaps, was the *Liverpool Oratorio*, with Paul McCartney. Written over two years at both of their houses, premiered in Liverpool Cathedral (conducted by Carl) in 1991: 'I did the writing down but it really was a collaboration. I won't be pressed into saying I did all the work. As Paul got more and more into it, he was able to give me more information.'

The most productive time was at the McCartney farm: 'Linda provided breakfast...he also has a lovely studio somewhere else that I daren't say.'

Another famous partnership at home: Carl is married to actress Jean Boht, the legendary Mrs Boswell of TV sitcom *Bread*.

They have recently uprooted from Barnes, where they were neighbours of Michael Ball, and bought not one, but two houses in Chelsea, one as home, the other as office: 'I walk from one to the other. Five minutes. The perfect distance. If it was any further, I'd probably not go. I'm really very lazy. On the way, I pass Waterstone's bookshop, Marks and Spencers, lots of clothes shops.' It helps what Carl calls 'that morning-fresh mind.'

The couple have two daughters, one working in theatre, the other in television. Carl and Jean met in 1970, working on a Joan Littlewood musical. Jean, who started out at Liverpool Playhouse, is presently in a London fringe play and about to tour in a double-bill of Stoppard and Shaffer dramas: ' I want her to be ambitious, do everything. Next spring, she's going to have a go at Miss Marple.'

When he comes to Liverpool for the Summer Pops, it's a two-week residency: 'I survive out of M and S and go to clothes shops to look for novelties. But mostly, I'm preparing. There are eleven concerts in quick succession. It's very demanding. And it's not just the concerts, it's meeting everybody.'

And there's something for everyone: from two nights of Michael

Ball, plus James Bond music, to concert for three sopranos (no tenors!) to a double whammy of 'Last Night' flag-waving in *Rule Britannia* mode.

'My New York background made me want to go across the board in music. Leonard Bernstein also fought an image problem in this way. And I've just decided I'm not paying any attention to it. I'm just doing what I like.'

[12.6.1999]

PAUL McCARTNEY

ORCHESTRAL MANOEVRES IN THE DARK

Paul McCartney is in wistful mood: 'I'm not afraid to shed a tear watching a sad film,' he admits. Is this - at last - the soft underbelly of historic Cavern Man? Not really. It's just that these things take time to surface.

'When I was younger, I would try to hide my emotions, ' he tells me. 'I used to have a problem with it. But these days, I'm more than happy to show them. I remember being in Africa hearing 30 musicians play music in a style I'd never heard before. The power and emotion of it made me weep - and I mean, really cry. I was gushing tears. But it was such a good feeling for me. It was a release.'

As a world audience converges on Liverpool for Beatles Week, Macca talks about the feelings behind his 'other' music: the classical stuff. Paul McCartney's *Liverpool Oratorio* is coming home for its 100th performance next month. The subject matter ranges from birth, marriage and death, to 'sagging off' from school and complaining about a late evening meal! And Paul will be in the audience at the Philharmonic Hall - a place he first knew for school speech days - on September 21.

Despite everything else that has filled Paul James McCartney's eventful 53 years, he still finds that particular prospect amazing: 'I've never got over the shock that people will actually sing my work,' he confides. 'I wrote the *Oratorio* because I was asked to for the Phil's 50th anniversary. I'm not sure I would have dared to otherwise. So I'm pretty encouraged that it's been performed in more than 50 cities around the world. I'm delighted that, by sheer accident, I'm in this incredible position that people will listen to what I do - without me having passed any exam.'

That said, he's ended up with a Fellowship of the Royal College of Music, handed over by Prince Charles. A certificate worth sticking on any wall. To Paul, it's as if classical music is something grown-ups do - and not having had a grown-up musical training, it still fills him with wonder: 'I've not come to this style of composing in the accepted way. I'm not academic and I don't have any academic training. I didn't pass any music exams at school - but then, I couldn't have done, because there wasn't actually a lesson. For us, studying music was just being a bunch of boys in a room for 45 minutes, listening to a classical record. The teacher would put on the record and leave the room. Being lads, that was fatal, because we just turned the music down and talked among ourselves.'

Consequently, when Paul composed his *Oratorio*, he would hum or play whatever came into his head, and the conductor Carl Davis - now director of Liverpool's classical Summer Pops seasons at the King's Dock - would write it down. It was a brave new world. And as Paul readily admits, he didn't know what an oratorio was, until he read the definition in *Newsweek*.

'That's true,' he says with a grin. 'And, when I wrote it, I just ad-libbed my way through, making up tunes.'

Not that tunes have ever been a problem: 'I've always loved melody and I've always had an easy time writing it. It may well be that a lot of modern British composers aren't writing melody - and that may be my role if I want to get out of rock 'n' roll. But I don't know where that ability comes from. It seems to come from nowhere. In fact, my most successful song, *Yesterday*, came to me in a dream. I woke up with the whole tune in my head. I even remember thinking: "Let's see what key it's in". And it was G. I didn't plan it that way.'

He immediately adds in a self-mocking way: 'Perhaps I shouldn't have said that. Maybe I should have said that it took me four months to write it in Tibet or somewhere…The thing is that the best melodies are often the simplest and, for a long time, I suffered from the belief that if something was simple, it was therefore naïve - and naiveté implies some sort of stupidity.'

Hardly; *Yesterday* happens to be the most played music track in the world.

'I use the term "orchestral" to describe my work these days,' says Paul. 'I don't actually like to use the word "classical" or call it "serious music". That infers that the whole Beatles' repertoire was a complete joke.'

At last, mention of the Beatles. And now he's brought it up…there were enough "classical" influences there to fill a book.

Says Paul: 'With the Beatles, we had this Ballad called *For No One* and, because I'd always loved the sound of a French horn, I asked George Martin (the recently knighted Beatles record producer) if he could get a French horn in on the song. So there I was, sitting in George's house, showing him the chords and I hummed the tune. But when we got to this one note, George said we'd gone off the range for the French horn. But that was the game. We stuck it in and - of course - the best players can reach that note.'

There was also the ending of *A Day In The Life* on the *Sgt Pepper* album, when Paul and John Lennon set out to use an orchestra in such a way that it broke all the rules. 'For me, it's interesting to see how musicians react to what you write for them. With *A Day In The Life*, John and I really got into the challenge of being very complex, with the big, swirling orchestral thing. We wanted to use a whole symphony orchestra, but George Martin was a little nervous about what we were asking them to do - to start playing the lowest note on their instrument and to reach the highest note in the space of 23 bars - and without any written music for it. That taught me a lot about orchestras. The strings did not like the idea at all, so they all stuck together and went up their scale together. However, the brass section was very happy. They liked the *avant-garde*. Put together, it gave us this great crunch of sound and that was what I wanted - to do what you shouldn't do.'

Well, Bach did the same. So did Mozart. So why not McCartney?

'I do like to break the rules,' says Paul. 'But that's how I tend to do things. I just fall in love with an idea - whether it's right or wrong.'

The Liverpool Oratorio has led to other classical pieces - a study called *Leaf* for piano and a commission to mark the centenary of EMI Records next year.

'I'm very excited by that,' says Paul. 'It will be about an hour long and for a big orchestra and, ultimately, for any orchestra and any conductor in the world. The word "symphony" is intimidating for me, because I feel then that I am stacking up against all the "real" symphonies. So I think of it as writing a functional evening's music. I realise that what we would call "classical" music was always turned on its head throughout history. I was pleased to learn that Stravinsky was booed at first. That gives me some encouragement - because his work is so accepted now.'

[23.8.1996]

JOHN LENNON

YOKO ONO'S HEAVEN - AND HELL

'It's a film that's made for you, not for me. I hope you like it...' Yoko Ono, Japanese actress and performance artist turned twentieth century enigma, joins me in the suite of a London hotel after the first showing of the film, *Imagine: John Lennon.*

As I awaited her arrival - delayed by the busy rush-hour traffic - I tried to imagine whether she would talk, or merely talk around, the issues which haunt her, and which stalk the ghost of her late husband. As it happened she was in candid mood. 'I can't see myself getting that involved again. It was beautiful. It was also heaven and hell, and the ending was terrible.'

No, not the film. She is opening up after eight years of widowhood, and months of putting together the celluloid testament to Lennon, which goes on screen across the country on Friday. 'There were times when we managed to have our privacy. We always felt we were using the media to plug peace, and because that was important to us, we felt we were on top of it. John was very much English, right up to the end. We would watch British films together, and he would say: "I went all over the world and I can't believe I came back to Liverpool." He thought New York was just like a big Liverpool, with its docks and piers.'

The film, which Yoko regards as the 'ultimate' life story of Lennon, has its genesis in Liverpool. There are all the usual places, with all the usual people: the Cavern days, Alan Williams recalling the wild excesses of Hamburg etc. There is the inevitable footage of four mop-headed lads oo-ing at screaming beehived girls, jumping around and getting up to silly antics. By the time the Beatles played for the last time together, on a London rooftop, they were all fur coats and plenty of nickers in the bank, and Yoko was already very much on the scene. Many of the fans blamed her for the break-up of the band.

Today, she says: 'We were engaging in such an intense exchange, that when people were accusing us, it all seemed to be in the distance. When you are totally in love, you tend to forget about it.' That intensity, with its bed-ins, did cool to several months separation - what Lennon later called his 'long weekend.' The film does not skirt the issue, but it underlines the final rebonding in a way that even the sceptical cannot doubt. Yoko says that although she set up the film, handing over much previously unseen material, she did not put it together. That's why she cannot say whether the other three Beatles were invited to appear in it, or whether they refused. 'I think the result is extremely moving,' she says. 'I don't think there is anything lacking. The important things are there, and close family members are making statements.' That includes John's first wife Cynthia and the son of that marriage, Julian. 'The most interesting thing about this film is that it doesn't have a point of view, whereas the Albert Goldman book presents everything from a point of view. You can imagine what I think of that book...'

Probably the same as she feels about much of the gossip: 'People said don't stay in New York. It's dangerous. I didn't take any notice of trashy books, but I wasn't going to sue them, as it would focus more attention on them. At the time, I was feeling defensive and emotional, and I didn't feel like doing a book myself. Then I decided to pool my energy and do something positive, especially as I had promised to do something about John and release something new every year up to 1990.' The next project may be some songs which she and John had envisaged for a Broadway musical. They are on cassette tape, not good enough to be reproduced for an album, but good enough to be published.

The film, based on more than 100 hours of Lennon interviews (which means he provides his own commentary) may have taken time, 'but the result is well justified by that. Since John's death, I have been in a strange position. I don't think anyone has been in the same position in history, actually. I have had to look at John's photographs, and look at John's tapes and videos. It is most painful, as you can imagine, but I think that I had to learn to block my emotions, and do it again and again. Still, this film was very hard to watch.

There may be other films made about certain periods of his life, but I regard this as the ultimate biography of John. It is a documentary. You can make up your mind about what you think about John by watching it. It's almost like we are still together, and I am enjoying it in that sense. People say to me: "Where's that feminist Yoko? What are you doing with yourself?" But I think because of the tragedy, I have changed a lot as well.'

Of Mark Chapman, the man who gunned her husband down outside their home, she says: 'I cannot be emotional with hatred towards him. It was beneath that. I never thought it would happen this way. One rainbow has been seeing Sean grow up. I think it is a silver lining - something that makes me smile and makes me laugh. I think there is some blessing in everything that happens to you, and the blessing is that both Sean and I are stronger for what we went through.'

What pleases her is that a new generation will see the work. 'Right now, that is my main concern: that younger people should be exposed to the film, and share in it. *Newsweek* just recently ran a cover story on John, and 14m people are listening to radio shows about him. So you see, they can't kill him.'

But there have been other tragedies for Yoko, like the loss of contact with her daughter Kyoko. 'In 1979, around Christmas time, there was a call out of the blue. She said she was coming for Christmas, and John and I planned a big dinner for her. But she never came.' Yoko Ono has never heard from her since...

But the future is the future. 'This year, Sean is moving to Europe, which means that I will have more time to be on this side of the Atlantic.'

Indeed, there will be no retirement for the widow of the young founding member of the century's greatest entertainment phenomenon; a musician, artist, writer, philosopher and poet, who, when he died, stunned the world into taking stock of his genius.

[26.10.1988]

ART

SALVADOR DALI

(REVIEW) TATE GALLERY

Everyone knows Salvador Dali: the mad Spaniard with the funny moustache, whose reproduced images sell in tens of thousands. It is, says Tate director Lewis Biggs, the pictures of Dali and Magritte which the public most asks to see. Now, their half-answered prayer sees a world class collection of 60 Dali originals on Merseyside until the New Year, with massive benefits for the local economy.

As you enter, there's a photograph of the artist working on a truly famous painting, *Metamorphosis of Narcissus*. Then you turn the corner and confront the actual picture. A thrilling experience. Here was the intelligent craftsman who went into showbiz, and kept the masses outraged and entertained right up to the time of his death a decade ago, aged 84.

A Dali painting is very Freudian, a Dali drawing even more so. Thus a comfortable relationship developed between draughtsman and psychologist, which explains the Tate's Sigmund Freud sideshow. What is most striking is how Dali kept re-inventing himself. He shared Wagner's belief that life was a play in which he was the central character and everyone else an extra. The notable exception was his wife, Gaia, who became (like Ono to Lennon later) a part inspiration and subject for Dali's creativity.

For all the weird imagery - including the obsession with phones, Hitler, matriarchal figures, and even the artist himself as Messiah - the most amazing single gift is the perspective Dali can give to a seemingly blank horizon. Even some of the smallest pictures have tremendous depth. You feel you could wander around inside them and keep going for ever, surrealism without end - Amen.

[28.10.98]

LAWRENCE ALMA-TADEMA

(REVIEW) WALKER ART GALLERY

A funny thing happened to me on the way to the Forum. I realised for the first time - albeit on a pre-Christmas package tour - that those famous capitols and columns one expects to make up the ruins of the great Roman meeting house were in short supply. In reality, the bulk of the architecture of the Caesars was composed of tiny, tile-like red bricks. Thus, most of what remains - even in the centre of modern Rome - has the appearance of an over-baked mud pie. Nevertheless, our common perceptions of Roman architecture come from those once-fashionable canvases showing everything from aquaducts to urns, and populated by diaphanous-gowned maidens and toga-clad senators.

This spring, Merseysiders will be able to enjoy the very best paintings evoking the glories of the Roman Empire in an exhibition at Liverpool's Walker Art Gallery. The largest show ever of the works of Victorian 'great', Lawrence Alma-Tadema, comes to Liverpool, direct from the Van Gogh Museum in Amsterdam. If you don't yet know the name, then at least recognise the effect. For Alma-Tadema is the chap who inspired the early movie makers. Without his particular vision, *Ben Hur* may have looked more Oxford Circus than Circus Maximus.

The Victorians were in love with the power building of the ancient world. Not surprising, therefore, that an artist who revelled in every last detail of Roman imperialism, would find favour at the Court of Queen Victoria. Enter Alma-Tadema, born in Friesland, Northern Holland, in 1836. The Dutchman had honeymooned in Pompeii and been instantly beguiled by the splendours of the Roman epoch. Overnight, as it were, they became the inspiration for the young artist's life work. Alma-Tadema studied every last detail of the era, combining the skills of artist and historian. When he moved to London in 1870, he found fame and fortune. He became a Royal Academician in 1879 - and having taken British citizenship - was knighted in 1899.

Alma-Tadema believed in the physicality as well as the spirit of his beloved Roman age. Not difficult, therefore, for him to make the journey into sensuous sensationalism, painting the nude form with abandon at a time of otherwise prudish moral values. As his style developed, he capped all these exotic visions with blue and sunny skies. Had he been alive today, he could have designed the Club Med brochure.

Julian Treuherz, Keeper of Art Galleries on Merseyside, and whose personal enthusiasm has led to the Liverpool exhibition, notes: 'Alma-Tadema was regarded as something of a joke until the 1960s, when interest began to revive. Now millionaires compete for his work in the salesrooms.'

The exhibition at the Walker - its only UK venue - will consist of 80 paintings, some water-colours and even some furniture. It opens on March 21 and runs until June 8.

[27.12.1996]

AUBREY BEARDSLEY

ART WITH A WILDE FLAVOUR
(REVIEW) WALKER ART GALLERY

It's not often nowadays that an art gallery warns of 'explicit and erotic' material. Still less so when the art comes from the 1890s.

Aubrey Beardsley was a lily-wearing aesthete, dead from TB by the age of 25. He never quite upstaged his elder contemporary, Oscar Wilde, as Man of the Moment, although a normal lifespan would have seen him living to the mid-part of this century. Goodness only knows how his art would have evolved beyond art nouveau into the age of cubism. He may have become old fashioned. Dying young, he remains a rogue.

Certainly, Beardsley the pen-and-ink artist, designer and book illustrator, packed immense achievement into a short life. His preference was to work on a small scale, sometimes with ultra simplicity, at others, cramming in dense eye-dizzying detail. A 'Beardsley woman' as the image became known, may have worn a pretty hat over a fine coiffure, but she could also possess the ripened corpulent body of an emancipated Grecian whore. His more gracious females had an Eastern promise, their delicate features like the suit designs for a revolutionary pack of cards.

Beardsley captures a wonderful mixture of madness and sex, ravings and cravings. Not only is he intrigued by the erotic, but more particularly, the sinful. Hence his ready identification with fallen grace - and the inevitable link with Wilde and Co, who considered immorality a high art form.

The Walker exhibition, already seen by more than 100,000 at the

Victoria and Albert in London, is hung beneath dimmed lighting 'to preserve the exhibits'. And, of course, the necessary whiff of decadence!

[17.2.199]

BLUNDELL DRAWINGS

OLD MASTER CLASS
(REVIEW) WALKER ART GALLERY

This really is a case of great art coming home. That is, if you believe our ancestors to be the rightful custodians of foreign art. The Blundells of Crosby are best-known for their 'marbles' - classical sculpture akin to the more famous Elgin Marbles, which the Greek government wants returned.

But Charles Blundell also amassed more than 400 Old Master drawings, half of them bought from the then bankrupt Liverpool merchant, William Roscoe. Three years ago, Merseyside gallery chiefs paid £3.2m for the lot, and 80 examples, including works by Mantegna and Rubens, have been framed and displayed to great effect. Because many drawings were stored in albums, they are marvellously preserved, full of stunning detail. Most intriguing are the silverpoint works, literally etched into chalk with a silver rod. No room whatsoever for error.

Other examples include sketches - and some mere doodles - from which artists later produced paintings or sculpture. Chief categories of interest, as may be expected in material dating back to the 15th Century, include Christianity, the human body, and virtually anything which involved suffering and mortality. There are also important copies, used as learning aids, most notably *Michelangelo's God Creating Adam*, by Rubens.

Like composers, most artists were male. The one woman represented (by a self-portrait) is Elisabetta Sirani, who died, aged 27, supposedly poisoned. The most extraordinary picture is Luca Cambiaso's *Christ at Pilate's House* - a cartoon sketch with futuristic Orwellian overtones. 1560, not 1984, I kid you not.

[1.7.1998]

JOHN MOORES 9

SOMETHING FOR EVERYONE
(REVIEW) WALKER ART GALLERY

The competition for good painting is now greater than ever. Public interest in visual art is also growing, although it is sometimes difficult to prove this in purely statistical terms. Yet amid the mass of exhibitions (they now spill from galleries into theatres and even onto the street), there are some milestones - some hinges for the future. John Moores' Liverpool Exhibition is one.

The ninth of these biennial exhibitions opens to the public tomorrow at the Walker Art Gallery. More than 23,000 people saw John Moores 8. This year, even more are expected to gaze up on the 90 selected works before the close on September 15.

Back in 1957, the first exhibition exploded upon Liverpool, violently denting some preconceived notions about art. Over the years, the John Moores has grown to be a substantial influence in the changing face of artistic expression which probably explains why the current show has the usual astonishing vitality and excitement.

Admittedly, time and patience are needed to understand some modern art; it is often much more personal than painting that purely depicts and makes a straightforward statement. But it is that feeling of being among fresh concepts and lively minds as one walks around which generates that marvellous atmosphere of the John Moores.

Many of the exhibitors over the years have been at the threshold of new horizons. Jack Smith, who won the first prize in the first show, gained an award three years later at the prestigious Guggenheim International. Richard Hamilton, joint winner in 1969, had a retrospective exhibition at the Tate the following year. The same theme with variations goes for other prize-winners and notably Bradford-born David Hockney.

But back to the present. The range is from the most abstract through to an almost photographic realism. It does as much to show the varying approaches of artists to each other as to the public. The £3,000 first prize goes to Bury-born Myles Murphy, now working in the south of France on a year's grant from the Lorne Award, for his *Figure Against A Yellow Foreground*. The figure is positioned against a series of vertical 'sections' that allow the eye to progress across the painting. First it is allowed in, then the path is blocked before it delves again for more detail. While it is certainly academic, there's also an engaging freshness.

Craigie Aitchison's *Daphne With Her Eyes Closed* (third), gives out a peaceful serenity. The more you look at it, the more magical it becomes, with its clever banding of colour set against the solitary figure. Sean Scully's *Subtraction Painting* (fourth) is clean, sharp and complex. It commands attention rather than chances upon it. John G. Walker's *Juggernaut II* (second) is easy on the eye. The bigness never overwhelms, but can scarcely fail to impress.

One of the 10 £100 awards this year goes to Maurice Cockrill, a lecturer in the Department of Foundation Studies at Liverpool Polytechnic. Two large petrol pumps - superb in claret - hold the centre of the canvas. Their sharp lines are highlighted by an outer stone wall, the detail of which is implied more than laid down. The foreground's simplified textural qualities also underline the central precision.

John Moores 9 offers something for everyone. And it's also an informative guide to trends in British painting in recent years.

[12.6.1974]

TATE GALLERY, LIVERPOOL

The infamous Tate Pile of Bricks (every tabloid front-page story, circa mid-70s) has arrived in Liverpool. There are, in fact, three of them, all firebricks, piled two deep in various combinations: what the experts refer to as 'factors of 60' (i.e.15 x 4; 20 x 3 etc). For your information, it's called Minimalism, which means anyone can do it, provided they follow the instructions. The sort of creativity which just exists.

As Shakespeare said: 'To be or not to be.' The question indeed. The important thing is having the idea. And an artist named Carl André had it in 1976. You can find the bricks - of course - at Liverpool's Tate Gallery, recent spawning of its controversial London counterpart. And in a local context, it makes a profound follow-on to the waxed 'slices of bread' sculpture, which was one of the fully-baked schemes which launched the Albert Dock-based gallery in company with Prince Charles last May.

Over to Lewis Biggs, who organises the exhibitions, and who spoke to me through the top of a beautifully knitted woollen jacket. (I shall try to keep the quotes Minimalist myself): 'You know about art by doing it, not looking at it... anyone can do a version of André's bricks.

It's just that he had the patent.' In the Tate's pristine non-smoking atmosphere, everything sounds other-worldly. The place is brimming over with people standing skewered on one leg giving their opinions. The good news, according to Mr Biggs, Kent born, Oxford educated, and previously working in London and Bristol, is that Merseysiders actually come clean about their prejudices on modern art. 'The public we have at this gallery is far more exciting than those I have had to deal with before. In Oxford, people thought they knew it all. People here like to talk about what they see.'

And what a lot of them there are! Only seven months after opening, the Liverpool Tate has already celebrated the arrival of its 500,000 visitor - the number originally anticipated for the first full year. By the summer, they expected one million people to have crossed their threshold, 60 per cent of them from Merseyside, and many of those on a second or third visit. 'People still come in asking to see the sliced bread,' says Biggs, who says that art is much more than simply painting or sculpture.

The Liverpool Tate's opening received fantastic international media attention, although the fear is that they could now become yesterday's news. London art critics' laziness, plus every Londoner's idea that what is happening in the great blue yonder doesn't matter, are important considerations. Hence the idea for yesterday's Open Day, to prove that life goes on...The message was quite simple: The decision to place the Northern branch of the Tate in Liverpool has paid off, and it is here to stay.

But new readers start here: at one time, most of Britain's finest art treasures were housed at the National Gallery. Then, in the 50s, the amoeba split. Things post-1860 were handed over to the Tate, marking the watershed between the old and new creative worlds. Yet there is a link between the oldest Roman sculpture, for instance, and the most modern work. It's just that for reasons of space and categorisation, there had to be 'contemporary' art. Other Merseyside galleries, like the Walker in Liverpool, and the Lady Lever on Wirral, already housed a lot of the establishment art. The Tate was something new, and, say the experts, offers the perfect complementary service. Of the new Minimalist exhibition, Lewis Biggs says, 'I hope people will react to the room as a whole. You can't go in without having a strong reaction to it.'

I know exactly what he means. I know exactly why I rejoice that Michelangelo didn't give the Sistine Chapel a coat of Wallpamur.

[22.3.1989]

SUPER LAMB BANANA

STATE OF THE ART

It's the height of a double-decker bus and will grace a street corner on the city waterfront. *Super Lamb Banana* is an inspirational hybrid of animal and vegetable, put together with a touch of ferrous mineral.

Detractors to date include the actress Jean Boht and the writer Alan Bleasdale. Politicians are also going bananas, bleating that Super Lamb is a waste of money, even before it leaves the old Bryant & May factory, where it's being prepared for public show. It will occupy the forecourt of the Mersey Tunnel ventilation building at George's Dock, near the Pier Head.

Instigator of the statue - which symbolises Merseyside's trading links, as well as how bio-technology could solve future world food shortages - is Lewis Biggs, boss of the Liverpool Tate Gallery. In turn, Super Lamb is part of Art Transpennine '98, featuring 70 commissions across the North, and made possible with £1.7m from the National Lottery. Both Lewis Biggs, overseer for the project stretching from Liverpool to Hull, and his staff at the Tate, are no strangers to the 'is it art or is it rubbish?' debate.

Shortly after the Tate opened a decade ago, the world's most famous pile of bricks - neatly stacked rows of fire-bricks arranged by artist Carl André - turned up in town. They had been the subject of tabloid derision ever since they went on show in London in 1974, and the intervening years had not mellowed the criticism.

The visual arts have their own set of problems: not least, the virtually blank canvases regularly produced for the biennial John Moores exhibitions at the Walker Gallery. But the boldest reaction has always been to 'outdoor' art - usually in the form of murals or sculptures. Edward Morris, curator of fine art for the National Museums and Galleries on Merseyside (NMGM) stoutly declares that 'public sculpture is the art gallery of the people.' Not least because it's seen by tens of thousands more people than ever bother to venture into galleries.

Adrian Henri, the Liverpool poet, painter and art critic, says *Super Lamb Banana* should be welcomed 'with an open mind, and, if needs be, a sense of humour.'

Time for a change of perspective, perhaps?

'I well remember the fuss back in the 50s about Epstein's statue of David over Lewis's entrance, ' says Adrian. 'Now people walk past and don't even notice.'

In that case, the complaints were over Boy David's lack of modesty. Not even a fig-leaf. Criticism nowadays is usually reserved for abstract sculpture. The public at large can still identify with the straightforwardly figurative - such as Tom Murphy's renderings of Littlewoods founders John and Cecil Moores in Church Street. Adrian Henri calls that 'Okay of its kind, but nothing to do with art in the larger sense of the word.' By which he means art that speaks for its own time, and the future. And he adds: 'I think we're a bit backward-looking in Britain. In France, for instance, there is a sense of imagination - which people aren't generally showing here where there's an almost a knee-jerk reaction from people who don't really think about public art and its purpose.'

Like Edward Morris, Adrian Henri accepts that 'because sculpture is public and can be pointed at, it is very vulnerable.'

Both he and Edward Morris have their favourite examples: for Adrian, they include Allan Jones's *Dancers in Concert Square* (relocated from the Garden Festival site), and, for Edward, the doors of the Co-operative Bank in Water Street (dating from circa 1900).

But conservation is as important as commissions. Adrian Henri is sad that Richard Hughes' 'buckets' fountain, dating from the 70s, on the Piazza opposite the Corn Exchange in Drury Lane, Liverpool, are in disrepair: 'They were really imaginative and marvellous to watch, filling with, and tipping water. Now they are just rusting away.'

More care, he hopes, will be shown for the John King statue, *Cases*, now being installed at the junction of Hope Street and Mount Street.

'There's a suitcase, a cabin trunk, a musical instrument case, and so on, depicting the student and artistic influence of that area,' says Adrian Henri. 'What's more, passers-by will be able to use it as a seat.'

There, one presumes, they may contemplate the state of the art. But a final note of caution from Edward Morris: 'People react more strongly for or against the art of their own time. But we should be pleased that new sculpture is being erected...and everyone has the right to make up their own minds about it.'

[24.4.1998]

LIVERPOOL OR BUST!

HAIL TO THEE, FAIR LIVIA!

My exclusive audience with the most famous - and infamous - First Lady of Rome, was a stony-faced affair. It may have had something to do with her journey to Liverpool, a place which, in common with our own Prime Minister, she probably regards as beyond the boundaries of civilisation. So, no gilded open chariot for the Empress. Instead, her minders had opted to sneak her into town in the boot of a Ford Orion. In turn, the Lady was encased in a foam-packed tea chest marked with nothing more special than large red capital letters proclaiming: FRAGILE.

But mark thee well. This particular Livia, the best of only four known surviving examples of an official portrait carved out in 10 BC, has a price on her head of £150,000. Her new home, after 2000 years of living in Rome and Cheshire, is to be Liverpool Museum, which has just saved her from the fate of export to Germany. And as their most expensive acquisition, she's to get pride of place in the museum foyer - the first face of history to be seen by the museum's thousands of annual visitors.

Certainly, Livia's pedigree matches up to her sustained VIP status:

- She was the wife of Octavian, who later became Augustus, Rome's first Emperor.
- Julius Caesar was her honorary father-in-law, having adopted Octavian.
- She was the mother of Tiberius, Roman Emperor during the lifetime of Christ.
- She was the grandmother of Claudius, immortalised in the book and TV series, *I Claudius*.
- And she was the great-grandmother of Caligula, also the subject of contemporary film making, who was enough of a nut to make his horse a Consul of Rome.

But if the family line became loopier and loopier, there is every reason to believe that Livia had her head (though not this one) firmly screwed on. Born in 58 BC, the daughter of a leading Roman family, she was 18 and pregnant by her first husband when she divorced him to marry Octavian, thus ensuring her role as Empress of the Roman Empire - the richest and most powerful woman in the world. When Octavian (then Augustus Caesar) died in AD 14, she made sure that

Tiberius succeeded him. Livia eventually left Rome in AD 26 and died three years later at the grand old age of 86.

But has history been fair to her? As portrayed in the TV series *I Claudius* by the actress Sian Phillips, Livia is seen as a murdering schemer. She was the chief character in a real life soap opera which would make an episode of *Dynasty* look like a remake of *Andy Pandy*. Her new guardian, Edmund Southworth, Keeper of Antiquities at Liverpool Museum, takes up the story: 'For forty years she lived an exemplary life as a wife and mother. This is the time when this official bust would have been carved, as the official portrait of the Empress to be shown to the Empire and displayed in important public buildings.

Although she would have been well into her 40s when it was commissioned, she looks only about 20, and she would have personally approved of this image. The quiff in the hair set a major style at the time, and we can find it in statues of other women from the same period. The ears are also pierced, and the Romans would doubtless have decorated the bust with jewellery and even pastel washed paints. So, like our own Princess of Wales, she was quite a trend setter. But, equally, there were Royal gossip writers around in her day, and this is where her later infamous reputation comes from.

Certainly, when Augustus died, there would have been many contenders for head of state, and she was determined that her son Tiberius should become Emperor. The fact that he did, and that she survived the intrigues, has led to the belief that she was personally responsible for the disappearance of rivals, although there is no solid evidence to support that. As it is, Tiberius was an absolute decadent, and went off to live on Capri - so he was quite a disappointment to her.'

Little is known about the actual history of the 30lb statue, until it was bought by James Hugh Smith Barry, an Irish aristocrat, and shipped to his home in Marbury Hall, in Cheshire in 1776. Barry paid £20 for it then, but when it came up for auction at Christie's in London last July, it was expected to fetch £50,000. Edmund Southworth, keen that it should remain in the North West, thought it would realise twice that amount, and managed to muster funds of £105,000. But he was unable to match a bid of £140,000 from a Munich sculpture museum. It was then that Arts Minister Richard Luce stepped in, and withheld the export licence, giving the British Museum three months to raise the same selling price. Southworth and his staff persisted. In the end they raised donations of £40,000 from the National Heritage Memorial Fund; £10,000 from the National Art Collections Fund, and £10,000 from the Wolfson Foundation, providing the balance from Liverpool Museum's own purchasing funds. After paying VAT and other expenses, the bust is now valued at £150,000, and is, says Southworth 'absolutely first division material, in keeping with our new status as a national museum.'

Of the four surviving examples, the Liverpool one is rated as the best. 'It is not only a high standard piece of art by any standards and from any era, but its importance lies in the fact that it was an official portrait, and we are delighted to have it in Liverpool on behalf of the nation.'

The Empress herself had nothing to add to that. One must assume that she approves.

[19.2.1988]

ARTHUR DOOLEY

HOME IS WHERE THE ART IS...

'I am a limited company,' says Arthur Dooley. 'Chairman, in fact.' For someone who was once a self-confessed anarchist, it's a state of affairs that matches up to the conversion of Saul to Paul. And one day - you mark my words - Arthur will be the patron saint of Renaissance Men.

Whatever happened to Arthur Dooley, the sculptor who used to wear a dirty bobble-hat and overalls, and appear all over 60s television with his head half inside a blast furnace? Arthur Dooley, the man who used to mould Dunlop tyres, and then moulded a new career for himself in art, while at the same time refusing to speak the pseudo language of artisan? Well, he went into limbo, had a nervous breakdown. For several years he was rarely seen around town, and shunned publicity. There were those who thought he must be sunning himself on the Costa Del Sol. But that's not the Dooley style anyway. No, he was living in Toxteth, and preparing for the second coming.

At 60 - 'a young 60 , mind' - he has re-emerged as head of the new Liverpool Academy in Seel Street, to pronounce : 'At my age you are only just maturing. Any artist under 60 hasn't really started.'

Arthur enjoys what he calls 'the only real type of industrial sponsorship in this country.' Liverpool Exhaust Supplies have given him the gallery space, a workshop and an office. He draws a salary and sells his work, and ploughs the cash back into the business. When it comes to book-keeping, he sits behind a desk surrounded by telephones and computer software, and proudly wears the blazer and badge of the Irish Guards, a calling which occupied nine of his three score years.

He has been in touch with Arts Minister Richard Luce, and plans to meet him in London shortly. 'I've got a plan to revolutionise art in this city. A whole new plan. I'd like Liverpool to be host to a National Congress of Artists, like it used to. Much better than festivals, which only last a week.'

So the revolutionary zeal is still there, even if at one time it was more political. Dooley supported the workers' take-over of the Fisher Bendix plant, in what now seems to be the looking glass of history. He campaigned for the revival of the South Docks and the demolition of tower blocks, in the days when it wasn't fashionable to criticise planners set on creating what they thought would be a brave new socialist world of egalitarian housing and shopping centres. All that took time and money, which explains more than anything else why Dooley, despite many commissions, was not a rich man. Once, he stood for the City Council in Everton, as an independent Save Our City candidate, getting just 250 votes. 'Lots of people thought I was a joke, and I was largely ignored. But perhaps someone was listening.' Now they've saved the docks, the tower blocks are being demolished and the chickens have come home to roost.

Arthur Dooley well remembers Old Testament Liverpool, when another Arthur - Arthur Ballard - was teaching at the Art School, and a disruptive John Lennon was lunchtime drinking in the side bar of The Crack. Adrian Henri was just beginning to paint and to write poetry with Roger McGough and Brian Patten. Then a chap called John Willet, a former assistant editor on the *Times Literary Supplement*, wrote a book called *Art in a City*, citing Liverpool as the prototype creative centre, with painting and writing and sculpture about to realise the rewards that pop music and football had already achieved.

But Dooley didn't arrive on the scene with one of the new-fangled fine arts diplomas, and even today he maintains: 'My degrees are in the work I have done.' He had relied on his own resources ever since he'd worked on the tugboats as a deckhand. He had also been a park keeper in Sefton Park, and like Dick Whittington, had once set off for London with little more than the clothes he stood up in. But it was a trip that was to change his life: he became a janitor at St Martin's Art College, cleaning up the mess left behind by aspiring students. And like Alan Bleasdale's fictional Yosser Hughes of a generation later, he decided 'I Can Do That.': 'Everyone's got eyes and hands and a sense of touch, which is why I still say anyone can be an artist.'

His first work was a figure of Christ, a subject wrought from his own faith and Catholicism, which has broadened into what he simply terms Christianity. And one cold winter's morning back in Liverpool, when he was on his way to Dunlop's, he decided to turn sculptor full-time. 'I could have gone on doing that same old job for 20 years.' For £4 a week, he got himself a small premises in Slater Street - just around the corner from where he has now put himself back to work. He installed tools, a bench and a bed, preferring to sleep on the premises for security reasons. At last he was in business.

In 1969 he put on an exhibition of bronzes at the University. They were sort of Henry Mooreish, but had Dooley's own distinctive angular style. Someone from the School of Architecture saw them, and he was asked to sculpt a Stations of the Cross sequence for St Mary's Church, Leyland. There are normally 14 stations, but Dooley, true to innovative style, added a Resurrection scene. As a result, he became associated with religious figuration, a theme which is still central to his work ethic: 'It's the most important thing in the world to me, and it has shaped my thinking throughout. Without an appreciation of the message of Jesus Christ, it would have been a waste of time. Everything else would have seemed a bit shallow.'

One of the troubles with young artists today, he says, is their lack of focus and motivation. 'Often, there's no philosophy and real sense of purpose. If you are going to do any work of art, then let's have a reason for doing it.' The greatest artists, says Arthur, were the engineers, the Stevensons and the Brunels. Although by definition, he must count himself a modern artist, much contemporary art leaves him cold. Had he been to the Tate at Albert Dock? A considered pause, then an answer. 'Yes. Petty bourgeoise anarchy a lot of it. The work of retarded juveniles. The Tate won't like me saying that, but too bad.' Perhaps a man who reckons to have been copied more than any other sculptor in the country can risk a controversial verdict.

Despite the executive air of Dooley's new office - 'things are very dictatorial here, I don't make any bones about it' - the sculpting work itself is as dirty and hot and time-consuming as ever it was. And the cost of the bronze and fibreglass resin are not exempt from inflation. The aim of the academy is to give a showcase to other artists rated highly by the boss. Paintings by Mike Lawson are just finishing a run, and shortly there will be a posthumous exhibition of water-colours by John Burns, who was a wartime student at the Liverpool College of Art.

Arthur Dooley's own work has yet to see the light of day there. All we have locally is a Resurrection sculpture in the Blessed Sacrament Chapel of the Metropolitan Cathedral; a Stations of the Cross at St Joseph the Worker, Kirkby; a Black Christ in Princes Road Methodist Church, and the Speaker's Podium at the Pier Head. But there's plenty going on behind the scenes, including a limited edition of Madonnas - how limited has yet to be decided - which sell for £75. 'I sold 120 of them last year,' he says.

Last October, Arthur Dooley put on a Reconciliation exhibition in the dungeons of Windsor Castle, at the invitation of the Dean and Chapter of St George's Royal Chapel. Thirteen of the 16 pieces sold, proving that there's still a big market for the man whose work graced the homes of TV personalities like Cliff Michelmore and Kenneth Alsop at the time of his initial 'discovery.' 'I sell everything I make. Equally, you could say for the past 40 years I have been messing about, and that the best is yet to come.'

[22.2.1989]

RALPH STEADMAN

DRAWING THE LINE ON A CANINE WORLD

Whoops! Mr Ralph Steadman, cartoonist extaordinary, has done a naughty. He's produced a book which every self-respecting savage dog will want to buy for his meek master. *Dogsbodies* is a collection of drawings showing all the things that make up any carefree canine's day, but which show their owners up as a self-conscious, easily embarrassed breed apart.

Not willing to stop there (is nothing sacred? Down, Rover), Wallasey born Mr Steadman demonstrates how man's best friend is often a mirror image of his owner. 'People match themselves with dogs like they do with cars.' One picture - a poodle lady walking a poodle dog - says it all. He adds that the whole series of cartoons are real life observations. 'If you overdo the satire or the humour, then you're no longer communicating with poeple and that's what it's all about. All these drawings are doing is laughing at the obvious. The cartoon device means that the images can be articulated in an immediate way.'

From the studio which Steadman built on the top of his Fulham home, he can see the gas works, and some high-rise flats. The streets below are milling with people ... and dogs. 'I don't have a dog of my own. There are already too many around. And anyway, they're a bloody nuisance. You can't go away or anything.' But if Steadman seems not too keen on bow-wows - except to admit that their eyes disarm him - his real venom is reserved for their custodians. 'The way they dress them up, force them into unreal domestic situations and parade them as exhibits, turns me off. Whatever the dog does is seen as a reflection of themselves. The dogs are the losers. They'll come back even if they're kicked up hill and down dale for misbehaving themselves.' What's all this then? Doggies' Lib? 'No. I'm not on any crusade with the book. Dogs have proved to be some of my funniest subjects. They involve so much heart-felt observation. I hope the cartoons help people to relax and not get angry.'

Whatever folk think of his doggy doodles, however, Steadman has plenty else to occupy him just now. He's working on two illustrated books (one about a beaver, the other a statement against war and violence); preparing for an exhibition of his drawings at the National Theatre and tuning in for a BBC TV *Arena* programme on his work on Wednesday. 'I find the writing part for the books very difficult. It's not like drawing where you see something being constructed before your eyes. You've got to keep referring back to what's already happened.'

His cartoons have graced the pages of *The Times* and *Rolling Stone*, *Punch* and *Private Eye*. What he considers as his strongest and 'best outcry' - a badly burned Vietnam baby against a black-cross - was published in *Oz*. 'It would never have been accepted by the National Press.'

The theatre, too, has seen his impact on set design. Liverpool Everyman recently used Steadman's graphic backcloths for three productions, including the controversial *One Flew Over the Cuckoo's Nest* and a children's play, *The Pig and the Junkie*, by Brian Patten.

Despite the accolades - and the criticism from certain quarters that he doesn't always know where to draw the line in confronting his public - Steadman still feels that cartoonists are underrated in the culture-cluttered world of visual art. 'We are not considered in the same light as an artist. That definition is built into the concept of carpeted galleries managed by men in pinstripe suits who hang frames on walls. But I would be lying if I said that I didn't think there was some genuine art in what I did.'

Right now, that art is concerned with that old definition of what makes news as Man Bites Dog. For that, Mr Steadman deserves a pat on the head.

[7.2.1977]

JOSH FISHER

EVERY PICTURE TELLS A STORY... YOUR *ECHO,* 1900

(REVIEW) SOUTHPORT THEATRE

And here is the news in pictures, as drawn by the *Liverpool Echo* staff artist at the turn of the century. For before the advent of the Press photographer, there was the quaintly titled 'Press Illustrator', the person who sketched the news either by rushing to the scene of a story, or by constructing a 'realisation' of events based on detailed despatches. Joshua Fisher was one of the pioneers in this field, and he worked for the *Echo* from 1899 to 1906, before leaving to pursue the prime love of his artistic life - water colour landscape painting.

These samples of his newspaper work, together with many others, have been unearthed by one of his grandsons, Mr Jeffrey Fisher, a technical consultant, who lives in Blundellsands. And it's a selection which shows the variety of tasks undertaken by 'Josh' in those days - everything from Royal Portraits to scenes of foreign wars and local events.

Josh Fisher, who died at his Wallasey home in November 1943, aged 84, was a leading figure in Merseyside's artistic life, and is perhaps best remembered today as a founder of the Liver Sketching Club. After a seven year apprenticeship, he went into business on his own, doing crayon portraits, water colours and general litho work. For several years, he painted all the advertising curtains for the Royal Court Theatre, the Shakespeare, the Alexandra (now the Empire) and the two Birkenhead theatres. He also designed and painted transparent signs for the then famous Reynolds' Waxworks.

When he joined the *Echo* as a pioneer illustrator, his drawings were made on the old Hoke Chalk Engraving Plates. 'Those were the days,' he recalled in a newspaper interview in 1932. 'There was a slab of steel covered with a film of chalk. I used to redraw the sketch straight on to the plate with an engraving needle. Then boiling water was poured on to the plate, and that's how we produced the first newspaper blocks for the up-to-the-minute illustrations.' He is said to have set up a record for illustration by this method, taking just ten minutes from the start of his sketch to the time that the paper was on sale in the street. The next method was by zincography, from pen and ink and wash drawings, which was much cleaner and healthier than the old way, when in Josh's words: 'I was covered from head to foot in white powder.'

Away from the *Echo* offices (then in Victoria Street), he had his own studio in Old Hall Street - a site now, ironically, occupied by our present building. Off duty, his favourite pastime was to paint in the Lake District and North Wales, and many of his works were hung in North West galleries, including Liverpool's Walker.

[25.10. 1980]

COMMENT

SHELLING OUT ON THESE
LATEST FASHION CRAZIES

*A Fashion is merely a form of ugliness, so unbearable
that we are compelled to alter it every six months* - Oscar Wilde

This week, I unearthed a photograph of myself so unbearable that I was compelled to assign it to the shredder. Marked 'Windermere, 1970', it gave the distinct impression that Burtons had sponsored the first manned mission to Mars. It shows a 20-year-old Riley - complete with head of hair which would have shamed Samson - wearing platform-soled shoes, flared trousers and a shirt with a penny-round collar. What a cool dude!

On holiday, in his first car. And, for some reason, holding a cassette of *Bridge Over Troubled Water*. How could this portraiture ever have been commissioned? Why were the eyes of the blind not opened? Perhaps because every other young male in Britain at that time looked exactly the same - give or take a Ben Sherman or a remaindered kipper tie. And so the years turned to decades...

In the past 20 years, shirt collars have been buttoned down, pinned down - even cut down. Trousers have been pleated, re-waisted, and now replaced altogether by designer-slashed jeans. And as for shoes, well, what are shoes these days?

In this age, when everyone remains a teenager until 30 (not least because so many are languishing at college, being post-post-graduates) the Young Male Hunter has found new clothing. But surely there's more to life than standing around with gelled locks, two days of stubble, and legs slightly splayed - holding a can of lager and bedecked in Hawaian T-Shirt, black denims and a pair of running shoes? Of course there is!

Salvation, for those with the imagination of Harry Cross at the dog track, comes in the shape of a Shell Suit - so-called because you have to shell out such a lot to obtain one. Indeed, as the new Littlewood's Autumn/Winter catalogue shows, it costs £89.99 (or up to 38 weeks at £2.37) to look like Gazza or Gary Lineker in their shell suits.

Bearing in mind that these outfits are aimed at grown men, what you actually end up looking like is a giant stick of Blackpool rock. Until you start moving. Then it's 'red and yellow and pink and green; orange and purple and blue.' Nowadays, nobody need settle for 'singing' a rainbow. You can actually become one yourself.

The August edition of *Esquire* magazine even goes so far as to suggest that the shell suit was invented here in Liverpool. As it happens, this is totally incorrect. It's like saying that Babylon is the home of the skimpy loin cloth. But when demand is such that even that bastion of good taste, Watson Prickard, feels compelled to stock these amazing Technicoloured Sheencoats, then any visiting London hack could be forgiven for thinking they'd found the supply source.

A better name, of course, would be Romper Suits. Or even, given our love of the vernacular, Incontinence Kecks. Deep in the urban psyche, it's all to do with pot bellies, elasticated and drawstring waistbands - and their close relationship to both nurseries and nappies. They remind us of things we wore before we knew how to do up buttons or fasten belts.

Of course, I am overlooking one remaining major item, apart from the outsize T-shirt. And that, of course, is the designer sports/training shoe. Which means that to really look like Gazza or Gary Lineker can cost you a further 90 quid! This means that, so far, the Dapper Dude, has spent nearly £200, and yet possesses not a single item of genuine clothing. Now, I'm not paid to advertise. But that would buy no fewer than15 assorted quality jackets - including tweeds - at say, Quiggins, in School Lane.

But each to his own - including George Bush. I could have sworn that when the American President announced the survival of democracy in the Soviet Union on Wednesday evening, he was wearing jeans. And what looked suspiciously like a Romper Suit top.

[23.9.1991]

MAKE MINE VEG!

Never again may blood of bird or beast,
Stain with its venomous stream a human feast.
- Percy Shelley

Just after 10 a.m. yesterday, with the government running around like headless chickens, I issued a unilateral statement to my anxiously waiting butcher. It read: 'Having consulted widely with my colleagues, I have concluded that the unity of my dinner parties and the prospects of peace in the household will now be better served if I stand down as a meat-eater, to enable vegetarian colleagues to enter their names on the menu.'

I stand by that even now - more than 24 hours later - as someone who has so far demolished two complete lentil roasts. Without splitting peas, I can already sense the wind of change. So, I believe, can my neighbours. For the next few days my mealtimes are to be shared by two vegetarian journalists. One eats fish, the other doesn't. The fact that Our Lord ate fish (and probably poultry) will not disuade them. Not that I intend to don a loin cloth and run along clifftops collecting berries.

But it is to be a new chapter of fruit, nuts and vegetables, although not necessarily in that order. Yet, if one of my literary heroes, George Bernard Shaw, could do it, so can I. For the first 25 years of his life, GBS was a meat-eater. Once converted to vegetarianism, largely through the poet Shelley 'who opened my eyes to the savagery of my diet', he lived on to be within sight of his 95th birthday. Two thousand years earlier, the Greek philosopher, Hippocates, had been caught scuffing his sandals through the sand declaring: 'Let your food be your medicine, and your medicine your food.' And so it has been throughout history. I even have a private theory that the great Johann Sebastian Bach was a veggie. He did, after all, compose *Sheep May Safely Graze*.

But I digress. Already my kitchen walls are becoming imbued with the smell of curry, in an effort to throw something vaguely warm over an assemblage of raw produce. Tis the depth of winter, and even working within the new kitchen cabinet policy guidelines, salads have been proscribed.

The prime reason is that the British salad is such an utter disgrace, consisting as it does of sheet upon sheet of rabbit's bedding (limp lettuce) soiled by unripened tomatoes, chunks of uninteresting radish, slices of decaying cucumber, a handful of cress, and perhaps a boiled egg. Once, in Paris - the undisputed gastronomic capital of the world - I saw a honeymooning veggie from Nottingham burst into tears because her French *Salade Verte* did not resemble the appalling plateful of garbage she was used to consuming back home. No snails for her. But had she tried tomatoes with vinaigrette and herbs, she would doubtless have been delighted.The French have a way with the simplest of things. Perhaps it's because their sun-kissed tomatoes are fresh, rather than fetched from the fridge. 'A tomato loses its flavour within six hours of being picked,' declares a well-seasoned cook of my acquaintance - someone who's reportedly never left chewing gum on their bedpost overnight.

At this stage, however, I am not counting my cutlets before they are snatched. I can remember my father, who worked for a time as an auctioneer at Stanley Abattoir, saying that if there were guided tours of slaughterhouses, the entire nation would turn vegetarian overnight. That said, we remained a meat-eating family: tripe and onions; liver and sausage casserole; steak and chips; leg of lamb. You name it, we ate it. A pig, apparently can be consumed in its entirety. If not at one sitting, then at several.

Indeed, a butcher's window can be viewed in several ways: as a garnished display of succulent cuisine; as the culmination of years of farming husbandry; as the proudly laid-out efforts of a shopkeeper trying to make no less an honest penny than an adjacent grocer; or as an open and unsanctified graveyard. Butchery is, after all, defined as 'wanton slaughter, massacre.'

Please do not address your letters of protest to me. Should I encourage that, then there will be others who claim that vegetables feel pain, and silently scream as they are pulled from the ground. Enough, at present, to adjust to my new diet. Tonight's feast is to be baked potato and cabbage pie with carrot croquettes.

But how long can it last ...? Unlike Bernard Shaw, I do not particularly wish to challenge morality. In truth, I could quite happily end this life slumped over a plate of bacon and eggs.

[23.11.1990]

OF CARNAGE AND CUISINE

'Man is, and always will be, a wild animal.'
- Charles Galton Darwin (1887-1962)

Life-and-death animal matters - whether for food, recreation or research - tend to infuse the Modern Briton with such a sense of guilt that more than a million scrawny folk now elect to survive wholly by way of vegetables and minerals Yet for the beefy Ancient Briton, there was no such crisis of conscience: give him a club and a cranium, and he'd cracked the problem of lunch.

Lest you misunderstand me, it must be said that in high summer I open windows to release back to the wild all manner of dragonflies, daddy longlegs, bluebottles, bees and wasps that threaten to crash land in my breakfast pot of Real Devon Honey. But I still draw the line at ants. And would do the same with mice, rats and cockroaches, if I had the misfortune to live in the sort of dwelling they found attractive. These latter creatures, being totally loathsome, have forfeited their right to domestic cover. For them, nothing less than salt, boiling water and fire, poison, snap-traps and pellets.

If that seems a trifle harsh to those planning a trip to the pantomime (where various raddled species of house-pests and vermin still get top-billing), for me, it marks a considerable journey down life's pathway of tolerance and understanding.

When I was 13, I used to shoot crows for fun, on the pretext that, being carrion eaters, they pecked out the eyes of young lambs. I also used to race frogs on pieces of string, and feed grasshoppers to lizards, pretending they were lions and gladiators. However, on a much more practical level, I would snare bunny rabbits and curry them - a thing that would never occur to me now, when you can buy them ready-skinned at the supermarket. It's merely a question of moral balance - one in which I try to remember that even Our Lord, while casting swine over cliff-tops, was partial to a good fish or chicken supper. I've had this textured spongey stuff that you pour sauce over and pretend is real meat. But it's no more like meat than Stork is like butter. For one thing, it refuses to bleed, which makes for lousy gravy.

I was contemplating this eternal tug-o-war between meaningless carnage and delightful cuisine only yesterday, when help and advice came from an unexpected quarter. The dog arrived home with a rolled up copy of *The Journal of Personality and Social Psychology*. The latest copy reveals how researchers at the State University of New York (in Buffalo!) have found that dogs can be of unflinching support when their owners arc under stress. Normally, a stiff drink of Lucozade would have done the trick. But for some reason, I couldn't find any. And as I was about to devour some *paté de foie gras*, having just seen a film about how it was obtained by force-feeding the goose, the canine presence was comforting. 'Look,' said the dog, fixing me with a verbal stare. 'If you don't eat it, I will. In fact, I'll have some anyway.'

'But,' I countered, 'this creature has suffered for the sake of a culinary whim. The dog ignored me, raced into the garden and attempted to slaughter a blackbird in cold blood. 'You see what happens when you bore me with trendy human philosophy,' said another verbal stare. 'Okay, you win,' I conceded, 'I'm on nodding terms with the blackbird. I never even met the goose.'

'Animal rights are one thing,' blinked the dog, 'but you can't discuss them seriously on an empty stomach.'

'Such logic,' I conceded, 'and from a supposedly dumb animal.'

[15.11.1991]

AAAGH -THOSE BALMY BARBIE SUMMER NIGHTS

God, having given us indoors and out-of-doors,
we should not attempt to do away with this distnction.
- Dame Rose Macaulay, novelist (1889-1958)

Barely was the ink dry on my recent ode to the joys (?) of picknicking in lay-bys, when I was invited to a barbecue. I had, of course, briefly touched on the subject in this same column, by offering recipes for Crocodile Bites and Sautéed Caterpillars. But no in-depth study of the British Barbecue has ever been undertaken. Until now.

One obvious reason is that barbecues are not British anyway. Indeed, there are those who believe that at latitude 60 degrees North, they are as socially relevant as an ice bucket in an Eskimo's cocktail cabinet. The true barbecue originates from Haiti in the Caribbean, and was devised for roasting hog and oxen whole. However, we are a nation of triers. And chicken drumsticks, lamb chops, sausage and beef-burgers will do very nicely, thank you.

But there's one big difference between a picnic and a barbie: whereas a picnic is a private function, lovingly prepared in advance, a barbecue is a public spectacle cremated in the presence of assembled friends, relations and colleagues. You might as well change the name of your house to 'The Joan of Arc Grill'. And you will need a house and garden, by the way. Or at least a back yard. The last person I know who attempted a 'balcony barbecue' was duly hosed down by large chaps wearing yellow helmets. Such was the vigilance of uninvited neighbours who feared for the safety of his flat.

Talking of which, neighbours play a large part in the planning of any barbecue. At the very least, they need be advised to wear earplugs, close their windows and take in the washing. And if they care for their dog, and don't want it mistaken for a kebab, they'll want to make sure it's safely indoors. From then on, you follow the usual timetable, bearing in mind that all accredited barbecues (like pantomimes) start at 7pm:

10 am: Tap barometer, If it's steady, proceed to shops for last minute miscellaneous nibbles.

11am: Go outside amd stick finger in air to check prevailing wind.

NOON: Make sure firelighters and charcoal are not damp. Put cubed cheese and pineapple etc on sticks in case meat becomes inedible.

1pm: Look at barbecue site and imagine 50 starving people queueing for their supper. Listen to weather forecast (too late to cancel now).

2pm: Put out glasses on trays. Cover to prevent midges landing.

3pm: Make punch. Put everything in it. If the guests are anaethetised by alcohol they won't know what they're eating.

4pm: Plug in electric organ on extending lead. Live music is another great distraction.

5pm: Tap barometer again. It could have been faulty earlier ('Just look at those clouds'). Test outside lighting, and electric organ. Sip punch.

6pm: Bash barometer. If it's falling, pour and consume large glass of punch.

7pm: Greet guests. Make conversation. Reminisce ad nauseam.

8pm: Attempt to light barbecue. Listen to unsolicited advice on how it *should* be done. Appoint biggest know-all as your assistant. Close all doors into house. Give assurance that acrid billowing smoke and paraffin fumes are temporary.

9pm: Relight barbecue. Douse excessive flames. Wipe soot from face. Place meat on grill. Commence feast.

10pm: A passing shower. Take paper plates inside, along with allegedly cooked meat. Wonder how it is that a chicken leg so crisp and black on the outside could possibly be so moist and pink within.

11pm: Shower not yet passed. Double strength of remaining punch.

MIDNIGHT: It's pouring down, but be jolly. Laughing a lot. Tell everyone: 'We must do this more often.'

1am: Go to bed resolving to put barbecue in car boot sale, and realisingthat you despise most of your colleagues, relations and friends.

Have nightmares about the feeding of the five thousand.

Wake up to realise it wasn't such a bad dream after all!

[19.7.1991]

EASTER MONDAY FROLICS

Easter, as you will have gathered, is a moveable feast. This year, it has arrived early, complete with an hour's extra daylight. A bonus indeed for what is generally decreed to be the start of the holiday season. Hoteliers in the Scottish ski resorts of Glencoe, Cairngorm and Glen Shee are rumoured to be down on their knees giving thanks for fresh spring snowfalls, after a winter decidedly off-piste, so to speak.

The Book of Common Prayer is where you'll find the key to the mysteries of the calendar. The table to find Easter day from the present up until 2199 AD gives the formula as 'the first Sunday after the full moon which happens upon a Sunday, Easter Day is the Sunday after.' So now you know. The easier calculation is that Easter Monday is always the next day.

But no way is it like Boxing Day following on from Christmas. Boxing Day is an excuse for a snooze in front of the telly. But Easter Monday - this very day - is a day of action: decorate the living room, mow the lawn, cast off the gloom of winter's hibernation. It's the day when you find out that your anorak no longer fits; when you discover that last season's worms have crystallised in your bait box, and that despite the usual mixed bag of weather, the roads are as busy as ever.

I spent much of my childhood in traffic jams at Queensferry. It was where I learned to play 'I Spy' as we returned from North Wales in first gear down Ewloe Hill. Those who gave up soon discovered that Ewloe had what passed for a castle over a stile at the bottom of a muddy field. And those with money to make decided that Queensferry was indeed a good place to build one of the first *Little Chefs*. Now it's all motorways and ringroads, but everyone still gets in a jam....

And if the family car was programmed to set off North, in those halcyon pre-M6 days, there was the queue at Milnthorpe for the Lake District, the drive through Kendal, and the sight, on rainy Bank Holidays, of sandbags outside houses on the banks of the River Kent. You see, we just had to go out. Holidays were to be used, not wasted, in those 1950 post-war days before the advent of package trips to the Costa Del Whatever. Indeed, you didn't just go out. You went on an expedition. And it seemed that half of Liverpool went with you, at exactly the same time.

One Easter Monday in Langdale, it rained so hard that part of the road was washed away: the waterfalls were white-ribboned torrents, the rivers muddy brown. All good stuff to put in a school essay entitled: 'What I Did Over the Holiday'. The grown-ups had all the bother, the kids all the fun. And how educational it was! You found out how lambs were born, because sometimes it happened in front of your very eyes. You found out that nettles stung. You built dens, fell out of trees, kicked a ball into the wrong field and found out that bulls didn't need a red rag to get angry.

There were set places for Easter Monday too: Moel Famau was a popular jaunt. Park in Cilcain, hear how they played host to a previous generation of evacuees during the Blitz, be fortified by ginger beer and a packet of crisps (the toy with the salt in a separate twist of blue paper), and then up the steep tracks to the ridge, from where the Vale of Clwyd looked like something out of a child's picture book. The monument on the top was falling down and had been in-filled with rubble. But in mist, it took on the appearance of a Gothic pile from a Hammer Horror movie. Then there was Loggerheads, a deep wooded cavern between two cliffs, full of echoes and mysterious sounds. Or Llangollen with its Chain Bridge; the Denbigh Moors with the ruins of the old hunting lodge; the ridges of Snowdon and the bustle of Beddgelert, complete with legend of Prince Llewellyn's slain dog.

As kids, we didn't know how lucky we were to have all this on our doorsteps. Nowadays, with hindsight, it's easy to see that living in other parts of the country does not give easy access to such a range of adventures. Merseyside could not be better placed to afford such benefits, and it still does. These days, I'm sorry to say, I take the easy way out, and stay at home on Bank Holidays. But somewhere this very day, some youngsters will be getting their first breath of good country air. The process is never ending.

A good day, therefore, to contemplate the environment afresh. The world is at last waking up to its self destruction. We've done more to damage the countryside in the past 40 years than mankind had done in the previous 4,000. But now there are, hopefully, a whole lot more Easter Mondays to come.

[27.3.1989]

WATCH OUT FOR WINTER

ON TIME AND TIDE OF PROBLEMS

Daisy the cow, Bobby the blackbird, Postman Pat and I all hailed the New Dawn today. In the twinkling of an eye, it was light at 6.30 am. (The same was true of Sunday, of course, but the world was having a lie in). It was only this morning that life truly brightened up for we Brits, as millions of commuters and livestock got down to the serious business of adjusting to Greenwich Mean Time.

They say that times in general change, and time in particular flies. But in this case, the sun reappears like some celestial conjuring trick. Likewise, it sets. Earlier. So tonight, you'll be stumbling home in the gathering gloom at 5pm, and falling over the cat in the pitch black, half an hour later. Why? Apparently, so that dairy farmers in the Shetlands and milkmen in Aberdeen can tell the difference between a teat and a gold top. So why couldn't we now stay with Standard Time? I hear you cry. And let those strange folk north of the border invent Scottish Summer Time?

The time lords at Greenwich tell me that when we tried a Standard Time experiment, from February 1968 to October 1971, it 'caused chaos'. There was a tidal wave of apprehension about schoolchildren milling around in zero visibility, looking for the nice lollipop lady. On a more personal level, a man in Hastings was awarded damages for doing battle with a lamp post, which required his head to be sewn together. A stitch in time, indeed. Questions were asked in Parliament. Schools began an hour later. While the cows kept to their own cud-chewing timetable. So Standard Time was scrapped.

Nowadays, the only victims of the Greenwich/Summer Time switch appear to be overnight rail and plane passengers, who have an uncanny ability to arrive at their destinations less than a minute after they set off. Many are said to require counselling.

Our great grandparents stood for none of this, of course. Summer Time was first suggested by a Colchester builder named William Willett in 1907, but it was not introduced until 1916 - and then only as a 'wartime emergency measure'. A wet summer followed. Someone visiting an 80 year old shepherd, half way up a Welsh mountain, remarked: 'Terrible weather.' 'No,' said Jones the sheep. 'It isn't the weather at all. It is God's judgement on us for altering His given time.'

The latest of the pressure groups for change - Daylight Extra - wants British Summer Time to become the norm from 1996, and for things to be totally in line with the rest of the Western Europe by 1997. That makes sense - especially for those in business and industry wanting to contact their continental counterparts. Let us take for example, Liverpool's twin city, Cologne. Many businesses there start work at 7am (when it is still 6am in the UK). When British office workers arrive (circa 9am), the Germans are thinking about lunch. By the time we take lunch, they are planning to go home. Net result: in some cases, little more than four hours of 'compatible business time'.

Besides, a survey shows that three out of four people want lighter evenings, not mornings. And the Royal Society for the Prevention of Accidents says continental-style times prevent 2,000 injuries on the roads each year. Meanwhile, if people who need extra daylight changed their working hours, it would have the effect of staggering rush hours in cities and saving the rest of us much irritation. Mind you, we'd have missed out on Sunday morning's extra hour in bed.

[24.10.1994]

TESTING TIMES!

*If I had no duties, I would spend my life
driving briskly in a horse and carriage* - Samuel Johnson

A friend of mine failed his driving test this week. What's more, he failed on the very point which the AA says defeats one in two learners: 'Lack of observation when pulling out of a junction.' I, of course, commiserated by offering to purchase a prize cocktail guaranteed to turn any set of Breathalyser crystals green. Soon, it was no longer the end of the world. Or the wheel. 'What,' I said, 'with the amount of traffic these days, and the unkempt state of some junctions...'

In a country with 500 test centres and 1,700 examiners, it seemed more than bad luck to have become a negative statistic. Of course, I didn't bring up the fact that when I took my test, it was still a case of 'Halt at Major Road Ahead.' (None of this hit-or-miss 'Give-Way' mullarkey). Nor that I should have failed - and not only by today's even tougher standards.

As chance would have it, I took that most public of examinations (which can lead to the most private of sorrows) behind the wheel of a Land Rover. Then, as now, they were billed as 'the world's most versatile vehicles.' So the hill start was a cinch: after all, with 12 forward-gear combinations to choose from, we could, if required, have gone through a ditch, across a building site, and up the side of a house. And the emergency stop was precisely what it claimed to be. The Land Rover didn't slow down. It stopped. In its tracks.

Being the era prior to safety belts, my examiner was thus propelled forward at meteoric speed, cutting his head on the independent windscreen wiper mountings which were then Land Rover features. I can still see him wiping his temple with a bloody handkerchief. Then came the dodgy bit - or so it turned out: reversing around a corner. To my horror, as I completed this manoeuvre, I discovered that both near-side wheels were fully on the pavement. But such was the bulk of the Land Rover and the shallowness of the kerb, that the examiner completely failed to notice (or perhaps he was still concussed?).

Anyway, I passed, and graduated into the world where petrol was 4s 3d (circa 21p) a gallon; where most car interiors still smelled of leather and many still had gear levers on the steering column. From an external point of view, little amber sticky-out indicators had not been abolished, and a buyer's chief concern was that a vehicle looked 'characterful', rather than merely aeronautically enhanced enough to be potentially capable of flight. And everyone, it seemed, could remember their number plates with greater ease. As a proud owner of Morris Minor 187 KD (£180 on the road), I headed for the open highway ... Just think what it would have been worth now (!).

But investment wasn't even a minor thought. The plan was to penetrate uncharted areas of the Lake District and North Wales - expeditions worth doing before the country was overrun with plastic cones and concrete motorways, smoke-belching lorries and thundering coaches. No skateboards flying off pavements, no kids on mountain bikes in high streets, and no one-way systems yet devised for each and every hamlet. You could even park outside the shop you wanted. And get to it without encountering a dozen sets of traffic lights and pedestrian crossings.

All this is not a description of life on the road in the wake of Samuel Johnson's love affair with the horse and carriage. It is of urban life 25 years ago. The only areas one may 'drive' now with any enjoyment are mid-Wales, parts of mid-Northern England, and in the Highlands of Scotland. Meanwhile, an incredible two million people continue to take the driving test each year in the UK. Quite what sort of stop-start touring they have ahead of them, goodness knows. My fortunate friend, who intends an early test re-take, will doubtless find out.

Whatever, that feeling of high-bound adventure, when a road was a highway to the freedom of the spirit, is virtually over. Bound up with countless rules and regulations. Have a good Bank Holiday. And take my tip: stay at home!

[25.5.1991]

THE SKY REALLY IS THE LIMIT

The Lord, in His wisdom, gave me a fertile imagination. One which, during extreme flights of fancy, contemplates metal fatigue and falling out of the sky. We all have our phobias: for Yours Truly it could simply be marked down as fear of flying.

As far as I was concerned, hurtling along thousands of feet up in a metal tube was a totally unnatural experience. This is where Douglas Ord, Senior Training Captain for British Airways, comes in useful. Douglas, 10 O levels, four A levels and a degree, as well as 22 years' flying experience, provides the counterbalance: the argument that planes provide the safest form of transport. Statistically, you would have to fly continuously for 99 years to be in line for an accident...

'Congratulations for being here,' says his colleague, Captain Peter Hughes, on welcoming 80 lily-livered non-believers to Manchester Airport for the fiftieth Fear of Flying Course. 'Let's rid ourselves of self-defeating, negative thinking.'

Just getting to the Airport, we are told, is the first major hurdle of the day. And we are over it. During the next six hours of listening (and learning to relax), we shall be transformed in the twinkling of a jet engine. Douglas, a chappie who thinks nothing of 30 take-offs and landings per week, is also human. He admits to going ashen in ski lifts. But in an aircraft, he feels on top of the world. And fit. You have to be. British Airways pilots have a medical twice a year. As a result, they are licensed every six months, and work on two weeks notice. Some are co-pilots for nearly 20 years before being given overall command of a flight.

'You're at school to-day and you must pay attention,' jokes Douglas. I paid enough attention to note down that he'd only been struck by lightning ten times. But even that's completely safe in a plane, which can also fly on one engine. But what engines! The 99-seater BAC 1-11 awaiting us on the runway has two Rolls Royce motors, each capable of providing enough power to light up the whole of London.

There are three basic fears:

- a sense of not being in control
- lack of knowledge
- claustrophobia.

There's not much you can do about not liking heights. To those like myself, who readily believed that planes plummeted, our leader explains that, bombs apart, aircraft can't fall out of the sky. 'It is wrong to think that there is nothing beneath you. There is a cushion of air. If you could dye it, you would see the aircraft floating like a boat. Except that it's safer than a boat.'

But the very fact that flying is a different experience, can make it scary....take off and landing; changes in the pitch of engine noise; the clunking of the under-carriage going up and down; the extension of the wing flaps; the reverse thrust, and in-flight turbulence. This 'bumpy ride' effect is caused by changing air pressure outside the plane. It can be quite dramatic, to the point of passengers having to refasten their safety belts. But it is quite normal, Douglas assures us. The planes are built to withstand much more than the high-level buffeting they ever get. So forget wings dropping off and what is often an apparent lack of momentum. Above the clouds, with nothing passing to relate to, a sense of 'speed' is academic.

Douglas, who started his career flying Chipmunks, and now commands some of the finest airliners in existence, says the forecast is good. He had been hoping it would have been a bit bumpier, as you get turbulence on about 50 per cent of flights. 'It won't stop happening. You've got to learn to love it. You mustn't spend your lives worrying about aeroplanes. There are lots more important things to think about, like the VAT man.'

Dr Lawrence Burns, Director of Psychology at Rochdale College, is at hand to train the brain. Apart from giving us some relaxation exercises, he tells us that avoidance of situations actually falsely maintains anxiety. 'I want you to say to yourselves: "My confidence will be sky high later today."'

Should we fail, Dr Burns has equipped each one of us with an elastic band to be worn on the wrist. The idea being that should negative thoughts arise, we twang the elastic on the bare skin as aversion therapy. Mediaeval monks were very good at self flagellation, and just to put history into perspective, we are also given two quotes. One from Sophocles, which runs: 'to the man who is afraid, everything rustles.' And from Julius Caesar: 'As a rule, what is out of sight, disturbs men's minds more than what they see.' Quite. It is now 3.15pm and our BAC 1-11 has been out of sight all day. Now it was being made ready for our flight over the Irish Sea.

There comes a point when theory has to end and experience commence. I didn't HAVE to get on the plane - and there it was, like a tame seagull, outside the terminal building. I felt terminal myself. Twang! A quick smack with the elastic band, and I'm up the steps and aboard. We taxi out, we get clearance from air traffic control ('Air traffic control in England is second to none'), we accelerate to 130 mph, and it's up, up and away...

Remarkable. I began to wonder what all the fuss was about. We climb gradually to 14,000 ft, and within 15 minutes we are over Liverpool and on our way to the Isle of Man. It's fantastic. Still, Douglas Ord is telling everyone every move: when the plane will bank (turn); how the sound of the engines will change, and as we return 45 minutes later, our landing is similarly explained. Some can be bumpy, which is why the tyres on a BAC 1-11, for instance, only do 20 landings a set. But our touch-down is absolutely smooth, as indeed the whole flight had been.

There is a lot of smiling aboard. Not out of relief, so much as pride. Phobias had been overcome, confirming the course's 98 per cent success rate. 'To not fly is to deny yourself so much,' says Peter Hughes, as he shakes my hand in farewell. 'You must be wondering why you've wasted the last 10 years being stuck on the ground.' I am.

[30.5.1990]

SCALING NEW HEIGHTS

Tis the year of the Matterhorn. And to help celebrate the 125th anniversary of the first ascent, I decided to represent Merseyside - to an altitude of 10,700ft. Had I continued by fixed rope to the summit - 4,000ft higher - I would have met up with a new statue of Saint Bernard, patron of mountain guides, complete with lightning conductor poking out of his head.

However, being a mere mortal, I viewed my own modest achievement as a corollary of life: have a nice time; get as far as you can; know your limitations and then get out of the way to avoid being trampled underfoot by weary folk on the way down. Incidentally, I was not sponsored. I did it because it was there. But for this most monumental of mountains - 'the noblest lump of geography thrust from the earth's crust' - it's business as usual, with 10 lives lost during the first month this season. The average death rate is one a week.

Ironically, Zermatt, the nearby resort built by Victorian British as the cradle of the 'new' sport of mountaineering, is also the grave of the adventurous. The town's neat cemetery has an entire section given over to those dashed to death on glaciers below the precipitous cliffs of the Matterhorn's notorious North and East faces. Some from the North West and North Wales. Attached to one head-stone - the last resting place of a 19-year-old - is a rusting ice axe. Beneath it the inscription: 'I chose to climb'.

It was the English climber, Edward Whymper, who conquered the arrow-head peak in the summer of 1865. His party made their way up the sheer arête, the Hornbill Ridge. But it was a triumph overshadowed by disaster. Four of Whymper's team died. In Elsie's Bar, a snug in Zermatt's singular high street, the controversial debate continues to this day: Was it a genuine accident, or did the ambitious Whymper cut the rope when his companions got into difficulties on the angular shoulder just short of the summit crest? Whymper's base had been the now plush Monta Rosa Hotel, named after a nearby higher mountain of lesser profile. But history has taken care of Whymper's profile. As one mountain guide told me: 'What Stanley did for Africa, Whymper did for Switzerland.'

Although it should be said at this stage that the Italians lay claim to the Southern flank of the Matterhorn. Which is why they call it Monta Cervina. The Swiss guides, who charge the equivalent of £320 to accompany climbers to the top, have pride on their side. There's not been a fatal accident involving one of their clients in 40 years. It's the inexperienced, the newcomers, or the loners who perish, often in blizzards which can rage at any time of the year.

'We cannot close off the mountain to amateurs,' bemoaned a member of the helicopter rescue service. 'Even in summer, the upper sections are coated in a treacherous layer of ice.' A single false move, and there's nothing but fresh air and the force of gravity between the ill-fated climber and the pyramidal base thousands of feet below.

I am not one to tempt fate. Nor do I court nightmares in which my assurance policies play the role of Banquo's ghost. But it's easy to see why this peak above all others has been a fatal attraction for so many. It's virtually purpose designed. Give a child a crayon and ask them to draw a mountain, and they draw this shape. As for scale...well, you've just got to be there. No photograph I've seen does it justice.

[17.8.1990]

WHO GIVES A FOUR XXXX
ABOUT THE BARD OF OZ?

*'The remarkable thing about Shakespeare
is that he is really very good'* - Robert Graves (1895-1985)

On the very day a survey showed that students are now able to gain degrees in English Literature without studying Shakespeare, British Television launched another glittering name into the academic stratosphere: Les Murray. Mr Murray - said to be Australia's leading poet - was the subject of Melvyn 'Sexpot' Bragg's *South Bank Show*.

Although still awaiting recognition from the Kangaroo Continent's Cultural Attaché to the Court of St James - the dribbling Sir Leslie Patterson - the other Les is hailed as a gem by dons Down Under. Actually, despite his half-moon specs and bald dome, Les's lineage marks him out as a bit of a rough diamond. His Dad chopped down trees and drove cattle through the creek with a whip - still constant sources of inspiration to the Bard of Oz. Les spoke emotionally about his childhood - 'lack of urban graces and underpants' - and read his work with the intensity of a man self-administering the Last Rites. Perhaps by the turn of the century, the entire world will not give a four XXXX for anything other than Les Murray.

Meanwhile, for the past four centuries, the world has been learning from Shakespeare - without needing to know whether or not he wore underpants. However, Dr Tim Cook of Kingston Polytechnic has found that three of Britain's biggest examination boards now offer A-Levels in English Language and Literature in which Shakespeare is not compulsory; and that several universities dish out English Literature degrees without insisting on the study of his plays. What's more, Cook identifies the culprits: 'Students are coming from schools which don't give them the background or mental equipment to interpret the difficult texts from the past,' he says. Thus, Chaucer and Milton are also suffering at the hands of trendy, ill-informed, wishy-washy educationalists - their works ever more displaced by Feminist writers, such as Margaret Atwood, Angela Carter, Toni Morrison and Alice Walker.

Set against this, one can even forgive John Major for picking a minor Trollope novel, *The Small House at Allington*, on *Desert Island Discs*. But while a balanced education is everything, what does it tell us about teaching standards? Circulating in many of our schools is a pugwash of a document - which cost £21 million of public money to produce -

advocating the study of 'linguistics' and 'dialect'. Language, argues the study, should be used 'appropriately' rather than correctly. Decoded, this means that the voices of the ignorant are heard above those of the truly educated. No wonder Education Secretary Kenneth Clarke wants to revive grammar schools - and good luck to the parents who insist on it.

Meanwhile, if you wish to be old-fashioned, reactionary - and well-informed, may I comment the Liverpool Everyman's current production of *Othello*. As one young member of the audience, now re-sitting O-Levels after the state education system failed him, said at the conclusion of this week's opening night: 'I don't know why people say they can't understand Shakespeare.'

Neither, my friend, do I. But what a curse that so many are being denied the opportunity to try - by folk with the intellect of a moist muffin.

[7. 2.1992]

PROFILES

HAROLD WILSON

Harold Wilson was an adopted Merseysider. Even if he never managed to lose his Yorkshire accent. As MP for Huyton, he became the Merseyside MP who bestrode the international stage of politics, but was equally at home supporting the Cavern Club, raising money for Liverpool theatres, or even lighting up on behalf of a local pipe smoking club.

'This is what they want to see,' he once told me, striking a match, cupping his hands and purposefully igniting a pipe full of tobacco. Like Churchill with his cigar, Wilson knew the power of pictures, years before the soundbite was officially invented. Cameras flashed. The crowd outside the Adelphi Hotel cheered. Harold waved and disappeared behind clouds of smoke.

In Huyton, they had known this worldly-wise, ultra-shrewd politician as their Member of Parliament since 1950. And he was to serve his constituents for the next 33 years - seven years after his shock resignation.

Wilson had shown debating skills ever since his family had moved from Yorkshire and he became a pupil at Wirral Grammar School. But he was not an elitist. His six years in Downing Street were 'The Harold and Mary Years', his wife being famed for her poetry. International money markets, the technological revolution, the Open University and the demise of Empire might have characterised his years in office, but he could take time out to enjoy the ordinary - and the extraordinary. Harold was a fan of the Beatles. He appeared with them on television, swapping jokes with John Lennon with as much skill as he had faced Edward Heath over the Dispatch Box at Westminster.

When the Everyman Theatre was rebuilt in the early 70s, Harold turned up to lend his support at an Adelphi fund launch. Indeed, he had only had to travel down three floors in the lift. For the Adelphi was a second home - and the place where he took refuge on general election nights. In Wilson's case, general elections were a speciality. He won no fewer than four, and lost only one - in 1970. At St George's Hall on election eve that year, he told a massed rally of supporters: 'There's only one party praying for rain tomorrow, and it's not us.'

He lost. It was one of the few miscalculations in an otherwise supersonic career that in 1947 had seen him become the youngest Cabinet Minister since Pitt the Younger. Down he may have been now. But not for long. By way of compensation, he was back in Downing Street in 1974. Two years later, his resignation - as spectacular as his entry into Parliament in 1945 - shook the world. Close colleagues like Roy (now Lord) Jenkins always discounted rumours that there might have been sinister implications. Most thought that Wilson himself had sensed the first failings of his legendary powers of memory and decided to go while the going was good. The man who once said that a week was a long time in politics, had been missing from centre stage politics for a generation when his death was announced this morning.

Harold who? anyone under voting age may ask. But Harold was the most successful example of that rare species called a Labour Prime Minister. He lived somewhere inside a Gannex mac, liked fish and chips, and disliked Ian Smith. Smith was the rebel Prime Minister of Rhodesia (now Zimbabwe), who had embarrassed Wilson's government by making a Unilateral Declaration of Independence (the infamous UDI) in 1965. Negotiating was a long process. Two years later, there were the famous Tiger Talks on board ship in the Med. Wilson told me later - during one of his many visits to the then Liverpool Press Club in Bold Street - that he'd rather have been on a Mersey Ferry.

Being little more than a cub reporter, I was in awe of such snippets from my 'mate' Harold. It was certainly time I started recording some of his thoughts for posterity, I thought. So let's go for something important. What do you think, I ventured to ask, is the most important single qualification to be Prime Minister? Harold beamed, lit his pipe, thought for a moment and said: 'A sense of history.'

Now, he has become part of that history. Not least the chapter headed The Pound in Your Pocket, devoted to his devaluation crisis. But history will generally view him kindly, as the undoubtedly charismatic politician who had no time for restrictive practices and who dragged the Labour Party - sometimes screaming - into the modern age.

[24.5.1995]

245

CLIVE BARKER

MASTER OF THE MACABRE

Last Friday, Clive Baker retired his mum five years early. Tomorrow, if the morning mail arrives on schedule, he could retire himself. By the way, Clive is just 32, and spent nine years on the dole.

Fantastic? Yes! True? Of course! For as the former Quarry Bank schoolboy has found out, writing horror stories, fantasy, film scripts and West End plays, pays big money. Witness the cheque for a six-figure sum for his latest novel, which is about to land on the doormat of his flat in London's Crouch End. And all for a story he hasn't yet completed - a fantasy set in modern Liverpool.

'It works out at about a dollar a word,' says Clive, on a visit to his parents' house in Mossley Hill. Add to that two films, one starring Denholm Elliott, Stephen Berkoff and Miranda Richardson (the Southport actress who has just starred as Ruth Ellis) and a West End play, with Denis Waterman and Rula Lenska tipped for the cast, and you begin to see that there's more than one source for Mr Barker's new-found fortune.

Resorting to cliché, I must tell you that I knew him when he had nothing; when he was presenting weird and wonderful mime shows out of season at the Everyman, with a group of amateurs, who called themselves the Mute Pantomime Theatre and later, The Dog Troop.

'Yes, the long days of the dole queue. Nine years of them, ' he remembers. 'In the end, they even called me in for one of those heavy interviews where they locked the door. I told them I wrote plays and produced a whole file of them out of a bag. I might not have been paid for them in those days, but I believed in what I was doing. I got so used to working like that, that I have no real intention of giving up now. The only difference is that people are suddenly prepared to pay me fabulous sums for it.'

He means he can now throw away the rent book and buy a place in London, pop a champagne cork whenever he likes and probably indulge in a couple of trips to Barbados a year. 'I like books and records. Fashions and clubs don't really interest me, although I have just ordered a new jacket for myself from a designer in Liverpool. It's a blue one. It's nice.'

He's getting used to the rather old joke of friends coming up to him and saying: 'Oh, we'll have to pay to speak to you now..."'

'Somehow, it has the effect of making other people feel insecure. But I hope I haven't changed all that much.' It did give a glow, however, to be able to come home and tell his mum, Joan, that she could ditch her job as a schools' welfare officer, if he made up her wages for the next five years. 'She liked the job, but she was tired, so she retired last Friday.' says Clive.

He says there is no mystery to his success. He simply made the right connections. Writing was nothing new. Getting an agent was: 'I'm not one of those people who knock agents. They are very useful. It meant that my first series of short stories were bought up.' Under the umbrella title of *Clive Barker's Books of Blood*, they hit the horror market in a big way here and in the States. Weidenfeld and Nicolson then brought out his first novel, *The Damnation Game*, a re-working of the Faust story, again with plenty of blood and gore.

'As far as horror is concerned, I've written myself out of the genre for the time being. Certainly, as far as short stories are concerned. But the publishers liked the novel and are putting it in for a Booker Prize. It probably doesn't stand a cat in hell's chance, but it is an indication of their faith in it and in me.'

Rave reviews in the right places - Radio 4, the literary mags, the 'heavy' press - have all cemented Barker's reputation in the business. 'Actually, I don't believe in the supernatural, and I don't like the sight of blood. I'm quite likely to faint, particularly if it's my own. And goodness knows why, when the photographers turn up, they all want me to go into the graveyard near my house and sit on a tombstone. It shows how misunderstood the whole horror thing is - as if we have come no further than the days of Bram Stoker.

It's all down to imagination. It's my greatest asset, I suppose. And yet, when fans turn up at book signings and identify with it, it can be quite creepy. To think that my fantastic imaginings can register in their reality.

The Liverpool book is a new departure, however. It's about the rediscovery of magic. And why shouldn't it be set here? Blake wrote about magic in Camden Town and Islington. It's just an example of how the extraordinary can be rooted in the ordinary.'

Coming back to his roots - admittedly with a copy of the local *A to Z* at his side - is what writers often do anyway: 'We used to live off Penny Lane…there will be a lot of my childhood in it.'

Indeed, his fascination with writing began as a schoolboy, when Ramsay Campbell, best known in these parts as a cinema critic for radio, went along to give a talk on gory literature. Yet in the States, Campbell himself is a cult figure in the horror stakes, with books like *The Doll That Ate My Mother* in the shops and book club catalogues. Even more relevant is the fact that in writing about Barker's books,

Campbell has called him, 'the most important new writer of horror since Peter Straub...the first writer to produce horror fiction in technicolour.'

Even the West End play *The Secret Life of Cartoons* has that added Barker imprint of the fantastic: where else would a cartoonist find his rabbit creation in bed with his wife?

'I try for new things all the time, although horror and sex and fantasy have played a large part in my output to date. When people meet me, I don't want to be treated as some Gothic reject. I'm an ordinary person, a nice enough guy, I hope.'

So what do mum and dad make of it all? 'Well, I think my father has read one or two of the short stories. But I don't think they've ever found my stuff to their taste, and that opinion hasn't changed. Actually, I don't think my mother wants to know that my mind works in the way it does,' admits Mr Barker - with a smile, of course.

[1.10.1985]

LAUREN BACALL

PUTTING PAID TO HER LEGEND

It was not quite your average day in the hack trade: I could have had lunch with James Bond, but I was not feeling sufficiently high-tec. So I chose instead to drop in on Lauren Bacall.

The former Mrs Humphrey Bogart is in Manchester, playing a raddled has-been of an actress in Tennessee Williams' *Sweet Bird of Youth*. It's the flip-side of the American dream philosophy, but Miss Bacall has lost none of her razzle. She sweeps up in a powder-blue Jag and climbs out in a yellow stripey outfit, which gave every impression of a wasp taking leave of a wedding bouquet. I'd thought up that little gem of prose before I found out that she really was in stinging mood.

Apparently, a copy of the *Daily Mail* had been delivered with her breakfast. She didn't like the bit about still building up her legend.

'Are you sober, now that I've left you for so long?' she asks. I put my thrice-filled gin and tonic glass - now empty - down on the table and scoop up a salted peanut...this is going to be a hard one to crack.

Ladies first: 'I am an actress. I am damn tired of being put into categories by the Press. I am a professional and have been for 40 years. I am appearing with distinguished actors, and being directed by a great writer (Harold Pinter). And having reached this stage of my life, I feel I can say what I like. They keep calling me a Hollywood 'quote' star. I mean, I haven't lived there for 25 years. I have been in the theatre steadily since 1966. The Press keep going on about this ageing film star stuff, as if after 35 you should cut your throat. I don't understand why people aren't meant to continue to produce in their lives. Especially in England, where actors are always respected much more so than in America. It's as if they don't understand that people are meant to get better and learn and grow...the attitudes here are becoming more like America...'

Well, that seemed to have cleared the air a bit. And blunted my pencil. Oh, for another G and T.

The mood grows softer. It's not me she's getting at, you understand. It's just all the legend stuff, which she thought she'd left behind. The voice is still sultry, so sultry in fact, you wonder why she didn't make all her pictures in asbestos. And she's looking just fine for a lady of

60. She'd come to talk business. And yet, she's not daft enough to think that the world doesn't still view her as the girl who became the new Garbo. The girl, who, in 1943 was an usherette in a New York Theatre, and within 12 months was co-starring with Bogart in *To Have and Have Not*. By 1945, she was his 20-year-old bride. He always called her Betty or Baby; she called him Bogie - just like everyone else.

The thing is, Bacall in '85 wants to move on. She will, of course, talk of Bogie: 'He was a man of tremendous qualities, he stood for good things. His standards were high.' But now, the play's the thing. Present tense, please.

Why did she choose a Tennessee Williams play?

'Look, I never choose parts. You don't in this profession. They are offered to you. I wanted to do a straight play. This is my first. I've only ever done comedy and musicals on stage. I did meet Tennessee Williams once. He said he'd like me to do one of his plays, and I told him it was one of my dreams.'

Working with Pinter as director has been a bonus too. She describes him as 'one of God's gifts.' There's an obvious integrity to her drift. This is a good play, a good part. Not just something to do. After all, they soon learned on the film lot back in '48 when Bacall refused to go before the cameras in a swimsuit, that she can in no way be compromised.

'I didn't think I was a cheapskate girl,' she recalls, mentioning with obvious displeasure the moguls' fascination for shooting semi-nude girls standing on iced cakes, etcetera. By this time, Miss Bacall is well thawed out. The sting has been retracted. She's done the lot. Her life has not been free of a little rumour running up and down Sunset Boulevard, but that's life.

'Moss Hart said you should shake your life up every seven years or so. I have - and I think I am wonderful to do this.'

We've cracked the nut. She's smiling - and not afraid of being a little self-mocking.

[12.6.1985]

JONATHAN BATE

MY KIND OF TOWN:
THE PROFESSOR WHO BELIEVES LIVERPOOL
PEOPLE CAN TEACH US ALL A THING OR TWO

Jonathan Bate is the chap who would rather educate Rita than Little Lord Fauntleroy. The 35 year old professor at Liverpool University is a favourite for the vacant chair of English Literature at Cambridge. He's also been offered an incredible £85,000 for a five hour week teaching in New York. But that's not his bag either - he prefers to stay in Liverpool with his loyal band of mature students, 75% of them women, like the hairdresser-turned-scholar of Willy Russell's famous play.

'Many of them have made huge sacrifices,' says Kent-born Jonathan, who lives in Toxteth. 'They have even sold houses to support themselves through a degree course because they are so motivated. Compare that to teaching a lot of callow public school children at Cambridge, and you can see why I don't want to leave.'

If that sounds trendy, don't be too readily kidded. Jonathan thinks that large sections of higher education have been hijacked by a 'lot of failed revolutionaries.' And of his own subject, he says: 'The problem is that instead of teaching English literature, they are pursuing political ends by other means.' Liverpool, he maintains, is more sinned against than sinning in this respect. Despite the city's reputation for being at the sharp end of politics, he feels his colleagues and students take a realistic view of life.

Since being appointed to Liverpool's King Alfred Chair of English Literature four years ago - he was then said to be the youngest professor in the country - Jonathan has raised his department's international profile and developed new courses. He has become famous as Britain's champion of the 'green' Romantic poets. Their message, he reckons, is appreciated by undergraduates becoming bored with Marxism and feminist tracts. He takes issue with those who see enjoyment of Wordsworth as irrelevant to modern life. 'What's gone wrong,' he insists, 'is that they have regarded an interest in nature as a form of escapism from the issues of society. But you cannot have harmony in life without an appreciation of nature. Coming as he did from Grasmere, Wordsworth thought that the greatest ill of city life was that people didn't know the names of their neighbours. Often that's still the case.'

What's needed is time to stand and stare. 'Ruskin said of

Wordsworth that he had taught us how to see. Nobody had ever looked properly at dry stone walls before.' Or a daffodil, perhaps ... ?

Jonathan's academic track record is pedigree stuff: grammar school followed by reading English at St Catharine's College, Cambridge. He then took a year's fellowship at Harvard 'funded by a philanthropist who got into oil when it was only used for lamps.' After doing his PhD, he taught for six years at Trinity Hall, Cambridge, where he was a Fellow. A professorship to the University of California, Los Angeles, followed. But what could have been a latter-day example of the infamous 60s British 'brain drain' failed to root. 'I tried it for a term, but the problem is that American academic life is confined to a conference circuit. You end up writing for other professors who speak to each other in impenetrable jargon.'

Chicago didn't capture the Bate imagination, nor did New York. Jonathan Bate says his job - as well as its benefits to students - is about the quality of life. 'The idea of full employment returning in a computerised age is unreal, but the arts can help people enjoy fulfilment. The ideal scenario would be a 20 hour week, not a 40 hour one.'

He also believes that if the Government wants more science graduates to drive the economy, it can only be achieved by expanding resources. 'You can't take students whose natural ability is in the arts and merely transfer them to science.' The bottom line, he insists, is to cut down on the paperwork and get on with the teaching. Says Jonathan, who is about to contribute a work on Elizabethan writers for the new Oxford History of English Literature, replacing the one by C. S. Lewis 'One of the greatest things about Liverpool is the large numbers of local mature students. I have absolutely no desire to leave here.'

[14.6.1994]

THE BEATLES' MANAGER

ALLAN WILLIAMS:
THE MAN WHO TOLD THE BEATLES THEY'D NEVER WORK AGAIN

Allan Williams is 69 next week and says the time has come to rewrite history. He is not, as the title of his autobiography suggests, *The Man Who Gave The Beatles Away* - 'I sacked them,' he insists.

There follows a gurgling chuckle like a sink emptying. Has life gone down the plughole for the Fab Four's first manager? Not at all. He travels the world telling tales of how it was - and how it might have been. The past 12 months have seen him in Mexico, the Dominican Republic, Cuba, Canada and Singapore. And now, clutching a vodka and lemonade, in a Liverpool pub.

'I have no regrets. Millions of people would still like to swap places with me. Just to have been a cog in the wheel that led to the greatest entertainment phenomenon of all time is marvellous.' A big cog, nevertheless: had Allan not taken the Beatles to Hamburg, there would have been no trained-up, hard-edged group for Brian Epstein, and more particularly, producer George Martin, to fashion. 'If you've heard the Hamburg Tapes, they're pretty rough,' says Allan. 'If you'd told me at the time that this was to be the world's number one pop group, I wouldn't have believed it.'

In those days, it was John, Stuart (Sutcliffe), Paul, George and Pete (Best). No Ringo. Allan Williams, ex-plumber and flogger of encyclopaedias, fridges and electric typewriters, was now selling a British pop group to the Germans: 'If the lads hadn't learned their trade in Hamburg, there'd be no Beatles today.'

Allan sacked the group after a revolt, led by John Lennon, which scrapped his 10% cut: 'They were getting £100 a session between the five of them, and becoming swell-headed. I told them I'd taken them on when nobody else wanted to know. I wrote a letter saying I was finished with them. I also told them they'd never work again. Well, we know what happened to that...there's only me now worrying about a pension.'

He last saw the Beatles together when they were recording *Let It Be*. 10 years earlier - in 1959 - he had first set eyes on John and Stuart when they chanced into his newly opened Jacaranda Club in Slater Street. Allan, no longer a plumber, had spent £350 recreating a continental coffee bar but the women's toilets were covered in obscene graffiti: 'So, as art students, I paid John and Stuart to decorate the loos.' He also paid them £100 to build self-destructing floats for the first Liverpool Arts Ball at St George's Hall: 'All the Beatles came in fancy dress. I had photos of John Lennon in a grass skirt, which I've lost.'

Their initial musical task under Williams' management was backing a strip act hired by Allan and his then business partner and still close friend, Harold Phillips - the legendary 'Lord Woodbine', who had come to Britain aboard the *Windrush*. The first official Williams/Beatles contract perished when another of Allan's ventures, the Top Ten Club, in Soho Street, burned down on its fifth day of operation. History going up in smoke. But the memories linger on.

None more so than the night the Beatles topped the bill at the London Palladium Royal Command Performance: 'That's when I really knew I'd blown it,' reflected Allan. 'I threw a cushion at the television. I wish I'd had a brick in my hand.'

He felt the same gut reaction when the group premiered their movie *A Hard Day's Night* at Liverpool Odeon: 'I only went as the guest of the writer, Alun Owen, who was a pal. I passed the VIP room and every socialite who'd never wanted to know the Beatles was there. I was so embarrassed. I left early. It was pouring with rain and the Beatles were getting into a car to be whisked away to the Town Hall,. I remember them smiling, waving through the half-steamed-up windows and shouting: "There's Allan." That really cut me up. They must have wondered what I was doing, standing on my own in the drenching night.'

The dream had become a nightmare? 'Actually, I don't think I could have handled it,' admits Allan. 'I have a mind like a grasshopper. I don't think I would have gone the whole trip with them. But I'd done my bit. I'd created them.'

Had Alan kept the Beatles under contract, he reckons he could have netted £25,000 back in 1961 for selling them to Epstein. 'That would have been a realistic price,' said Allan, who had been brokering deals since he was a teenager. His father, Dickie, was a joiner by day and promoter by night. His son and heir followed suit.

Allan's first promotion was a dance matching the lads from Bootle Tech with the girls from neighbouring Johnson's Dye Works. He could have been an entertainer: 'There was a group called Stefani's Silver Songsters. I passed an audition in my lunch hour, bought a one-way ticket to Morecombe and had my bags packed. When I got to the bottom of our road, my father burst out crying and so did I. So I didn't go. I was only 14.'

Instead, Allan, born in Percy Street, Bootle, February 21, 1930: educated at Beach Road and Central schools, Litherland: evacuated to Chirk, and returned home as 'uncontrollable', daily pushed a plumber's handcart down Hawthorne Road to repair war damage: 'I was so small, people thought the cart was running away on its own.' He says the early trauma of finding out his mother was actually his stepmother 'has affected me throughout my life'. 'My real mother died when I was one year old, giving birth to twins, who also died. Her name was Annie Cheetham and she came from Waterloo. I only found that out comparatively recently.'

Allan met his wife, Beryl, when he was in the Bentley Operatic Society and she was a visiting dancer from the Birkenhead Operatic for a production of *Merrie England*. They married when Allan was 26, separated seven years ago, but remain friends. Their son Justin is 35, daughter Leah, 24. Beryl was on that first trip to Hamburg when Woody nearly killed them all when the car got stuck in tracks in front of an oncoming tram. The rest really IS history.

Allan is still promoting. Next up is a St Patrick's Night do at Bootle Town Hall on March 17: 'I've had some disasters though. The last one, a Sinatra tribute in Wigan, had more in the orchestra than the audience.' A gambler to the last. Does he have a favourite Beatles' track? '*Fool on the Hill*,' he laughs. 'Honestly.'

[13.2.1999]

CILLA BLACK

Our Cilla has kept up her Liverpool connections: why else would she have a picture of Derek Hatton hanging in the downstairs loo of her Buckinghamshire home?

'Me family can't stand him, but Bobby and I met up with him at the Cup Final. He seemed perfectly charming...Liverpool's answer to Richard Gere.'

And Bobby, husband of 17 years, was at her side, always willing to fend off the more overbearing fans, when the uncrowned Queen of Scottie Road came home to lay early plans for a 1986 Christmas season that will see her starring in *Aladdin* at the Empire Theatre.

There were things she'd planned to say, and things she thought she might say. But even a star who's about to enter the busiest 12 months of their career, can be thrown off cue. 'Hello, I'm from the *Catholic Pictorial*, ' says a voice. 'Do you still go to church?'

'Oh...er...no, except at Christmas. Although if I did go to church, it would have to be a Catholic church. I wouldn't know where to put the money anywhere else. But I still pray - if only to say "God, why have you been so good to me for so long..."'.

It was a line of questioning quickly exhausted. Then it was Cilla's turn to exhaust everyone else with a mixture of anecdotes and wacky nonsense. Stories of how life used to be at No. 380 Scotland Road, a flat hovering twixt a Chinese laundry and a bank. 'There was the time they thought me dad was trying to commit suicide. He was standin' on the window ledge with the police and fire brigade telling 'im not to jump and all the people from the pubs just lookin' up like. And all he was doin' was tryin' to find out if I was all right. I'd fallen asleep on mam and dad's big bed and they couldn't get the door open.

I mean, that's the place I always think of when we talk of home. Our little place with the outside loo and the back yard with the coal in it. Me mam doesn't to this day really like the house I bought her in Gateacre. She said it should have been by a bus stop. I mean, that's what we were used to: the sound of traffic day and night. It would lull you to sleep. Now we've got this house in 17 acres, and when she comes to stay with us, she says the sound of the birds in the early morning drives her mad.'

Cilla's Mum, also Cilla, is now 74, but still has her stall selling nylons in the market along Great Homer Street. 'I think what she does is buy them off other people's stalls and then ups the price a bit,' giggles her famous daughter. 'But it's her life. You couldn't ask her to stop now.' Nor, it seems, can you ask Miss Black to change all her ways. 'After, I'm goin' to see if I can find that place off London Road where they used to deep fry Holland's steak and kidney pies with the chips. Do you know, I put on 'arf a stone last time I came back to do a book signing session. And at the Atlantic Tower, where we stayed, they put out some buttered bread for me, a plate of chips and a bar of Cadbury's chocolate.

I probably wouldn't 'ave left Liverpool if things had been different in the early days. But the roads were so bad. It used to take seven hours to get to London. Nowadays, we can be up 'ere - illegally - in three hours.'

So why not come back for good? Well, she says, sons Rob, 16; Ben, 12; and Jack, 5, are now 'Southernised'. Rob is at Merchant Taylors' School in London. 'The wife of George Martin, who produced records for myself and the Beatles, asked me ages ago what school I had 'is name down for. I got all these brochures, and the only name I knew was Merchant Taylors' - because of the one at Crosby. It was where all the posh and clever kids went to when I was at St. Annie's.'

In those days, immediately prior to Priscilla White changing her name to Cilla Black as the only girl in Brian Epstein's legendary pop stable, the 'in' words were 'Fab' and 'Gear', and they were dancing to the Noddy and the Monkey down at the old Cavern.

And today, there's a 43-year-old mum called Mrs. Willis - for that's what they respectfully call her at the grocers and the butchers in Denham - who's madly trying to keep up with certain new developments.

'Our house is murder at the weekends. They've all got stereos - hand-me-downs they are - and they're all blasting away. Rob has even got his own group. He sings and plays the bass. At least he's learned something from me...'

Cilla's own schedule is busier than ever. After a week at the family home in Marbella - 'we had a break-in, and I'm going out there to see everything is all right and to buy new curtains,' - it's off to Scarborough for a summer season. Then, before the panto, there are new series of *Surprise, Surprise* and *Blind Date* to do for the telly. 'It was either that or get pregnant again,' she jokes. 'But I'm probably too old for that now.

People sometimes ask me why I haven't been back more. The last time was for panto in 1978, and the time before that was 1966, to appear with Gerry and the Pacemakers. But they seem to forget - you've got to be asked.

I've certainly seen the Empire stage door more than any other star. I was the original Stage Door Johnny, collecting autographs of people like Frankie Vaughan, Norman Wisdom and Dickie Valentine. And I remember Bob Hope waving to the crowds from the circle bar window. It was a day out to see 'im.' But there were no Beatle autographs: 'When you're mates, you're mates. I was never in awe of the Beatles. They were family. For a night out, we'd go to the Shakey. The Empire was too expensive. Or to the Homer or Derby picture houses and envy Doris Day. There's always been something of the actress in me.

But I'm not nervous about coming back, like I was last time. I just took six steps out on to the stage and the whole place erupted. It was a great welcome home.'

[12.12.1986]

PATRICIA ROUTLEDGE

PEDALLING DOWN MEMORY LANE

Those glued to Granada tomorrow night for an intake of culture will see a woman in a floral frock, pedalling away on one of those post-war iron-framed bicycles with a shopping basket on the front. Tis none other than all-round entertainer, Patricia Routledge, riding around Wirral recapturing her youth.

Thus, *Celebration* (10.30pm) goes by the name of *Birkenhead Revisited*, albeit distinctly a notch down from *Brideshead* and Castle Howard. But Hamilton Square is beautiful, the antidote to the hammer-head cranes of Cammell Laird's, which, when Ms. Routledge was a gal at Birkenhead Park Council School, gave birth to the *Ark Royal*.

She was born, according to legend, 'in a gentleman's outfitters.' So perhaps it was her formative proximity to cobbled-street capitalism, that gives her an uncanny air of the grocery shop sense of urgency endemic to M.Thatcher. 'Now you've asked me a question ....are you going to allow me to finish?'.

The Diary was joining in the melée at Granada's Liverpool studios, as Ms Routledge was produced, in advance, to mix with the masses at one of those sausage-on-a-stick soirées, which actually ran to bacon-wrapped-around-cocktail-cherries-on-a-stick. Our encounter came somewhat late in the day, as my avowed intention at such functions (during the course of any one financial year) is to consume the equivalent of the television licence in food and drink. And while I am fully aware that the cash goes to the BBC, the television's the television when it comes to signing cheques.

As it happens, Ms Routledge was being seized upon to sign a lot of autographs as the circulating star of the show. Plunging my raw carrot into a dish of taramasalata, I advanced, taking a slightly circuitous route so that an old dear with a Brownie Instamatic could capture the right side of Ms.Routledge's head for posterity. Did she like the end *Celebration* result? 'Oh I think they've done a marvellous job,' said the lady who, as a nipper, had danced the polka the whole length of the new Mersey Tunnel the day before it was officially opened by George V in 1934. The public had been allowed to walk through as a special treat, and now Ms Routledge was walking through her early years as a treat for the viewers.

Back to school, and back to the site of the old Argyle Theatre (now a car park), singing all the way. 'The songs featured in my one-woman show I devised for the *Festival of Comedy* last year. I said I'd never do a show like that, but my home town has asked me back four times, and to refuse would have been churlish.' So singing it was, in a vibrant contralto sort of way. And a little acting on the old school stage, re Mr Pickwick. Her first taste of theatre had been in those gymslip days, playing the hare in *The Hare and the Tortoise*. There were memories of Mr Kettlewell and Mr Jones as 'The Ugly Sisters'. She went on to Liverpool University, read English, and was going to be a teacher. But fate beckoned.

Still on her bike, she is seen going along Broadway in Bebington, a journey she took every day. But how could anyone have known that her future included Broadway, New York? At last we see her at the old box office at the Liverpool Playhouse, where she made her professional debut (on the stage, not in the box office!) 'This is where it all began,' says Ms Routledge. Seconds later the programme ends with the sort of abruptness usually associated with the outbreak of war. Still, that leaves plenty of scope for *Birkenhead Revisited 11*.

'Thank you all for coming. It's so lovely to see you all here,' Ms Routledge tells her private audience. A fitting gesture, it seems. For across the eyes, Ms Routledge has the look of our own dear Queen. Everyone applauds. And across the crowded room, I espy my dear friend Carl Hawkins, now Granada's stylish Chester reporter, and formerly chairman of the Playhouse. Carl has seen them all come....and go, and has the dog-eared programmes to prove it.

P.S. Ms Routledge's pianist, also present, goes by the most memorable name of Chuck Mallett. Perhaps he could make an appearance on *That's Life?*

[1.11.1989]

ADRIAN HENRI

THE MAN WHO MADE POETRY THE NEW ROCK AND ROLL

One day, I'm sure, there'll be one of those blue plaques outside a house in Mount Street, saying: Adrian Henri, poet and painter, lived here. For poet and painter is what he proudly proclaims on his income tax return. The poet has sold more than a million tomes; the paintings change hands for up to £35,000 a picture. Meanwhile, Liverpool's single most enduring everyman as artist, drags his would-be 19th century self perilously close to the 21st century.

In between is the reality. A man of 66, already famous, and living in a terrace directly opposite Paul McCartney's juvenile Fame School. An artisan surrounded by books and things in wall cabinets: one full of preserved moths and butterflies; another with stuffed birds and a squirrel. On the mantle, a bowl of glass tulips and the sculpture of a carton of milk being poured into a glass, half obscures a post-card of a pig in a nun's habit. All is presided over by Ruby, a glitzy art deco dummy, who knew better times as a wig stand in a hairdresser's window.

Welcome to Bric-a-Bracsville: 'This historic thing with poetry is one of my quarrels,' says Adrian, 'The achievement of people like Roger McGough, Brian Patten and myself is that we actually convinced people that a poet was a quite modern and important thing to be.' Alfred Lord Tennyson, he reminds me, was an incredibly senior figure, scribing rhymes in *The Times* about the Crimean War et al. What Adrian and the Mersey Poets of the 60s (when Toxteth was known nationally simply as Liverpool 8) managed to do, was reach the public: 'by playing with pop music, television, and the whole business of image, to show how poetry had to reach people, and not just in a few slim volumes.'

At the time, Adrian himself was anything but slim. Rather, a 20-stone roaming rotunda, taking an evangelical cue from the mediaeval troubadours. *The Mersey Sound* became the biggest-selling poetry anthology of all time. Tough on Tennyson. No wonder Mo Mowlam suggested Adrian as the next Poet Laureate. In which case, the honour would be all Birkenhead's. For that's where Adrian was born, one April morn in 1932. For five years, because his father had no job, he lived with his grandparents in Tranmere. When his dad did find work at a holiday camp, the family decamped to North Wales. And, because of the Blitz, that's where Adrian stayed - apart from a week in an uncle's air raid shelter, which he calls 'an intense experience.'

The young Henri failed the 11-plus at junior school in Rhyl, being redeemed by the newly established 13-plus and then dispatched to St Asaph Grammar, where he flourished. There followed a fine arts degree at Kings College, Durham, and coming up to speed, a Fellowship from the Liverpool John Moores University. At last, the prophet poet honoured in his own country. But looking back at his youth, Adrian admits: 'I was a square peg in a round hole. So bad at woodwork and metalwork, they put me with the girls to do "commercial" which was shorthand and typing, and which I also couldn't do. I was a lonely child. The usual fat boy with glasses who gets bullied. I never did things like go to the snooker hall. Instead, I went to the library. One thing that saved me was the children's theatre in Rhyl. I learned a lot of basic skills as a performer at 12 and 13.'

During warm summer days, he also started the first of 10 seasons as a fairground worker, something he still includes on his c.v. to prove he has lived in the world that gets you dirty. A world where the smell of engine oil mingles with that of fried onions. Enough to turn your stomach on the dodgems.

'Terrific training for life. You have to talk to total strangers,' says Adrian. 'Resting actors, villains, low-life. A place with its own language and traditions. I was honoured to be part of it.'

He returned to Liverpool, never to leave, in 1965, because of a girl who worked on the opposite stall and had a book of poetry by Louis Macneice. 'She looked like a dream. Black ski pants and polo neck sweater, black eye make-up and long blonde hair. Her boyfriend was an artist from Liverpool.'

Adrian also got to know the Liverpool painter Don McKinlay, who had been working in Rhyl as a street photographer.

In early life, Liverpool had been a great and exotic foreign place. Now it was the Promised Land. 'Going to Lewis's was like going to Heaven.' Adrian had met his future wife, Joyce, during a brief teaching spell at a Catholic boys' college in Preston. Their 12-year marriage ended with the couple throwing a joint divorce party. 'Radical in its day,' concedes Adrian. Joyce went on to become Adrian's best friend, tragically dying of cancer. He has since immortalised her in a picture of skeleton dancers in Hope Street. Her death was but one tragedy in his life. 'In early 1970, my grandmother, grandfather, mother and father all died within five weeks of each other, all by chance.'

The Mersey Poets scene disintegrated. 'A lot of acrimony - money, women, the usual things. I was also feeling quite ill. I went to see the doctor and was told that I'd had a heart attack. I was in bed for three months.'

But there was to be solace. Adrian's relationship with Catherine, a French academic, who teaches American literature and art history at the Sorbonne, is, he says, the longest of his life. While other couples dally over a Chinese takeaway, they meet regularly in Oxford, Paris, New York and Strasbourg. There is even a small apartment in Paris. 'Even if I had a permanent base there, which is an option at the moment, I'd still like to keep this house. I don't think I'd ever leave it now.' And he adds: ' I don't want to make it sound like some incredible sacrifice. I've stayed here because I like it.'

He does, however, believe that 'poets are people who have never quite grown up. They still see things in the way that children do. That's why doing readings for kids is such a pleasure. It's a licence to be nine years old again. When I was at school, it was all talk of wandering through daffodils. It didn't really connect with me at all. Hopefully, kids nowadays will grow up thinking of poetry as perfectly natural.'

And his testament to a lifetime's dedication with pen and brush? 'Some people say we've trivialised things. As it happens, I think not. I've tried to make whatever I like part of my life.'

Who can say better than that?

[23.1.1999]

PETER TOYNE

UNIVERSITY CHIEF A FIRST AMONG EQUALS

After a hard day at the office, Peter Toyne goes home and plays with his train set. Or he may sit watching *Coronation Street* and *Brookside* while munching a bar of Cadbury's Dairy Milk. Other favourite options include playing the piano - 'mainly hymn tunes'; cooking a meal 'with lots of messy sauces' or 'mowing and hacking' his three-quarter-acre garden.

They're all ways of turning off for the Yorkshire butcher's son who wanted to drive a steam engine but ended up in charge of Liverpool John Moores University, and has just been declared Liverpool's chief Millennium planner. In nine days time, he installs Cherie Blair as new Chancellor of the JM. For Peter Toyne's own official titles of Vice-Chancellor and honorary Professor, read also chief executive: running a £100m-a-year budget, employing 3,000 staff, tutoring 20,000 students. Without the JM, he reckons, there would be no Cream or Nation club scene in Liverpool; no Hardman Street bar quarter; a huge population pumping back millions into the city economy. 'Twice as many people as in the city of Ripon, where I went to school,' he likes to point out.

Peter Toyne progressed to teaching geography at Exeter University, a degree which must now pay dividends in finding his way around the 26 outlying buildings of his Liverpool empire. 'Here we have to walk through the streets. You go past the *Big Issue* sellers and the dereliction. A city struggling with itself and coming to life again. That's damned good for every student.'

He looks out from his Rodney Street executive suite at the blackened, half-wrecked edifice of the Church of Scotland: 'That's the next one I really want,' says the man whose interest in expansion and real estate has led to the JM being called the 'Rapid Hardware University'. The restoration of the North Western Hotel in Lime Street and the Bull Ring flats in St Andrew's Gardens testify to what Toyne calls 'the twin attack on buildings for academic use and student residence.'

Now commercial developers are getting in on the accommodation game: the university runs the halls for no profit - but someone else pays to build them. However, there is profit in expertise: 'We sell virtually everything around here.'

The grandest scheme to date is the Liverpool Telescope being constructed by the JM in the Canary Islands. Scientists from four continents are queuing to buy time. Back to earth, and Toyne wants to turn the Scottish Church into a library and art gallery. Only years away is the old convent chapel in Mount Pleasant, about to be made into a University Great Hall.

Peter and Angela Toyne's son Simon (Eton and Oxford) was an organ scholar - part of a family liking for the Church Omnipotent. Peter Toyne jokingly calls Liverpool Cathedral, where JM graduations are held, 'the grandest university chapel in Christendom.' But there are now sufficient Far Eastern students to warrant graduation ceremonies in Kuala Lumpur. 'I go out there and sell the university to them,' he says. 'We sell Liverpool as well, with pictures and videos. If I go, it means a hell of a lot more than sending a recruiting team. They meet the person in charge.'

Peter Toyne personally fronts the university's image - captain of a flagship enterprise that has to raise £35m a year in addition to grants and fees. There's no financial tie in with the family of the late Sir John Moores, after whom the institution was named. 'No megabucks…and we didn't even ask,' insists the professor. 'What we wanted for a role model for this generation. John Moores is the guy who did it for himself and that's exactly what we're about.'

So how about university standards and league tables?

'I think people are on to a very stupid debate there. You can argue the toss forever and never get a sensible answer. What is certain is that degrees are different from what they were, and so they should be. What matters is that we are still taking people to the maximum of their capability and I'll argue till the cows come home that is what we do. A first is still a first. A degree is a degree.'

Although older universities still select from the highest A-level grades, Peter Toyne argues that the newer ones recognise how people developed during their course. Astro-physics, general engineering and sports science now put JMU in the international super league. Realistically, the JM is 'two thirds of the way through the universities - at the top end of the new universities.' He says the job is to respond to change. Better still, anticipate it: old physics out, new physics in: old English out, Media Studies in. And so on. Even Oxbridge had been guilty of dropping entrance standards when they wanted certain sportsmen 'who couldn't do a damn thing.'

'I don't like elitism that is bred of privilege. I have no problem with elitism on merit. That's fair.'

The ceremonial mace that precedes him in the still-fanciful processions - that ironically have their roots in the Oxbridge tradition - was made by an unemployed Kirkby man who started off with an HND certificate in Design Technology and ended up doing a full degree. 'I'm so proud of that. It's the epitome of what we stand for.'

But he was even prouder of being declared Businessman of the Year for transforming an ailing old polytechnic of just 4,000 students into an institution, which, although not without criticism, cannot be ignored. Peter Toyne had come to Liverpool in 1986 when the Poly staff had just been issued with redundancy notices. Both city and college were on their knees. The key was ditching local authority control in '88. 'There was a real field to be ploughed.' The geography degree was about more than ice-capped mountains and oxbow lakes. Toyne's specialisation was the location of retail business and customer behaviour; how to respond to markets and at what price. But student loans remain a vexing issue.

'Quite frankly, had this happened 40 year ago, when I was about to go to university, I don't think I'd have gone there. I come from a very ordinary family, an only child, and I was the first to go to university. I was regarded as slightly weird - Old Weirdo Toyney.'

He says he can still smell the engine oil of the rail sheds at Doncaster.

'Everyone else in my village worked down the pit. That background is something that stays with me and why I was happy to come to Liverpool and make all this available.'

[16.1.1999]

MERLIN HOLLAND

OSCAR WILDE'S GRANDSON

On Christmas Eve, 1881, Oscar Wilde sailed from Liverpool aboard the good ship *Arizona* to famously 'declare his genius' to America. At 27, he was an international celebrity. But little more than a decade later, he faced imprisonment, bankruptcy and disgrace, dying in a Paris hotel on November 20, 1900.

As his centenary year dawns next Tuesday, Wilde is back in fashon and once more fêted as a literary giant. That's something which makes his grandson, Merlin Holland, extremely proud.

It could once again become the family which dares speak its name. Merlin Holland has spent more than half a century being Oscar Wilde's grandson, mostly with consenting adults, in private. His grandmother, Constance, changed the family name to Holland to protect the innocence of Merlin's father, Vyvyan, and elder brother, Cyril, after the once lionised Wilde was sentenced to hard labour and dispatched to Reading Gaol for gross indecency with London rentboys.

Holland was a distant maternal family name, taken from a Major Holland Watson. It guaranteed anonymity. Only in October 1954, when they put a heritage plaque on Wilde's Chelsea house, did young Merlin, then eight, wake up to the fact that grandad was a celebrity: 'I was taken out of school and brought up to London,' he recalls. 'There was a big lunch at the Savoy. I remember having to scribble my name on peoples' menus.' But then there was a family shutdown once more: 'There were deeper reasons,' reflects Merlin. 'My parents thought I might somehow try and cash in on or emulate Wilde. And in those days, of course, the whole question of homosexuality was something that was very thorny.'

Two generations down the line, Merlin talks of his ancestor as either 'Wilde' or 'Oscar' or sometimes 'Oscar Wilde.' But never, during the course of our lengthy meeting, as 'my grandfather.' The apparent distancing is due to the way he now works - editing, writing about and lecturing on Wilde.

So what of the surname - referred to by Oscar himself in the biographical *De Profundis* as 'that made great in the history of my country (Ireland).' Wilde's father, Sir William, was the leading Irish surgeon of his day, who invented the operation to remove cataracts. His mother, Speranza, was a nationalist poet and campaigner. 'If I do ever revert, I would do it for the Wilde family, rather than just for Oscar. One tends to forget them, and that shouldn't happen,' says Merlin. 'But a change would take a lot of personal courage.'

He then gives me the first full account ever of his feelings on becoming Merlin Wilde. 'I think in England I would store up a load of personal snipers and whingers. Whereas on the Continent, people regard Wilde foremost as an artist, with his sexual preferences as his own affair. Here, almost every article starts off: "Oscar Wilde, gay playwright...' I just shrug my shoulders and think it's Britain.

I used to say that to keep Holland would serve as a permanent rebuke to Victorian morality. But this whole business of being Wilde's grandson is something I found difficult to accept. The first 45 years of my life was very much *not* as Wilde's grandson. I was putting it off. But it was obviously going to go on being unfinished business, and unless I found a niche somewhere, I was going to carry on feeling uncomfortable. The only way to come through was to be accepted by the academics and scholars as someone doing serious research. I neeeded to be able to talk and negotiate from a position of strength, so I can stand on the same side of the fence as them, and look at Wilde as they do, rather than grinning inanely like a monkey in a cage. That I refuse to do.'

And so it is. Personal mementos of Oscar include a copy of his first published work, the poem *Ravenna*, and a first edition of *Dorian Gray*, in Latvian. After five years 'selling paper to the Arabs, travelling the Middle East and Africa at someone else's expense', 10 years with an academic publishing house and a further 10 years running a ceramics import business with his wife, Sarah, Merlin Holland is hard at work editing Oscar Wilde's letters. He has also discovered 12 more poems from the great man.

What started off as a six till nine Saturday morning job, answering letters from Wilde fans worldwide, has become full-time. So much so, that he has given up his wine column for *The Oldie* and *Country Life* magazine. And there is an apostolic succession. Like Oscar, Merlin Holland went to Magdalen College, Oxford - and it gets better. Merlin's own son, Lucian, is currently in his third year at Magdalen, holding the college classics scholarship, and - wait for it - occupying the same rooms Oscar Wilde had, at 71 High Street: 'It wasn't a joke by the College or anything,' says Merlin. 'Especially as Wilde's biographer, Richard Ellmann got it wrong.' Another claim by an Oxford hotel, that 'it was here Oscar Wilde discovered women weren't his thing,' is less beguiling.

'It's rubbish, and it makes me furious,' says Merlin, who is also working on a book about his grandmother, Contstance. 'I have looked in great detail at her last years, and there are some astounding surprises,' he tells me. 'Constance knew that she didn't come up to Oscar's level intellectually, and she could not give him the stimulation he needed. But she could give him a great deal of affection and love, which she was still prepared to do when he came out of prison. But I'm afraid to say it was friends and family who kept them apart. I'm not saying it would have lasted, but it might have done something for him.' And he confirms the mere guessing of others over the years: 'Not only did Constance suffer, but she was desperate to get back with Oscar.'

Merlin refers to Wilde's upcoming centenary year as 'the bunfight'. It is but part of a gradual Wilde renaissance that has seen his plays back in the West End and on Broadway. '*A Woman of No Importance* has very strong feminist overtones. *An Ideal Husband* has all the political sleaze.' Topical stuff. Typical Oscar.

'He undoubtedly started the cult of the individual,' says Merlin. 'If he were here today, he'd be a permanent chat show guest, rather than the host. But he will never allow himself to be kidnapped by minorities. He was sufficiently generous of spirit to say that if he could help, he would, and then move on. And I think that's the way he should be treated by the gay movement. If people can come to an understanding of the subject through the sympathy they have with Wilde, then I think he will have performed a vital function for us to go into the next century with.'

More generally, he says of his grandfather: 'If there is one single figure of the last 100 years who cannot stand having his life separated from his work, it is him. I think we turned the corner with the publication of the first letters in 1962. They showed Wilde as a man of considerable thought and humanity, rather than as a two-dimensional cut-out funny man. His life is the play he never wrote. And now his work is being taken more seriously. Now he has that extra dimension.'

Is there a question Merlin Holland would like to ask Oscar Wilde?

'*Yes* - why the hell did you sue Lord Queensbury for criminal libel? I think it was absolute madness. It started the calamity.'

[26.11.1999]

BRIAN LABONE

FOREVER BLUE

Brian Labone and I have one very obvious thing in common: we're both twice the size we were when our paths first crossed 30 years ago. 'I've lost about three stones of late,' he insists, making an immediate defensive tackle.

However, he remains, on aggregate, a tad bulkier than when he captained Everton and led them out on the Wembley turf during the glorious Catterick years. Nowadays, the Labone waistline is in the lunchtime care of the Pig and Whistle - or any decent city centre pub that hasn't been wrecked by a juke box. Weekends are mainly teetotal 'unless there's been a bad result and I have a heavy Saturday night.' Sundays are often taken up playing golf at Ormskirk (handicap 14), occasionally giving old pal Ian Callaghan a run for his money.

'I also do a lot of reading,' says Brian, nowadays divorced from his wife, Patricia, and living in Lydiate. 'I'm mainly into history and biographies.' Perhaps he should write his own and bring us up to date? 'My daughter, Rachelle, is 28 and the love of my life. She works for BT at Skem,' says a still very proud dad. 'As for work, I flog insurance. You can be posh and call me a financial adviser, if you want. I've been staggering around doing that for the past 20 years and I suppose I'm a bit of a landmark.'

He says the pub, like the golf course, remains a good place to do business: 'You make a lot of contacts. I like going around town - and I still like talking football. I just think they're tinkering around with the rules too much now. I know they've got to, to get winners of competitions but it's very sad when a cup final or the World Cup can be decided on penalties. I can't understand why they get away with so much cheating,' he says. 'And it is cheating - people pretending to be tripped and getting penalties.'

Never short of an opinion, Brian - or 'Labby' as die-hards still call him - says he 'used to be a very biased Evertonian, but I've mellowed a bit.' Today, he does PR work for Everton on a Saturday, arriving at Goodison around 10.30am and leaving at 6.30pm. He knows all the present players and they know him - of course. Nevertheless, Brian has just stumped up eight quid for a ball for the first team to sign for a business client: 'You don't get anything free from Everton,' quips the skipper of old. 'A lot of chaps still come up to me with programmes from when I was young and slim and dark haired and ask me to sign them. I suppose there's a little bit of ego to it when people still recognise you.'

And in his case, they do. For big Brian Labone remains one of the great local heroes. One of only three guys - along with Neville Southall and Dave Watson - to have made more than 500 first-team appearances in the royal blue shirt: 533 according to the record books, 532 according to the man himself. In the Age of the Striker, it's worth recalling how Labone had little interest in straying upfield in search of goals: 'Besides, we had Roy Vernon, Joe Royle, Alec Young,' he says modestly. Brian only scored twice in a 14-year career. At centre back, his job was to stop the other side scoring. Which is exactly what he did, using his height to head off an attack.

'This change to the new ball, when will it all stop?' he wonders. 'Apparently, the new ball is very difficult to control.' But what about the old, heavier ball being dangerous? 'I headed thousands of them. Whether I'm going loopy, I don't know. Some ex-players do develop trouble. There's quite a high incidence of them becoming forgetful.' Everything is different. Not just the ball, but the kit and even the grass. Only the goals at either end are the same now.'

Born during the Blitz, Brian says football was the only thing that kept Liverpool kids going. 'That was all we had, kicking a ball at Walton Hall Park. There were wide open spaces. Days when your mother would give you a bottle of water and a jam butty in the morning and say she didn't want to see you till six o'clock.' The Labone home was No 1 Saxonia Road, Walton - 'I still meet an old neighbour, Bill Roberts. Prime conversation was always Everton's fortune. My father took me to some early games but by the time I was 10, I used to go to the boys' pen for threepence or fourpence.'

If that seems laughable today, what about the wages? 'When I signed for Everton in August 1957, the ceiling pay for a footballer was £20,' recalls Brian. 'I got £7 a week - very good for a 17-year old. When I was reserve for the first team, on a couple of occasions I actually got the £20. There was a £2 win bonus, and a £1 draw bonus, and that was that.' There was also eventual anger. The players were considering a strike. They all met at Belle Vue, with Jimmy Hill chairing the meeting. 'The test case', says Brian, 'came in 1960 with George Eastham's transfer from Newcastle to Arsenal. Things improved, but not madly. If a man was earning four figures, he had a good job. Even by 1970, I was earning £100 a week, which, if the average earnings were £30 to £40, wasn't a dramatic difference. Not like today. Even I can't imagine going to my bank every week and having £10,000 going in. When I left the game, you didn't have half a million pounds in savings, and there were no pensions. So you had a few bob - but you had to work for a living."

IIe says hc has no hang-up about losing out on the mega-bucks. 'Only in the late 70s and 80s did it go crazy. I would think players who just missed it might feel differently, but when you're playing football, you don't really think of the money. I think players are a bit mercenary now but I also think they do their best.'

But even to Brian, it seems an age since an Achilles tendon injury put paid to his career in 1972. Normally, he could have expected three or four more seasons and then perhaps drifted into soccer management but it was not to be. Labone was just 32 - with a very uncertain future: too young to become a manager, no longer fit enough to be a trainer. A partnership in an electrical company didn't work out: 'I'd always had the cushion of knowing I could go into my father's central-heating business when I finished football but he died in 1969, aged 51.' Norwest, who'd taken over the firm, said they couldn't find a position for Brian: 'I hit a brick wall,' he admits. 'I got a phone call from a pal who played for West Ham, who offered for me to go out to South Africa but I had to turn it down because of my injury.'

And so, approaching the Big 60, he continues to work. 'I can't afford to retire. Besides, some of the stuff they put on telly now would drive you to work. I have had an exciting and full life. I only ever played for Everton and I was in the first team most of the time. Somebody said to me that once you make one move, you are prepared to move a dozen times. But I have never wanted to move out of Liverpool.'

[30.1.1999]

MARGARET SIMEY

A LIFE PREOCCUPIED WITH LIVERPOOL

Margaret Simey was, as she put it, 'camping out' in the lounge of her sprawling Liverpool 8 Georgian terrace, I find her working off trays and trolleys, eight chapters into a book written in pencil script. When finished, it will sum up the politics of her 93 years: the difference between theory and reality, the fight for justice and the relish for argument or as she puts it 'The difference between Tony Blair and his third way and what actually happened in Toxteth.'

For Toxteth is how history itself will remember Margaret Simey. The voice crying in the wilderness - but this time being heard. A broken hip, now mending, has brought a new perspective: 'I think we are all misled by the Queen Mother. She gets up two days after her hip operation, but nobody says she wouldn't be able to walk. That takes months. And now I've come back that much older,' says the woman who enraged Margaret Thatcher, Michael Hesletine and Kenneth Oxford.

Born in Glasgow, educated in London, and living in diverse places from the West Indies to West Kirby, Margaret Simey has spent most of her long life in L8, as a city (and later county) councillor representing the people of Granby. 'My whole life's preoccupation has been in Liverpool. I don't care if it's the police or housing, or whatever. Liverpool is tops.'

She came here at 18 when her father was appointed principal of the old College of Commerce. It was a journey Margaret Simey made from the posh world of kippers and high tea and public school, where she had sat in class with Churchill's daughter and been taught by musical luminaries such as Gustav Holst (of the *Planets* fame) and Vaughan Williams. 'We had nothing but the best,' she recalls. The magic of Liverpool, she proclaims is 'that it isn't England. It hit me with such a wallop that this was a real place. We are global and have learned to tolerate and respect each other's traditions. As such, we are a national asset.'

Margaret Simey was Liverpool's first female graduate in the then new subject of Social Science - a subject her late husband, Tom, taught as professor here. She remembers women not having the vote: 'I was an easy victim for emancipation. I worked so hard trying to get Eleanor Rathbone elected as an MP that I very nearly failed my degree.' To this day, Rathbone still heads the list of women like Fanny Calder, Maggie Bevan, and most famously, Bessie Braddock, who shaped the Simey vision: 'I was trained by Bessie - one of her local secretaries. A real apprentice. Much of the trouble today, starting with Blair downwards, is that they were never apprenticed. They arrive as lawyers or whatever, whereas I was trained to be a politician and have never been anything else.' Margaret Simey rubbed shoulders with the formative Liverpool movers and shakers: the Crawfords, the Holts, the Bibbys - 'all gone now. They took over where sturdy Viking origins, followed by a Presbyterian upbringing, left off. I like the right to be ourselves,' she insists. 'You don't get that in the churches now. They're all about worship, not how I cope with my conscience.'

Her pleasure reading remains the lives of the great reformers: Marx, Lenin, Knox: 'If I had them in a row on my bookshelf, the Bible, about Jesus, would be in their company. Of all the doctrines I've come across, his and John Knox's are the ones I like the best. I long to have a political approach to Jesus.'

Praise is not a polite matter, of course, for Margaret Simey, as former Chief Constable Ken Oxford found to his cost. 'All that stop and search row. One law applied to the white boys, another to the blacks. The riots were the moment of revelation to me. They were not demanding housing or money or jobs, but justice. When I encountered Kenneth Oxford, I wanted police accountability. The word had not been used. before. Now it's everywhere. But he, being excessively English, couldn't take that. A middle-class wife didn't argue with the police.' Not unless the Chair of the police authority was called Margaret Simey, who then turned her fire on Michael Heseltine, the Minister personally dispatched to Merseyside post-riots by a dismayed Margaret Thatcher. 'I kept telling him that if he just listened to Toxteth, they could teach him. But he told me there was no room in his plans for anyone like me. So I belted him, verbally. He paced round and round the room while I bawled and shouted at him.'

There is now a procession of callers who queue to benefit from Margaret Simey's accumulated wisdom: 'That's what the elders of the tribe should be for,' she says. But never, never call her Lady Simey: 'I've never forgiven Harold Wilson for making my husband a peer. It was when he was packing the House of Lords because of the huge Tory majority. My husband accepted on those grounds, but I decided I wasn't going to be a Lady. I said I would go on as plain Mrs and Wilson countered that he couldn't care a damn. Ever since, to this day, I am sickened by the way some people lick my boots. They can't resist the pleasure of writing a letter to Lady Simey. That's typically English and I won't have it.'

And she adds: 'If I had my time again, I'd be far more radical. It wasn't until I was 80 that I grasped what it was all about. If I could begin again, then, by gum, we'd get this city moving.'

Now there speaks a politician you can actually believe.

[6.1.1999]